CAPE TOWN
WINELANDS &
THE GARDEN ROUTE

John Bradley, Liz Bradley,
Victoria Fine & Jon Vidar

Atlantic Ocean

Brandvlei

Garies

R355

R353

R358

R355

N7

R355

Loriesfontein

R355

R63

Nieuwoudtville

R27

R27

R364

R27

Calvinia

Lutzville

R27

Vanrhynsdorp

R363

R355

U P

Vredendal

N7

R362

Klawer

R364

R354

Lamberts Bay

R364

Graafwater

R364

Clanwilliam

R365

Cederberg Wilderness Area

Sutherland

R366

R365

Citrusdal

N7

R355

R356

Aurora

R355

R356

Paternoster

Velddrif

R399

R354

Saldanha

R27

Picketberg

R303

Langebaan

R45

Hopefield

Porterville

R356

Moorreesburg

R365

Saron

R307

R45

R311

Tulbagh

R46

N1

Darling

R44

Wolseley

R315

Malmesbury

De Dooms

Atlantis

R304

Wellington

N1

Worcester

N7

R27

Paarl

N1

R318

Kraaifontein

R45

R60

Montagu

Cape Town

Franschhoek

Robertson

R62

Barrydale

Stellenbosch

Bonnievale

R60

Hout Bay

Khayelitsha

Genadendal

R317

Swellend

Muizenberg

M17

Somerset West

R43

R406

N2

Simon's Town

Grabouw

R406

N2

R316

Caledon

R317

R319

R32

Hermanus

R44

R326

Napier

R43

R320

R316

Bredesdorp

Port Beau

Gans Bay

R43

Arniston

Pearly Beach

R317

R319

Agulhas

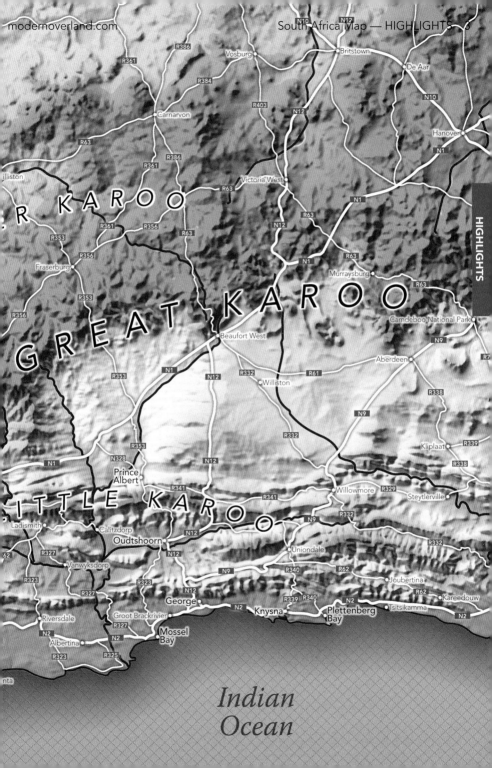

R386

R361

Vosburg

N10

Britstown

N12

De Aar

R384

Carnarvon

R403

N12

N10

Hanover

R63

R361

R386

N1

illiston

Victoria West

R63

N1

R KAROO

R63

R353

R361

R356

R63

N12

R63

Fraserburg

N1

Murraysburg

R63

R356

R353

GREAT KAROO

Camdeboo National Park

R356

Beaufort West

N9

R7

Aberdeen

R353

N1

N12

R332

Williston

R61

R332

N9

R338

R339

Kliplaat

R332

R338

N1

N328

Prince
Albert

R353

Willowmore

R329

Steytlerville

ITTLE KAROO

R341

R341

Ladismith

Calitzdorp

N12

N9

R332

R332

Oudtshoorn

N12

Uniondale

R62

Joubertina

Vanwyksdorp

N9

R340

R62

Kareedouw

62

R327

R323

George

R340

N2

R62

R323

N12

R339

Plettenberg
Bay

Tsitsikamma

Riversdale

Groot Brackrivier

R327

Knysna

N2

N2

Albertina

N2

Mossel
Bay

R323

R325

nta

*Indian
Ocean*

HIGHLIGHTS

Make an Impact Where You Travel

Savvy travelers understand that as global citizens, we impact the earth as we explore it. At Modern Overland, we take a practical approach to making a positive difference in our world. We make it easy for you to identify stops along your route that are working hard toward a better world. We seek out and highlight businesses and organizations that are socially and environmentally responsible so readers can actively choose to support these progressive establishments. These enterprises are marked with an **IMPACT** throughout both our print and digital guidebooks so you can decide to positively affect your world as you go.

10%
Give Back

Ten percent of the profits from this Modern Overland guidebook go back to community education initiatives within South Africa, Lesotho and Swaziland through the Modern Overland Foundation. To learn more about what we are doing and how you can get involved check out *www.ModernOverland.org*.

Sustainability

We print our books on paper that is certified by the Forest Stewardship Council.

Research, Plan, Book and Explore at:
ModernOverland.com

TOP EXPERIENCES

Winelands, Western Cape – p. 127

Enjoy some of the world's best wines while touring vineyards that overlook rolling hills and dramatic mountains. From chic showcase tasting rooms to historic cellars and gourmet restaurants, this region captivates wine enthusiasts from around the globe.

Langa – p. 116

Take the time to explore an oft-overlooked but vibrant part of Cape Town in the township of Langa. To really immerse yourself in the township lifestyle, spend a night at a guesthouse, eat at a local restaurant, and have a Langa resident show you around.

Table Mountain – p. 82
Hike up or take the cable car to the top of this iconic 1,080-meter-high Cape Town landmark for views of Robben Island and the city and harbor below.

Ostrich Riding, Oudtshoorn – p. 161
Hop on the largest bird in the world and hold its wings for dear life as it bolts in any direction. Keeping your balance atop these awkward and fast moving birds is not as easy as it looks.

Shark Cage Diving, Hermanus – p. 150

Face your fears and jump into a metal cage as Great White Sharks come within feet of you. Up-close encounters with these magnificent animals make for a good adrenaline rush – just keep your hands inside the cage.

Mzoli's Meat Party, Gugulethu – p. 122

Every Sunday locals from the Gugulethu township descend upon Mzoli's and meld with university students, Capetonians and visitors for a daylong street party over meat, beer and music. If you are in Cape Town on a Sunday afternoon, this event is an absolute must.

Paternoster – p. 186

Watch fisherman haul in their early morning catch in this quaint fishing village of traditional whitewashed houses before enjoying some incredibly fresh and tasty seafood.

Whale Watching, Hermanus – p. 150

The cliff-side town of Hermanus is a top spot to sight large Southern Right whales, primarily during the July-October calving season when they come into the bay and teach their young to swim alongside them.

Table of Contents

OVERVIEW

CAPE PENINSULA
Cape Town to Cape Point and back
Distance: 145 km / 90 mi
Suggested Time: 1-3 days

If your schedule allows for time to get out and explore beyond the city limits, one of the best trips is to tour the Cape Peninsula.

There are a handful of small towns that dot the coastline on either side of the peninsula; each with their own unique appeal. Heading south from Cape Town via the M3, you will first hit the ocean when you reach Muizenberg (p105) where you can soak up the sun on the beach or rent a board and catch some of the best waves in the area. Just beyond Muizenberg is Kalk Bay (p105) an old fishing town that is small enough to get around on foot with a selection of superb cafes and guesthouses. Boulders Beach in Simon's Town (p110) is also worth a stop to get up close with one of the largest colonies of African penguins.

Covering the southern end of the peninsula, the Cape of Good Hope Nature Reserve (p114) is home to ostrich, baboons and a variety of antelope. At the very tip of the peninsula is the Cape of Good Hope, the southwestern most point of the African continent, and Cape Point where you can hike up to the old lighthouse built back in 1860.

Returning to Cape Town via the western side of the peninsula along the M6 will bring you past Chapman's Peak Drive (p78) a 10km stretch of narrow road carved into the side of the mountain with spectacular views. This route will also bring you into Cape Town's neighborhood of Camps Bay (p69), which is a great place to enjoy a sunset cocktail overlooking the ocean.

WINELANDS & THE GARDEN ROUTE
Cape Town to Plettenberg Bay - *Distance: 1000 km / 621 mi*
Suggested Time: *1-2 weeks*

After a few days exploring Cape Town (p52) and possibly a day or two in the surrounding Townships (p115) and the smaller towns dotting the Cape Peninsula (p105), head a short distance east to the historic winelands. The vineyards surrounding Stellenbosch (p133) and Franschhoek (p141) offer not only a selection of the countries best wines but also some superb dining experiences. If you have a few extra days in your itinerary, this is a great place to spend them.

From the winelands there are two main routes to head east to the Garden Route: the more costal N2 or the more inland and hilly R62 that cuts through a number of quaint towns. If cage diving with Great White Sharks or seeing huge Southern Right Whales appeals to you, then head down to Hermanus (p149). Alternatively, head into the Little Karoo along the R62. Stop in Montagu (p155) for a taste of a small town South Africa. Continue along the scenic R62 to Oudtshoorn (p159), where ostrich is served up for breakfast, lunch or dinner. After a hearty meal head on out to one of the many ostrich farms where those who are confident in their balance can mount one of the gigantic birds and go on an ostrich ride. The small and relaxing town of Prince Albert (p166) is a short distance away but getting there is half the fun and requires navigating over some steep and tightly wound mountain switchbacks.

The Garden Route hugs the coastline from the rough and tumble city of Mossel Bay (p168) to posh Plettenberg Bay (p179). In between the two cities is the more leisurely lagoon town of Knysna (p173) where you can live it up outside of the city on one of the islands or spend a few days with the House of Judah Rastafarians in the neighboring Khayalethu South Township (p177).

OVERVIEW

🏛 HISTORY

Sixty million years before dinosaurs roamed the earth, prehistoric mammals inhabited the dusty terrain of South Africa's interior. Proto-human remains found at the Cradle of Humankind World Heritage Site in the Gauteng province are evidence of the hominid ancestors that called the region home nearly two million years ago. But it wasn't until roughly 100,000 years ago that our stone-age ancestors transformed into modern Homo sapiens and began walking their way into the future.

Nomadic San hunter-gatherers are South Africa's indigenous peoples. Their rock art can be found adorning caves and mountainsides throughout the country from Johannesburg to Cape Town. Some of these paintings date as far back as 30,000 years when the San roamed freely between South Africa, Namibia and Botswana. San that chose the more rooted lifestyle of sheep and cattle herding were later referred to as Khoikhoi, meaning "men of men." The San and the Khoikhoi are not racially different as was once thought; the differing terms merely reflected the divergent lifestyles of South Africa's indigenous population. Together the San nomads and the Khoi pastoralists became jointly known as the Khoisan, or by the European-imposed terms "Bushmen" and "Hottentots."

The Great Bantu Migration

Between 500 and 1200 A.D. a wave of Bantu-speaking peoples descended from central Africa and settled South Africa in what later became known as the Great Bantu Migration. These Bantu-speakers had much darker skin than the indigenous Khoisan and were composed of four distinct language families. The Nguni-speakers, the largest group, settled in the fertile regions east and south of the Drakensburg Mountains. They lived in dispersed farming and cattle herding communities and are the ancestors of the present-day Xhosa, Zulu, Ndebele and Swazis. The Sotho-speakers, the BaSotho, Tswana and Pedi, settled in the Drakensburg Mountains and westward in

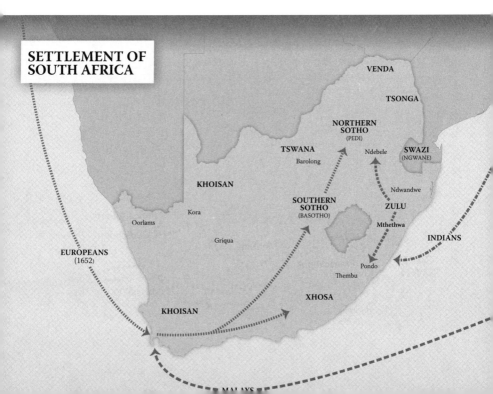

SETTLEMENT OF SOUTH AFRICA

the flat plains of the interior and Highveld. They lived in highly organized farming communities and worked primarily as iron and coppersmiths. Venda-speakers and Tsonga-speakers established themselves in the northeastern part of the country along the Limpopo River and developed refined metalworking skills, specializing in gold sculpture and jewelry.

Indigenous Khoisan living in the eastern parts of the country were largely absorbed into the migrant societies, their legacy remaining in the distinct Khoisan clicks heard in the Zulu and Xhosa languages. Migration slowed as Bantu-speakers opted for the fertile lands in the east and stopped short of the dusty southwestern plains, allowing the Khoisan of the present-day Western Cape and Northern Cape to maintain their distinct culture and language. Interaction between the different groups was largely peaceful and based on trade. Widespread violence that emerged in later years was either a direct result or byproduct of the arrival of Europeans in southern Africa beginning in the late 1400s.

Early European Encounters

Portuguese sailors and explorers had long dreamed of a sea passage to reach the riches of Asia, but the windy southern African tip thwarted early attempts. In 1487, Portuguese explorer Bartolomeu Dias finally rounded the cape, only to be blown ashore in a violent storm. He returned to Portugal with stories of the 'Cabo Tormentoso' (Cape of Storms) and the copper-colored men he saw along the shore herding cattle. However his princely sponsor, Henry the Navigator, had a more positive name for the fated cape - it would be called the Cape of Good Hope. Ten years later, Vasco de Gama followed Dias' route and successfully reached India. The seaway to the Indies was officially open.

Throughout the 1500s, European sailors regularly rounded the southern tip of Africa on their way to trade with the East Indies, modern-day India, Southeast Asia and Indonesia. Cape Town was used as a halfway point to replenish supplies, get fresh water and buy meat from the local Khoisan herdsmen on the slopes of Table Mountain. For years the Khoisan had engaged in long-distance overland trade with the Tswana and Xhosa in the east, however they soon preferred the ease of trade with passing ships. But tensions between the local Khoisan and the European traders emerged when sailors began to demand more meat

than the Khoisan were willing to sell. Seeing no consequences for themselves, many sailors stole livestock and sailed away. Khoisan retaliation was meted out against the next unsuspecting ship. In the eyes of the Europeans, trade in the Cape soon became unstable and expensive.

The VOC's Cape Colony

In 1652 the Dutch East India Company (VOC) sent a delegation of workers to the Cape to establish a small, permanent settlement on the southern shores of Table Bay. Their mission was to secure a more stable halfway point for their trading vessels and thereby surpass their competitors. To this end, they set out to regularize trade with the resident Khoisan, grow fresh vegetables to sell to passing ships and build a hospital for sailors. Initially, they were not interested in establishing a colony. But as the settlement grew, VOC Commander Jan van Riebeeck succumbed to requests to allow workers to expand beyond the confines of Table Bay and establish small farms to increase production.

The encroachment of these first free burgher "Boers" (Dutch for famers) on Khoisan grazing land was not a welcome development. In the first Khoi-Boer War of 1659, the Khoisan had early success pushing the free burghers back, but they were not strong enough to take the entire fort, which resulted in a stalemate. The VOC then capitalized on the relative lack of unity between the disparate clans and a year later defeated the Khoisan. From then on the free burghers considered all Khoisan land to be theirs for the taking and continued to spread deeper into the fertile rolling hills of the Western Cape.

Life in the Cape Colony was heavily influenced by the Dutch Reformed Church, a conservative branch of Calvinist Christianity. Most of the original VOC employees were members of this religion. As the colony grew, the VOC encouraged more European immigration to the Cape, mainly other Dutch Calvinists, French Huguenot refugees and Germans. However not everyone came to the new Cape Colony willingly. Within the first 10 years of settlement, the VOC began importing slaves to build Cape Town and work as servants or laborers on Boer farms and vineyards. Slaves were mainly imported from the eastern African coast including Madagascar and Mozambique, India, Malaysia and Indonesia. In total, over 60,000 slaves were imported to the Cape under VOC rule. As a company geared towards profit, VOC

OVERVIEW

considered slaves merely as a labor supply and was not concerned with the well-being of the slave population. The company therefore did not invest any time into converting their slaves to Calvinism, a fact which later allowed Islam to flourish among the "Cape Malay" population.

European Expansion

Cape Colony expansion posed difficulties for early European farmers and was often fatal for the resident Khoisan. Owning farmland became a status symbol for the Boers and soon wealthy whites bought up rich agricultural land in the valleys just beyond Cape Town. Poorer Boers were forced to trek farther into the interior. They obtained cattle and sheep from rival Khoisan by either warfare or trading, but lacked the necessary labor to work the vast expanses of farmland they claimed. Displaced Khoisan were understandably unwilling to work for the invaders; they preferred to retaliate by raiding white farms and stealing back their cattle. The Boers, in turn, formed their own militia "commandos" and hunted the Khoisan "Bushmen" to near extinction.

Ongoing warfare with Boer colonists forced many Khoisan to retreat north into the arid desert. Those who fled later became known as the Kora, Oorlams and Griqua. Many of these groups were joined by freed or runaway slaves and whites rejected by colonial society. The mixed-race renegades were able to maintain a measure of independence as they raided the interior on horseback. Khoisan who weren't killed or forced to flee were subjugated as underpaid workers on Boer farms. Khoisan allowed to stay on newly claimed Boer land were paid very little and ended up assimilating into the Dutch culture of their masters. They, along with the descendents of slaves imported from the east, laid the foundations for the future "Cape Coloured."

As the colony expanded farther east they encountered a more formidable opponent. The Xhosa, the southernmost Nguni-speaking peoples, densely populated the fertile region beyond the Gamtoos River, present day Jeffreys Bay. At the same time that the Dutch Boers were moving east, the Xhosa were expanding west in search of more land for their growing population. The Xhosa had heard of white settlers in the far southwestern Cape, but initially did not view their presence with much alarm. They saw the new white colonists as fellow pastoralists, who, like

the Khoisan before them, could in due course be absorbed into the growing Xhosa society. The collision of these two expanding peoples exploded into conflict over grazing land and cattle in the late 1770s, leading to the outbreak of the first of nine so-called Frontier Wars that would ravage the Eastern Cape throughout the 1800s. Both the Xhosa and the frontier Boers suffered tremendously in these early wars. Sore from losses to the Xhosa, lack of support from the colony and resenting heavy VOC taxes, the Boer trekkers rebelled. They expelled all VOC officials and established short-lived independent governments in interior towns such as Swellendam and Graaff-Reinet.

The Brits Take Over

British seizure of the Cape Colony from the Dutch in 1795 was more a defensive than offensive move. Napoleon Bonaparte was making great strides across Europe and the British did not want to lose the strategic African port to the French. However by the time Napoleon was defeated, the British decided to stay on as the colonial power for other geostrategic and political reasons, not the least of which was pressure from abolitionists and missionaries.

The change in colonial administration meant a social and economic transformation in the Cape. Missionaries flooded into the country to "modernize" the African populations and soon became champions of the plight of slaves and Africans. British liberal reforms included the abolition of slavery in the Cape Colony in 1834. More than any other reform, Boers in the Cape saw abolition as a direct attack on their rights and way of life. Poor Boers were unable to afford to pay full wages for workers, and wealthy Boers resented the fact that they weren't properly compensated for their lost "property." In their frustration, many Boers began to distance themselves from British colonial power and traveled east.

The presence of a standing British army in the Cape was initially met with mixed reactions by frontier Boers who were in losing battles with the Xhosa in the east. The British sent reinforcements to stabilize the frontier and support white settlers. Prior to British occupation, the Frontier Wars between the Xhosa and Boers were largely fought as a type of guerilla warfare. The Xhosa were shocked by the organization and strength of the British army and were driven east of the

Fish River, while Boers applauded British colonial expansion and the clearing of new land for white settlement. But after farther extension of the colony's boundary in 1835, the British came to realize that they could not just eradicate all Xhosa, and probably more importantly, did not want the administrative costs of a new province. They handed part of the annexed land back to the Xhosa a year later. The relinquished land was unforgivable in the eyes of the Trekboers, who packed their wagons and headed north to join their Boer brothers in the Great Trek.

Nguni Kingdoms and Mfecane

As the British were solidifying their colonial rule in the west, warring northern Nguni kingdoms were vying for dominance in the east. Throughout the 1700s, a number of chiefdoms began to expand, subjugating smaller chiefdoms and absorbing them into their ranks. These growing kingdoms required increased land for grazing pastures. The Portuguese presence as a new profitable trading partner to the north increased the impetus for heightened competition over the region's resources. By the end of the 1700s three major military states reigned – the Ngwane (later known as the Swazis), the Ndwandwe and the Mthethwa.

Severe drought at the end of the century plunged the region into bitter warfare for decades. These tumultuous years became known as the mfecane (Zulu for "the crushing") and forever changed the eastern shores of South Africa. Violence intensified between 1816-1819 and the Ngwane, under King Sobhuza, were expelled north of the Pongola River and established what today is one of the longest reigning monarchies in Africa: Swaziland. The Ndwandwe and the Mthethwa remained for the final showdown. With the death of the Mthethwa leader Dingiswayo, the Ndwandwe appeared victorious. However, a new leader, Shaka, king of the smaller Zulu tribe incorporated into the Mthethwa federation, soon rose to challenge Ndwandwe domination. As a former commander in Dingiswayo's army, Shaka proved to be a skilled and ruthless military force. His highly trained regiments defeated their

enemies and drove the broken Ndwandwe from the lowlands. They fled across the Drakensburg Mountains spreading death and destruction throughout the Highveld, the Zulu army nipping at their heels.

Difaqane in the Highveld

The reverberations of the mfecane were soon felt throughout the interior, giving rise to the difaqane (Sotho for "the scattering"). In the early 1800s, numerous Sotho and Tswana chiefdoms populated the Highveld in small, quasi-urban stone-walled settlements. Their sophisticated economic and political organization far outstripped that of their

OVERVIEW

militarized Nguni neighbors. They were skilled craftsmen and engaged in long-distance trade with other southern African societies. But all that came to an end with the spread of the difaqane. Attacks from renegade bands of Nguni warriors including the notorious Ndebele clan led by Mzilikazi, as well as far-reaching factions of Shaka Zulu's army, wreaked havoc on the people of the Highveld. Thousands of Sotho and Tswana were killed and displaced. Those who did not perish fled west or took to the hills for sanctuary.

The BaMokoteli clan of the Southern Sotho took refuge on the mountain plateau of Thaba Bosiu in the Drakensberg Mountains. From their elevated haven the great Moshoeshoe proved to be an adept leader and statesman. He bolstered his numbers by offering protection to smaller Southern Sotho chiefdoms and incorporated them into his kingdom. He made strategic alliances with white missionaries and appealed to them for horses and firepower in order to protect his people. Moshoeshoe was a skilled diplomat and sent gifts and tribute to appease the mighty Shaka and drove out other Nguni aggressors from his impenetrable stronghold. The growth of Moshoeshoe's powerful Sotho kingdom brought a measure of stability to the mountain region. However, soon another belligerent force invaded the highlands – white Voortrekkers hungry for land.

The Great Trek

Boer resentment of British colonial administration in the Cape had steadily grown throughout the early 1800s. The imposition of the English language and the abolition of slavery were seen as direct affronts to the Boer way of life. The apparent inability or unwillingness of the British to extend the borders of the colony eastward and provide more land to Boer farmers proved to be the final straw. Fueled by a desire for land and freedom from British control, the Boers packed their wagons and began the Great Trek into the interior in the 1830s and 1840s. The great exodus of Boers from the Cape became a romanticized moment in history, when Trekboers became pioneering "Voortrekkers" (meaning "front trekkers") and invaded the Highveld of present-day Orange Free State and the Transvaal.

Unbeknownst to the Voortrekkers, their Great Trek coincided with the difaqane. Land recently or temporarily depopulated due to violence was seen as free for the taking. Voortrekkers were able to exploit hostilities between tribes to their own benefit and easily found displaced tribes willing to ally with them against their Ndebele and Zulu aggressors. It was only with the help of these allies that bands of Voortrekkers defeated the Ndebele near present-day Pretoria, pushed them north into Zimbabwe, and in their wake settled in the Transvaal.

Battle for Natal

While some Voortrekkers settled around Bloemfontein and Pretoria, others continued eastward into the fertile lowveld of present-day Natal. Under King Shaka, the Zulus had previously tolerated the presence of white British settlers and gave them leave to build the small settlement of Port Natal (now Durban) in 1824. But in 1828 Shaka's half-brother Dingane assassinated him and usurped the Zulu throne. Dingane lacked the military deftness and leadership qualities of his brother, but it is uncertain if even the mighty Shaka could have better negotiated the Boer invasion.

Dingane initially appeared deceptively welcoming to the Boers migrants, only to unleash his regiments on a delegation of invaders led by Voortrekker leader Piet Retief in early 1838. Later that year the Boers retaliated. Protected behind a tight circle of wagons, the Boers used their superior weaponry to mow down more than 3,000 Zulus. The disastrous Battle of Blood River was a decisive battle and an important victory for the Boers as it reinforced the Voortrekker delusions of pioneer destiny. Dingane's army was weakened as it fled north and the Boers declared their new republic of Natalia, laying claim to the British settlement in Durban and establishing Pietermaritzburg as their capital. However this republic was short-lived and the British seized Natal from the Boers in 1842. Embittered Voortrekkers, refusing to live under British rule, recrossed the Drakensberg Mountains and returned to the Orange Free State.

The Zulus, having retreated north, deliberately avoided further conflict with their white neighbors to the south. After the Battle of Blood River, civil war had broken out in the Zulu kingdom and in 1840 King Dingane was killed. Under rule of his brother, Mpande, the Zulu kingdom diverted their attention away from the British and instead focused on strengthening their northern boundary, largely at the expense of the Swazis.

The British were quick to develop their new colony of Natal and established a lucrative sugar cane industry based around Durban in the 1860s. Unable to persuade Zulus to toil on their plantations, they began importing thousands of indentured laborers from India, laying the foundations of KwaZulu-Natal's large Indian population.

Boer Republics

In the 1850s, the Boers established two independent republics – the Oranje-Vrijstaat (Orange Free State) and the Zuid-Afrikaansche Republiek (ZAR), claiming vast expanses of land as their own. In theory, territorial claims encompassed present day Gauteng, the North West Province, Limpopo, Mpumalanga and the Free State. Yet the reality of their jurisdiction was much more limited.

Moshoeshoe's kingdom meted out early embarrassing defeats to the Boers who tried to encroach on the expanding Sotho empire. But a series of subsequent wars chipped away at Sotho

OVERVIEW

territory. In 1868, Moshoeshoe was forced to request British protection to save the remnants of his mountain kingdom from complete annihilation. Boer attempts to wrest control of the northern regions of the ZAR from the powerful Pedi kingdom were less successful. The Pedi-Boer War of 1876 nearly bankrupted the young ZAR republic. A year later the British annexed the weakened ZAR, and began its own military campaign against the Pedi stronghold in the north. With the help of the neighboring Swazis, the British were able to overpower the Pedi and usher in colonial domination.

The Boers refused to be subjected to British rule yet again and rose in revolt in 1880, in what later became referred to as the First Anglo-Boer War or the Transvaal War of Independence. In a decisive battle in 1881, the Boers regained control of the ZAR. Soon, the discovery of gold in the Witwatersrand and the heavy taxes they levied on the gold mining industry afforded the ZAR with a powerful standing army that sent punitive military expeditions against the remaining African chiefdoms that defied Boer authority. By the end of the century, the Boers had conquered the northern Venda and made good on their territorial claims as far north as the Limpopo River.

Despite the setback in the First Anglo-Boer War, the British continued their campaign towards federation. The Zulu kingdom was seen as the last standing African impediment to complete colonial control. In 1879 the British army invaded Zululand. Zulu king Cetshwayo sent the full might of his army against the British and won a handful of decisive battles. But the Zulu forces were no match for the thousands of British reinforcements that flooded the region and captured King Cetshwayo. The British implemented its tried and true practice of divide and rule and the mighty Zulu kingdom was reduced into powerless artificial chieftaincies.

All That Glitters is Gold... And Diamonds

The discovery of a shiny pebble near Kimberley in the western Orange Free State in 1869 forever changed the South African interior. The promise of diamonds attracted hordes of money-hungry prospectors who flocked to the region in hopes of striking it big. However, before the Boers could capitalize on the diamond fortune in their republic, the British convinced the resident Griqua to request protection from Boer advances. In one fell swoop, the British established Griqualand West and brought under British control the world's largest diamond mine of the day. Soon the infamous imperialist Cecil Rhodes consolidated ownership of the diamond mines and became the world's greatest diamond baron.

The harsh working and living conditions of the Kimberley diamond mines set the future standard for a system of migrant labor that persisted throughout the next century. Barrack-style, single-sex dorms were set up for black migrant laborers recruited from far and wide to work in the dangerous depths of the mines. White prospectors were often given less dangerous jobs and employed as managers. Many Pedi and Zulu traveled to the diamond mines in hopes of earning enough money to buy weapons to defend their kingdoms against Boer and British attacks. Wages were kept low to deter migration of entire families to mining towns, perpetuating a system

where men were forced to migrate alone to earn money and then return intermittently to their women and children who remained behind in rural areas.

The Boer republics soon recovered from their loss of the diamond mines when large deposits of gold were discovered deep within the reefs of the Witwatersrand near Johannesburg in 1886. The subsequent gold rush transformed the country as thousands of prospectors from other parts of the colony as well as from Europe and North America flooded into the region. Johannesburg soon boomed as southern Africa's wealthiest and largest city. The influx of "uitlanders" (foreigners) and wealthy British mine owners into the ZAR undermined the Boer's already tenuous control of the republic. To deal with their insecurity, the Boer government levied heavy taxes on the mining industry, restricted voting rights only to the Boer population and instated a series of laws that controlled the movement of black African miners.

The British resented Boer control over the wealth of the Witwatersrand. Uitlanders resented the heavy taxes and their lack of rights in the Boer republic. Forever driven by imperial pursuits, diamond baron Cecil Rhodes, then Prime Minister of the Cape Colony, colluded with gold miners in the Transvaal to overthrow the ZAR government in 1895. The Jameson Raid coup attempt failed horribly and Rhodes was soon forced to resign as Prime Minister. The coup attempt made ZAR President Paul Kruger acutely aware of British designs for his republic. He convinced the Orange Free State to enter into a military alliance, and with assistance from German suppliers, Kruger began a campaign of mass armament. In 1899 he issued an ultimatum to the British Empire to withdraw colonial troops from the border region. When they refused, Kruger declared war.

South African War

In 1899 the Boer republics declared war on the British Cape Colony and Natal. A highly mobile Boer army had several early successes capturing towns such as Ladysmith, Mafikeng and Kimberley.

However, the Boers could not have anticipated the amount of resources that Britain was willing to put into South Africa. Thousands of British Imperial reinforcements were shipped in to relieve its besieged cities and overtake Boer capitals. By the end of the war, Britain imported some half a million troops to secure the region.

Outnumbered, Boers fought as bands of commandos using guerilla-style warfare against the Imperial Army. But ruthless British scorched earth tactics and the use of unsanitary concentration camps to detain Boer women, children and black Africans proved devastating. An estimated 40,000 people perished from disease in the concentration camps. Both sides had employed black scouts and spies. However the majority of blacks sided with the British, hoping for better treatment if they prevailed.

Boer forces were finally subdued by 1902. With the signing of the Peace of Vereeniging, the ZAR was renamed the Transvaal and, along with the Orange Free State, became property of the British Empire. Notably, this peace treaty excluded the possibility that any part of southern Africa would belong to the African populations.

Union and Segregation

In 1910, the British finally realized their dreams of federation and consolidated their colonies as the Union of South Africa. Unity was tenuous, however, and the British remained preoccupied with placating Boer discontent and inferiority complexes. Language in the Union agreement introduced racial segregation and paved the way for a series of discriminatory laws.

OVERVIEW

Early in the century, public health measures were used as justification to clear black populations from city centers and relocate them in newly designated African "locations," forming the first government-sponsored townships in South Africa. The Native Lands Act of 1913 restricted land ownership along racial lines, reserving a mere 7 percent of land for African occupation. Africans were pushed off designated white land unless they were in direct employment of the landowners. The 1923 Native Urban Areas Act aimed to further remove blacks from city centers. Housing and labor was segregated and pass laws severely limited African movement within cities. To curtail black political mobilization and demands on the state, the 1927 Native Administration Act defused national organization and decentralized political power to chiefs in African reserves. Cooperative chiefs and headmen were appointed as the sole intermediaries between the state and African society.

African and Indian Mobilization

Early missionaries established schools for Africans throughout the country, and by the turn of the century, a growing African educated elite class was well versed in British law and customs. Acutely aware of their political exclusion in the formation of the Union of South Africa, a small group of Africans came together in the outskirts of Bloemfontein in 1912 to form the first modern African national political party, the South African Native National Congress (SANNC). The party later changed its name to the African National Congress (ANC) in 1923. Workers unions served as a vehicle for national organization, protesting segregation, poor working conditions and the imposition of a colour bar, which reserved high paying jobs for whites only. Some politicized Africans also began to take to Communist ideals and formed the South African Communist Party (SACP).

As Africans became more politicized, so too did the oppressed Indian population in the east. Indians were well established in Natal, but lacked cohesive unity as a minority population. Indians had come to South Africa under a variety of situations. Some had been imported as indentured laborers on sugar plantations beginning in the 1860s. Others came as free laborers, merchants, businessmen or on holiday. Regardless of their status or background, all Indians were treated as second-class citizens. In 1893, a young Indian lawyer named Mohandas Gandhi arrived in South Africa and embarked on a journey that would forever change his life, his country and the Indian minority in South Africa. After he was expelled from a train in Pietermaritzburg, the racism and prejudice Indians in South Africa faced ignited a fire of social justice in Gandhi. He mobilized the Indian population and led them in a non-violent campaign of protest against registration and pass laws. In return, he and thousands of Indians were beaten and imprisoned for defying the government.

Afrikaner Nationalism

In the early years of the 20th century, a wave of Afrikaner nationalism swept over the country. Beginning in the late 1800s, the Boer intellectuals in the Cape Colony began to refer to themselves as Afrikaners and campaigned for the recognition of the Afrikaans language as separate from Dutch and on par with English. After the South African War, Afrikaners were determined to ensure the protection of separate identity; language and culture would be protected by law. A secret society of white Afrikaner men, the Broederbond, formed to infiltrate national power circles and advance Afrikaner interests in politics. Poor Boer farmers whose livelihoods were destroyed during the war were especially concerned with defining themselves as superior to the coloured and black populations. They demanded protection against the rising black elite as well as cultural insulation from the assimilating forces of the British Empire. The Union government obliged with policies that reserved better education, employment and housing for whites.

Afrikaner nationalists began making considerable political headway when General J. B. M. Hertzog formed the racially conservative National Party (NP) in 1914. The NP had close ties with the Afrikaner cultural movement, and with mainly Afrikaner support, won the 1924 national elections. Reassured by his victory, Hertzog developed a political platform based on racial domination and independence from the British Empire. But when he allied with more moderate political forces to form the United Party, ultra-conservative factions split from the NP. Under the religious and political leadership of Dutch Reformed Church minister D.F. Malan, the Purified National Party was born.

The rise of the Nazi threat in Europe caused

fractures in the ruling United Party government. British South Africans were largely in favor of supporting the Allies. Afrikaner nationalists advocated for non-involvement. Many Afrikaners could sympathize with the Nazis' agenda of white supremacy and the idea of the chosen race, and as ardent anti-imperialists, wanted nothing to do with helping the British Empire. This wartime tension split apart the new United Party, and Hertzog was deposed for his views on the war. Jan Christiaan Smuts, a seasoned soldier, became Prime Minister of South Africa for a second time and led the country into WWII. Hertzog's ousting from the coalition undermined the party's claims that they represented Afrikaners, and radical pro-Fascist military groups emerged in protest, such as the ultra-conservative Ossewabrandwag (OB), which targeted and sabotaged South African army posts.

One thing both British and Afrikaner South Africans could agree on, however, was that they did not want to give blacks guns. Non-whites served only in non-combat roles during the war. But with whites away at war, the booming wartime economy allowed many blacks to step into manufacturing jobs previously reserved only for whites. Rapid urbanization and organization of strikes for improved labor conditions accompanied the transition. Postwar white backlash against the growing affluence of the black population along with Smuts' seeming inability to solve the labor shortage and control black urbanization led to the election of Malan's ultra-conservative National Party.

Beginning of Apartheid

The National Party narrowly won the 1948 election on its platform of apartheid (literally meaning "apartness" in Afrikaans). Building upon past racially charged legislation, it advocated for separate development of the races and for each race to take control of its own culture and management. Strict, centrally enforced segregation through legislation would ensure this separateness. Interracial marriage was first to go, followed by the devastating Population Registration Act in 1950, which classified people according to their race, dividing them into white and non-white and then further subdividing non-whites into coloureds (mixed-race), Indians, and "Bantu" (black). Following the tried and true tactic of divide and rule, the black population was further divided into ethnic groups: Xhosa, Zulu, Tswana, Venda, Sotho, etc., as a deliberate attempt to weaken national African unity. The Group Areas Act then determined where certain races were allowed to live. These two acts caused enormous confusion and misery, with many uncertain cases and split families.

The NP attempted to win the support of the coloured population by deeming the Western Cape a "coloured preference area," ensuring favor for coloured people over blacks in employment. However, Group Areas still proved devastating for coloured and Indian communities. As blacks were forcibly removed to remote African "homelands" and newly developed townships, an estimated 600,000 coloured and Indian people were also removed from their homes in the city centers of Cape Town, Durban, Johannesburg and elsewhere.

Group Areas legislation was reinforced by the 1952 Urban Areas Act to control urbanization. Strict laws were imposed to determine who was eligible to live in urban townships and work in urban areas. Africans had to show that they had either been born in town or had worked continuously for one employer for 10 years. Those who did not qualify were "endorsed out," with a mark made in their ID book requiring them to leave the area and move to a rural settlement. The final straw of the first wave of apartheid measures was the 1953 Bantu Education Act. Mission schools were closed for focusing too much on English and overeducating Africans with liberal ideas. Education was transferred to state-run schools which emphasized ethnic awareness and aimed to teach blacks no more than the bare necessities needed to serve the white population.

Opposition and Protest

With the election of the National Party and the emergence of apartheid legislation, the African National Congress (ANC) resurged as a countrywide mobilizing force. ANC membership was newly emboldened by the creation of the ANC Youth League, led by the young attorney Nelson Mandela, Walter Sisulu and Oliver Tambo. Younger, radicalized Africans rejected the conciliatory tactics of the "old guard" and successfully organized mass protests. In 1952, Mandela organized the Defiance Campaign and all around the country people refused to

OVERVIEW

carry passes and thereby risked imprisonment. Rural protest in the newly created homelands or "Bantustans," was also on the rise. Homeland residents denounced local chiefs as puppets of the national government and the ANC was able to garner strong support in the countryside.

The ANC was also able to make key alliances with the South African Indian Congress, the Coloured People's Congress as well as with progressive whites. National coordination of groups calling for equality and civil rights culminated with the Assembly of the People, held in Johannesburg's largest township, Soweto. Here the Freedom Charter demanding "The People Shall Govern!" was born. Its call for a non-racial South Africa remained a key element of the ANC platform over the years and much of its contents regarding equal rights were incorporated into the new Constitution of South Africa.

However by the late 1950s, some activists felt that the ANC was being undermined by coordination with non-Africans and that the party's tactics were not radical enough to exact change. In 1959, more radical factions of the ANC split to form the Pan Africanist Congress (PAC). Led by Robert Sobukwe, the PAC advocated for liberation for Africans by Africans and adopted a Programme of Action. In 1960 a PAC-organized anti-pass demonstration attracted international attention and outcry. A group of unarmed civilians had left their passes at home and non-violently presented themselves at a police station in the town of Sharpeville. Reactionary police opened fire, killing nearly 70 protestors, many of whom where shot in the back as they tried to flee.

In the aftermath of the Sharpeville Massacre, the government began to clamp down on opposition. Under the auspices of the Suppression of Communism Act, the ANC and PAC were banned and their members were forced to go into exile or underground. Public gatherings were outlawed; people were detained without trial and often beaten in police custody. A year later, the National Party realized their dream of independence and the Union of South Africa succeeded from the British Commonwealth of Nations and became the Republic of South Africa.

While not abandoning organized protest and mass actions, the ANC and the PAC finally agreed that an armed struggle was necessary. Mandela, Walter Sisulu and Joe Slovo of the South African Communist Party formed the military wing of the ANC called Umkhonto we Sizwe (meaning "Spear of the Nation") and began a series of sabotage campaigns, targeting government offices and police stations. The PAC's military wing, Poqo (Xhosa for "pure" or "alone"), adopted more violent tactics and aimed to destabilize the country by any means necessary, including murder. In 1963 the high command of Umkhonto we Sizwe was arrested at a farm outside of Johannesburg. Mandela, Sisulu, Govan Mbeki and six others were tried in the famous Rivonia Treason Trial, and the majority of those charged were sentenced to life imprisonment on Robben Island.

Black Consciousness

The dark days of repression in the 1960s left open a political power vacuum that organized labor and radicalized youth would come to fill. Students emerged as a powerful political vanguard as the Black Consciousness Movement swept through universities and intellectual circles. Led by the charismatic medical student Steve Biko, Black Consciousness rekindled black determination to realize freedom and equality without the help of whites. Within the context of the liberation struggle, "black" came to refer to anyone non-white, including the coloured and Indian populations.

Workers unions also created crucial openings for defiant strikes and protest. However white voices continued to dominate schools and labor. In 1969, black students broke away from the multiracial National Union of South African Students and formed their own South African Students Organization (SASO). In 1973 the Black Allied Workers Union was launched. Student protests and union strikes had a measure of success, but increased government repression peaked after student protest turned into student insurrection.

The Soweto Student Uprising marked a turning point in the struggle against apartheid. Sparked by inequalities in Bantu Education and the introduction of Afrikaans (considered the language of the oppressor) as a teaching medium in black schools, the South African Students Movement (SASM) organized school boycotts and a march through the streets of Soweto. Police first used tear gas to disperse the crowd, but then opened fire, killing a 12-year-old boy. Violence ensued. Riots spread throughout the country during the following year. Attacks on government property, police informants, municipal beer halls and local shebeens reached a new level of intensity as students clashed

Black Homelands

CISKEI — Independent Homeland

Lebowa — Dependent Homeland

········· — Provincial Borders

BOTSWANA

VENDA

Lebowa

Gazankulu

MOZAMBIQUE

TRANSVAAL

KwaNdebele

Kangwane

Johannesburg

BOPHUTHATSWANA

SWAZILAND

NAMIBIA

Upington

Kimberley

ORANGE FREE STATE

Qwaqwa

NATAL

KwaZulu

LESOTHO

Durban

Atlantic Ocean

CAPE

TRANSKEI

Indian Ocean

CISKEI East London

Cape Town

Mossel Bay

Port Elizabeth

N

200mi
500km

OVERVIEW

with police. President Vorster responded with increased repression. Hundreds died, people were imprisoned and beaten, and many organizations were banned. Black Consciousness organizer Steve Biko was arrested, tortured and killed at the hands of the police.

Homelands

Central to apartheid policies of "separate development" was the promotion of ethnic reserves, or "homelands." Blacks, who comprised over 80 percent of the population, were restricted to roughly 14 percent of the land, unless they were in direct employment of whites. In 1963 the Transkei, in what today is the Eastern Cape, was the first of 10 created "autonomous" homelands to be granted self-governance. The theory was that blacks would become self-sufficient in homelands independent of South Africa, however the reality was much different. Homelands largely did not have enough resources to support their growing populations and became dumping grounds for unemployment and poverty. Migrant laborers continued to be dependent on the economic opportunities in South African cities. Foreign investment was prohibited and homelands

lacked the infrastructure and industry needed to generate gainful employment.

In the end, only four of the 10 homelands became independent states – Transkei (1976), Bophuthatswana (1977), Venda (1979) and Ciskei (1981). The black population, regardless of whether they lived in the homelands or in urban squatter settlements and townships, were effectively stripped of their citizenship and became foreigners in South Africa. Many local African leaders with political aspirations embraced the homeland structure and were complicit in the system for their own political gain, such as Zulu Chief Mangosuthu Buthelezi in KwaZulu. However the international community refused to recognize the independent status of these "puppet states," which were known to be politically fabricated products of South Africa's racist agenda.

State of Emergency, State of War

Economic recession, increased opposition and international pressure during the 1980s marked the beginning of the end of apartheid. Internally, the unemployment rate for black Africans skyrocketed, fueling the political turmoil that engulfed the decade. Pass laws and influx control proved increasingly unable to slow rapid urbanization; townships and squatter settlements grew exponentially. Anti-government resistance expanded. Unions emerged as an effective mobilizing force and a vanguard for resistance as they organized protests and "stayaways" where participants would refuse to go to work and stay at home. The Black Sash, a group of white women of conscious, campaigned against human rights abuses in the country. Civic organizations increased collaboration and unity, culminating in the formation of the United Democratic Front (UDF) formed in the Cape Flats in 1983.

Violence increased both on the part of militant youth "comrades" and local vigilantes opposed to national civic organization. Vigilante groups aimed to curtail the influence of the ANC and the UDF, and to enforce loyalty to local black township and homeland authorities. Black on black violence was especially severe in KwaZulu-Natal, where the Inkatha National Cultural Liberation Movement attacked ANC supporters. Evidence later surfaced that the South African security services were covertly bankrolling Inkatha in support of its destabilizing violence.

In the face of violence and opposition, the South African government, led by President P.W. Botha, both increased repression and eased some "petty apartheid" measures in the hopes of co-opting Indians, coloureds and black allies. In 1984, a white-only referendum established the new "Tricameral Parliament," which presumed to extend representation to the coloured and Indian populations while expressly not extending further representation to blacks. However neither the Indians nor the coloureds could be fully bought out. Conciliatory measures broke with the core principals of apartheid and caused a backlash by some right-wingers, leading to the rise of white paramilitary factions such as the Afrikaner Weerstandsbeweging (AWB or Afrikaner Resistance Movement).

In 1985, Botha declared a State of Emergency, the first of many in the coming years. State security services amped up their repression of the "black menace." In the midst of increased criticism, the state kept a tight grip on media and imposed an information blackout within the country. At the same time, South Africa continued to fight losing, expensive and increasingly unpopular battles against the communist "red menace" in Angola and Mozambique. The diffusion of Cold War tensions by the late 1980s undermined South Africa's claim as the last bastion of anti-communism in the region. It became increasingly popular for foreign governments to be anti-South African, and an international divestment campaign further exacerbated the economic recession. It is estimated that the South African economy lost roughly one third of its strength due to divestment.

Dismantling Apartheid

The momentum of the tumultuous 1980s made radical transformation inevitable. By the end of the decade the ailing Botha stepped down and F.W. De Klerk replaced him as president. The younger De Klerk accepted that reform was necessary. Within the first year of his presidency, he released political prisoners and unbanned political associations, including the ANC, PAC, and the Communist Party. On February 11, 1990, Nelson Mandela became a free man after 27 years in prison. ANC leadership returned from exile to join him and the armed struggle was suspended in exchange for negotiations. Over the course of the next few years, De Klerk repealed the racist laws that formed the cornerstones of apartheid.

In 1991, the Convention for a Democratic South Africa (CODESA) convened with representatives of various political groups. However violence and disagreement on basic principals continued to mar negotiations. The ANC and the UDF struggled to transform their liberation movements into viable political parties. Cooperation between ANC leaders educated abroad while in exile and those who had remained in the country to struggle and languish in prison proved challenging. Factions within the National Party found it difficult to comprehend the idea of a single, unified state, and there was much anxiety and concern over the protection of wealth and private property. The KwaZulu-based Inkatha Freedom Party threatened non-participation as it continued to attack the Xhosa-controlled ANC and its supporters. Conservative factions of the National Party split and aligned with the AWB neo-Nazi paramilitaries who physically invaded the negotiations in 1993. Between 1990-1994 it is estimated that roughly 14,000 died due to political violence. Despite the upheaval and interruptions, Mandela and De Klerk's role in the negotiations won them the Nobel Peace Prize in 1993. In 1994, negotiations concluded with South Africa's first-ever non-racial democratic elections.

Rebuilding the Rainbow Nation

In April 1994, millions of South Africans of all races and walks of life waited in long lines to cast their votes in South Africa's historic democratic election. In the end, the ANC won 62.6 percent of the national vote. The National Party won 20 percent and the Inkatha Freedom Party 10.5 percent. As leader of the ANC, Nelson Mandela was inaugurated as president. In an effort to continue movement towards reconciliation and unity, Mandela formed a coalition with other political parties to create the interim Government of National Unity. The interim government was charged with writing a new constitution. F.W. De Klerk and Thabo Mbeki were appointed as deputy presidents. Former homelands were dissolved and incorporated into the newly delineated South Africa.

Along with the presidency, Mandela inherited a plethora of challenges. Externally, Mandela sought to bolster the failing national economy by rebuilding international relationships and encouraging reinvestment from Europe, the Americas and Asia. Internally, he faced racial inequalities, poverty, and a crisis in housing, health, and education. A Reconstruction and Development Program (RDP) was initiated to build affordable housing and address deficiencies in healthcare and access to clean water. Restrictions on land ownership were lifted and the government set up a program of subsidies and loans for people to purchase land. The Restitution of Land Rights Act of 1994 allowed people to reclaim land that had been seized from them since the 1913 Native Lands Act. Education was desegregated. Quotas were imposed on the business sector to promote affirmative action hiring practices.

Additional challenges were posed by the rising health concerns surrounding HIV. The first death from HIV/AIDS was recorded in South Africa in 1982. By the mid-1990s, tens of thousands of people were suffering from the disease. Miseducation, social stigma and the perpetuation of South Africa's migrant labor system all contributed to the spread of the epidemic.

In 1996 the new South African constitution was signed. In an unprecedented campaign of public participation and collaboration, the South African constitution became one of the most progressive the world has seen. The Women's National Coalition was especially instrumental in ensuring that the rights of women were institutionalized, and that protections against discrimination based on gender, pregnancy and marital status were codified under law. They also successfully lobbied for a large percentage of women to hold parliamentary seats in what was previously a highly patriarchal government.

By the end of his tenure, Mandela emerged as a skilled statesman who garnered international respect for his humbleness, dedication and commitment to reconciliation and unity over all else. Though many of his efforts to address inequalities fell short of their goals, in his brief time in office he set an exceptionally high standard for future presidents to live up to and restored respect for the South African government at home and abroad.

Truth and Reconciliation

In 1995, the Government of National Unity established a Truth and Reconciliation Commission (TRC) to investigate and expose human rights violations and crimes under apartheid. Archbishop Desmond Tutu was charged to lead the commission in an effort to confront, understand, forgive and hopefully unite a fractured and pained society. Amnesty was offered to perpetrators who were willing to come forward and confess their crimes in their entirety. Victims were invited to tell their stories, confront their aggressors, extend forgiveness and apply for reparations. Those who did not confess to past crimes faced the possibility of criminal prosecution.

Chilling details about the actions of the police and security forces as well as heinous individual crimes surfaced. However critics of the process point out that few high-level government officials came forward, which for some cheapened the whole process. Former President P.W. Botha was notably absent. Others were opposed to amnesty for murderers, and problems with the allocation of reparations left many unfulfilled. Yet the TRC remains an unprecedented step towards national reconciliation and healing.

The New South Africa

In 1999, Thabo Mbeki succeeded Mandela as president of the ANC. Concerns about Mbeki's ability to fill Mandela's shoes abounded, but support of the ANC actually increased and they won over 66 percent of the national vote. The New National Party collapsed. Unable to reinvent itself and garner broader, non-racial support, it ended

OVERVIEW

up receiving less than 7 percent of the vote. The new liberal Democratic Party emerged as the largest opposition, with the Inkatha Freedom Party a close third.

Though not the revered, charismatic Mandela, Mbeki proved to be an adept politician and diplomat. He appointed Jacob Zuma as his deputy president and appointed key Inkatha adversaries to prominent government positions. The cooptation of Inkatha successfully defused violence between ANC and IFP supporters. He

The Basics

CAPITAL - Pretoria (executive), Cape Town (legislative), Bloemfontein (judicial)

POPULATION - 50.1 million

LANGUAGE - Zulu 24%, Xhosa 18%, Afrikaans 13%, Sepedi 9%, English 8%, Setswana 8%, Sesotho 8%, Xitsonga 4%, other 8%

TIME ZONE - GMT +2

BORDERS - Botswana, Lesotho, Mozambique, Namibia, Swaziland, Zimbabwe

VISA - Most foreign nationals do not need to arrange for visas prior to travel and are issued entrance permits upon arrival for no charge that are valid for 90 days.

MONEY - $1 USD = R7.4, £1 GBP = R11.1, €1 EUR = R10, ¥1 JPY = R0.08

The Rand is the name of the currency used in South Africa. Many people in neighboring countries will accept Rand bills, but outside of the southern Africa region it can be difficult to exchange for other currencies.

TIPPING - 10%-15% is customary for restaurants and bars.

PHONE - Country code +27. Cell phone coverage is available throughout most of the country.

INTERNET - High speed Internet is available throughout the country, although slightly more expensive than in most developed countries. GSM modems that allow users to connect anywhere within the coverage range of a cell phone tower are quite popular.

ELECTRICITY - 220V/230V AC, 50Hz using three-pin plugs with round terminals that are not widely used outside of South Africa. European two-pin round plugs are also commonly used for smaller appliances.

EMERGENCY - Police 10111 (112 from a mobile phone), Ambulance 10177

made use of his international education while in exile and emerged as a diplomatic voice in international issues and regional African conflicts.

HIV/AIDS and corruption allegations marred Mbeki's presidency. He came under international criticism for his denial and inaction regarding the HIV/AIDS crisis. His administration was berated for its failure to implement a national treatment program and make antiretroviral medicines publically available. After his reelection in 2004, a corruption scandal forced Mbeki to dismiss his deputy president Jacob Zuma from office. Zuma's dismissal caused a split in the ANC. Rape charges against Zuma and his confession to knowingly having unprotected sex with a HIV-positive woman, coupled with his statement in court that he took a shower immediately after having sex with the woman because it "would minimise the risk of contracting the disease," did little to deter his supporters.

Infighting in the ANC led Zuma to replace Mbeki as Chairman in late 2007. His corruption charges were dismissed on a technicality, and a year later, Jacob Zuma became the third president of the Democratic South Africa. As a populist with strong ties to trade unions and the South African Communist Party, Zuma's socialist leanings, personal life and sordid history have come under constant scrutiny. However he maintains widespread support from youth and rural populations.

Looking Forward

The outlook of the rainbow nation's future prosperity is met with varying degrees of optimism and skepticism. South Africa currently faces some very serious issues, and the ability of the country to adequately address them in the coming years will weigh heavily in defining the success of the new South Africa. Serious economic, unemployment, crime and inequality problems cause many citizens to question the competence of the ruling ANC. Racial and social tensions have come a long way, but are still quite thick. Rampant corruption, HIV/AIDS and an inadequate education system are driving forces behind much of the country's shortcomings.

But for a country that created a free democracy out of the repressions of apartheid and made presidents out of its former prisoners, it has an impressive will and ability to overcome obstacles. The past two decades have been nothing short of

an amazing transition, and today there is a vibrant energy throughout the country that warrants a sense of optimism. Many city centers that were once deserted are in a full swing of regeneration. A successful hosting of the 2010 World Cup helped improve infrastructure, focused international attention on the country and promoted tourism and a sense of national pride. The younger generation that grew up within South Africa's free democracy is coming of age. They are beginning to influence the country's direction and affecting positive change. Right now is another one of South Africa's pivotal moments in history and there is much to be excited about.

GEOGRAPHY

South Africa sits at the southern tip of the African continent with a coastline that stretches nearly 3,000 kilometers along the Atlantic and Indian Oceans. The coastline spans an array of arid desert, rocky cliffs, lush forests, rolling grassy hills and marshy wetlands. The country's interior is equally varied. Much of the west and central part of the country is a vast basin of mostly dry semi-desert scrubland that gives way to rocky hills. Running along the eastern corridor is southern Africa's highest mountain range, the Drakensberg Mountains, with peaks reaching up to 3,482 meters. The Drakensberg Mountains form an iconic escarpment that transitions into grassy foothills extending to the eastern coast. The eastern coastline is a lush semi-tropical forest region that levels out into a large wetland extending into the interior near the border of Mozambique.

The country is administratively divided into nine provinces, some of which were recently formed in 1994 under the new democratically elected government. There are three capital cities within the country, each the seat of one of the branches of government. Pretoria is the executive capital, Cape Town is the legislative capital and Bloemfontein is the judicial capital. The country's smallest province by size, Gauteng, is the country's largest province by population, encompassing both Johannesburg and Pretoria. In contrast, the country's largest province by size, the Northern Cape, is the country's smallest province by population, accounting for just over two percent of South Africans.

South Africa shares its borders with six other countries, the most unique being Lesotho, which is located entirely within South Africa. Other bordering countries include Swaziland to the east and Botswana, Mozambique, Namibia, and Zimbabwe to the north.

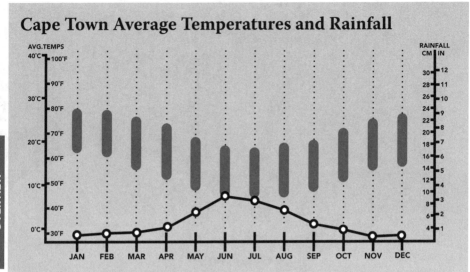

CLIMATE

South Africa is best known for its warm summers filled with sunshine but its climate is just as varied as its geography and can range from blisteringly hot desert to snow-covered mountains. Outside of these extremes, the country's climate is fairly moderate, a result of its subtropical location and proximity to the ocean. The summer season runs roughly from November to March and the winter season lasts from June through the end of August. The central and northern parts of the country receive most of their annual precipitation during the summer months while the southern coastal region tends to get most of its rainfall during the winter.

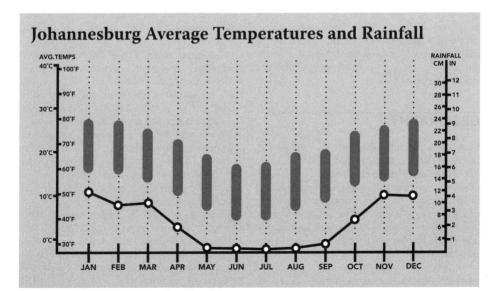

Cape Town and the surrounding area has a Mediterranean climate with comfortably warm, dry summers and afternoon temperatures around 24°C / 75°F. The winters are relatively mild with daytime temperatures around 16°C / 60°F although it gets chilly in the evenings. Frequent fog and rain are characteristic of Cape Town winters.

The Johannesburg region has a mild subtropical highland climate with summers that are similar in temperature to Cape Town and winters that are only slightly cooler, with an occasional dip below freezing over night. Almost all of the annual precipitation in this region occurs during the summer.

during apartheid are slowly fading, they remain a significant social force. The four general categories that were used to describe South African citizens during apartheid continue to be used today, but within each category are important sub-groups distinguished chiefly by language.

Africans (commonly referred to as blacks) are by far the largest and most diverse group, representing almost 80 percent of the total population. They are the descendents of the Bantu migrants who came to Southern Africa during the first few centuries A.D. Though they represent nine of the 11 official languages, they originally stem from four different linguistic

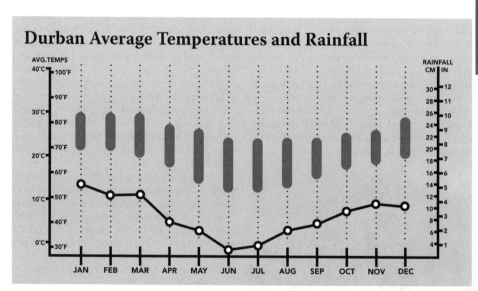

Durban touts yearlong sun and warm temperature as one of its attractions. The region's subtropical coastal climate is tempered by the ocean with occasional summer showers and a much warmer winter season, with most days topping 21°C / 70°F.

PEOPLE

Desmond Tutu is said to have coined the term "Rainbow Nation" to describe South Africa. Its population of roughly 50 million people represents a vast diversity of cultures, languages, traditions and attitudes. Though the racial divisions established

families: Nguni (Zulu, Xhosa, Ndebele and the neighboring Swazis); Sotho (Northern, Southern and Western Sotho, also called the Pedi, BaSotho and Tswana); Tsonga; and the Venda.

Zulus represent the largest ethno-linguistic group; almost a quarter of South Africans speak Zulu. The Zulu nation, concentrated on the eastern coast, underwent a cultural renaissance under apartheid and formed its own national political party, the Inkatha Freedom Party, which draws heavily on Zulu cultural pride. The second biggest group, the Xhosa, largely hails from the Eastern Cape and represents roughly 18 percent of the African population. Nelson Mandela and many other influential ANC politicians are Xhosa. The

Pedi (Northern Sotho), Tswana (Western Sotho) and BaSotho (Southern Sotho), who also form the basis of the population in the neighboring Lesotho, each account for just under 10 percent of the population. The Tsonga and Venda represent a small portion of the national African population but are prevalent in the northeastern-most part of the country.

Within these large ethno-linguistic groups there are cultural and historical differences, and strong allegiance to one's specific ancestry is common. The apartheid government tried to highlight these differences as a tactic to prevent national black unity. To counter this, African leaders have sought to encourage solidarity rather than tribalism.

"Coloured" is perhaps the most difficult category for foreign visitors to understand. Reflecting the arbitrary nature of racial division during apartheid, the term refers to South Africans of mixed-race descent. Although coloureds – about 9 percent of South Africa's total population – may trace their varied ancestry to indigenous Khoisan, African, European, or South Asian roots, a specific sense of identity within the community is strong, cemented by the common use of the Afrikaans language. Coloureds occupied a unique position during the apartheid era. They were given slightly less horrific working and living conditions than blacks but were considered inferior to whites.

The Western Cape is the only province where coloureds make up over 50 percent of the population. Cape Malays, descendents of Malaysian, Indian, Indonesian and East African slaves, are a major sub-group within the coloured population and comprise much of the Western Cape's Muslim community. Their vibrant legacy in the region can be experienced through eye-catching festivals and aromatic Cape Malay cuisine.

Whites, comprising approximately 9 percent of the population, are ethnically and culturally split between Afrikaans and English speakers. Afrikaners, who trace their roots to early Dutch, English, German and French Huguenots, began their presence in South Africa as pioneers and farmers. Today they dominate most of South Africa's rural areas and have the difficult task of balancing acknowledgment of the atrocities of the apartheid system with attempts to preserve and celebrate their own distinct language, culture and history. Much of Afrikaner rural life is heavily influenced by the teachings of the Dutch Reformed Church.

Non-Afrikaner whites include descendents of British immigrants, approximately 70,000 Jews of eastern European and German descent, and small Greek and Portuguese communities. "British" South Africans, by far the largest of this group, tend to consider themselves more liberal and secular than Afrikaners, while Afrikaners pride themselves on their strong sense of tradition.

Asians, of which 98 percent are of Indian descent, represent the smallest of South Africa's chief racial categories with a population of around 1.2 million. KwaZulu-Natal is home to the largest Indian community outside of India, many of who are the descendents of indentured laborers brought to Natal to work on sugar plantations beginning in the 1860s. The city of Durban in particular is renowned for its South Asian cultural influences. The majority of South African Indians are Hindu, though Muslims make up 20 percent of the Indian populace. Other South African Asians include a Chinese community numbering roughly 200,000.

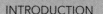

LANGUAGE

Since 1994, the Constitution of South Africa has recognized eleven languages officially and equally (prefixes are used by native speakers when referring to their own language): English, Afrikaans, Zulu (isiZulu), Xhosa (isiXhosa), Swati (siSwati), Ndebele (isiNdebele), Northern Sotho (Sepedi), Southern Sotho (Sesotho), Tswana (Setswana), Venda (Tshivenda), and Tsonga (Xitsonga). Before the dismantling of apartheid, Afrikaans and English had been the country's only official languages, Afrikaans displacing Dutch in 1925. While only spoken in the home by 8 percent of the population, English is the country's lingua franca, so except in the more rural, remote areas of South Africa, English will get you by. Afrikaans is nevertheless very present throughout the country, and is used on signs and other public postings.

There are nine indigenous languages in South Africa, and knowing the basics of a few, and where to speak them, will always be appreciated, even if your pronunciation is laughable. The indigenous languages are split into four groups: Nguni (Zulu, Xhosa, Ndebele, Swati), Sotho (Northern Sotho, Southern Sesotho and Tswana), Venda (Tshivenda) and Tsonga (Xitsonga). Most black people in South Africa speak languages in the first two groups. Nguni languages and Southern Sotho contain clicks, which can be difficult to master, but if you're planning on staying awhile in the country, Zulu, the mother tongue of South Africa's majority, can be particularly useful.

During apartheid, separate language governing bodies were created for each of the nine indigenous languages, in attempts to impose strict ethno-linguistic divisions. But after 1994, the Pan South African Language Board was established to uphold linguistic rights and promote multilingualism. Besides the official languages, there are groups of people in South Africa that speak Khoi and San languages, as well as Arabic, Hindi, Urdu, Tamil, Gujarati, Telugu and Hebrew.

CULTURE

Though discussions of South African society tend to focus on differences, certain common themes bring everyone together. One of the first things to understand about the people of South Africa is that they're used to being labeled. The lingering effects of apartheid, during which racism and inequality were institutionalized, are obvious: neighborhoods are, with some exceptions, racially designated, locals tend to refer to race frequently in conversation, and mixed-race dating is a topic of hot debate.

A blatant division between the haves and the have-nots is perhaps the largest obstacle to social integration. A stroll through Cape Town drives this point home: just minutes from the leafy, lush suburbs where well-off Capetonians reside, enormous townships cram thousands of extremely poor non-whites into neighborhoods rife with crime and poverty. Few white South Africans make an effort to visit these townships and witness what is, for the majority of their countrymen, a typical living situation. (cont. p42)

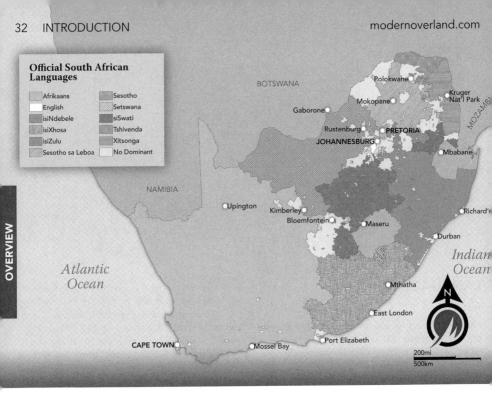

South African English:

The predominate language of business, media and government, South African English, like many former colony linguistic varieties, has a flavor all its own. While only 8 percent of the population speaks English as a first language, English is spoken as a non-native tongue by about half of the population, a fact that has contributed to the language's vibrant variety and flux. More akin to British English than American, South African English also incorporates vocabulary from the country's indigenous languages.

Babalaas	Serious hangover
Backpackers	Hostel
Bakkie	Pick-up truck
Big Five	Lion, Elephant, Buffalo, Leopard & Rhino
Biltong	Cured meat (similar to jerky)
Bonnet	Car hood
Boot	Car trunk
Braai	Barbecue
Bunny Chow	Curry stuffed in a loaf of bread
Cool Drink	Soda
Cozzie	Swimsuit
Eina!	Ouch!
Filling Station	Gas/Petrol station
Howzit	Hello/How are you
Izzit	Really
Jol	Party/Good time
Just Now	Soon
Kombi	Minivan
Lekker	Cool, lovely, delicious
Now Now	Soon (more immediate than "just now")
Pissed	Drunk
Robot	Traffic light
Rubbish	Garbage
Sharp	Everything is good
Shebeen	Informal drinking establishment
Sundowners	Sunset cocktails
Sweets	Candy
Township	Suburb (often underdeveloped living area for non-whites under apartheid)
Tuned	Told someone
Vuvuzerla	Plastic trumpet

Afrikaans:

Afrikaans is a variation of Dutch, but has undergone many transformations from the High Dutch of 17th Century Boer settlers, including incorporating some vocabulary from French, English, indigenous African languages of the Khoi and Bantu peoples and even some elements from the languages of East Asian slaves. Until 1925, English and Dutch were the official tongues of the Cape, but with the Union of South Africa, Afrikaans was recognized as its own distinct language. Today, Afrikaans is the majority language in the Northern and Western Cape, and in the Free State. Afrikaans is also spoken in nearby Namibia, where it is considered a national but not official language.

Afrikaans is the mother tongue of 80 percent of coloureds and 60 percent of whites. That said, from the late 19th century onwards the Afrikaans language was used as a means of constructing an exclusive white Afrikaner ethnic identity, and later furthering the segregationist policies of the apartheid government. During apartheid, many black South Africans saw Afrikaans, in the words of Desmond Tutu, as "the language of the oppressor." In 1976, the uprising at Soweto occurred as a reaction to the Afrikaans Medium Decree, which forced all non-white schools to implement Afrikaans as an equal language of instruction, alongside English. The sociolinguistic legacy of Afrikaans is recorded in many of South Africa's museums, but is specifically prevalent in the Western Cape city of Paarl.

OVERVIEW

Pleasantries

Hello	Hallo
Goodbye	Totsiens / Baai (informal)
Please	Asseblief
Thank you	Dankie
How are you?	Hoe gaan dit?
I'm fine	Goed
What is your name?	Wat is u naam?
My name is ___	My naam is ___
Where do you come from?	Waar kom u vandaan?
I come from ___.	Ek kom van ___ af
You're welcome	Dis 'n plesier
Good morning	Goeiemôre
Good evening	Goeienaand
Good night	Goeienag

Timing

What is the time?	Hoe laat is dit?
Today	Vandag
Yesterday	Gister
Tomorrow	Môre
Next week	Volgende week
Now	Nou
Sunday	Sondag
Monday	Maandag
Tuesday	Dinsdag
Wednesday	Woensdag
Thursday	Donderdag
Friday	Vrydag
Saturday	Saterdag

Necessities

Yes	Ja
No	Nee
Excuse me	Versikoon my
Do you have ___?	Het jy ___?
I am sorry	Ek is jammer
How much ___?	Hoeveel ___?
Where is ___?	Waar is ___?
Where is the bathroom?	Waar is die toilet?
Internet café	Internetkafee
Beach	Strand
Church	Kerk
City/Town	Stad/Dorp
Office	Kantoor
Pharmacy	Apteek
Police	Polisie
Street	Straat

Numbers

One	Een
Two	Twee
Three	Drie
Four	Vier
Five	Vyf
Six	Ses
Seven	Sewe
Eight	Ag / Agt
Nine	Nege
Ten	Tien
One Hundred	Honderd
One Thousand	Duisend

The Nguni Language Group

South Africa has four official indigenous languages that belong to the Nguni group. Historically, the pastoral Nguni, part of the larger grouping of Bantu people, slowly migrated south with their cattle from the region around the Great Lakes. All Nguni languages contain clicks, a result of historical interaction with the Khoisan people. Although they share similarities and to some extent mutual intelligibility, the Nguni language group is anything but a monolith, comprised as it is of diverse ethnicities, and a multitude of distinct languages, each with their own unique dialects.

OVERVIEW

Zulu (isiZulu):

At 24 percent, isiZulu, the language of the Zulu people, is the most widely spoken mother tongue in South Africa, and is understood by around 15 million people. Like all indigenous South African languages, isiZulu was an oral language until the 19th century, when it was written down in the Latin alphabet by European missionaries. While isiZulu can be heard throughout the country, it is primarily concentrated in KwaZulu-Natal, and also the eastern Free State, southern Mpumalanga and Gauteng.

The Zulu language is tonal, and makes use of three different click sounds – the dental (c), the alveolar (q), and the lateral (x). Sentence structure is governed by the noun.

Pleasantries

Hello	Sawubona (singular)
	Sanibonani (plural)
Goodbye	Hamba kahle (when remaining)
	Sala kahle (when leaving)
Please	Ngiyakucela
Thank you	Ngiyabonga
How are you?	Unjani? (singular)
	Ninjani? (plural)
I'm fine	Ngikhona ngiyabonga
We are fine	Sikhona
What's your name?	Ngubani igama lakho?
My name is ___	Igama lami ngu ___
Where are you from?	Uphumaphi?
I come from ___	Ngiphuma ___
Nice to meet you	Ngiyajabula ukukwazi

Necessities

Yes	Yebo
No	Cha
Excuse me	Uxolo
Water	Amanzi
Food	Ukudla
How much ___?	Kubiza malini ___?
Where is ___?	Likuphi ___?
Where is the bathroom?	Likuphi ikamelo lokugezela?
Would you like to dance with me?	Uthanda ukudansa nami?
Mobile phone	Umakhalekhukhwini / icell
Bus	Ibhasi
Train	Isitimela

Timing

What's the time?	Sikhathisini?
Today	Namhlanje
Yesterday	Izolo
Tomorrow	Kusasa
Sunday	Isonto
Monday	uMsombuluko
Tuesday	uLwesibili
Wednesday	uLwesithathu
Thursday	uLwesine
Friday	uLwesihlanu
Saturday	uMgqibelo

Numbers

One	Kunye
Two	Isibili
Three	Kuthathu
Four	Okune
Five	Isihlanu
Six	Isithupha
Seven	Isikhombisa
Eight	Isishiyagalombili
Nine	Isishiyagalolunye
Ten	Ishumi
One Hundred	Ikhulu
One Thousand	Inkulungwane

Xhosa (isiXhosa)

Spoken as a mother tongue by approximately 8 million South Africans, isiXhosa (pronounced with a lateral click) is the country's second largest language. IsiXhosa is primarily concentrated in the Eastern Cape, but can also be heard in the Western Cape, particularly in and around Cape Town.

Pleasantries

Hello	Molo (singular)
	Molweni (plural)
How are you?	Kunjani? (singular)
	Ninjani? (plural)
Please	Nceda
Thank you	Ndiyabulela
I am well	Ndiphilile
What is your name?	Ngubani igama lakho?
What is this?	Yintoni le?

Timing

Sunday	Cawe
Monday	Mvulo
Tuesday	Lwesibini
Wednesday	Lwesithathu
Thursday	Lwesine
Friday	Lwesihlanu
Saturday	Mgqibelo

Necessities

Yes	Ewe
No	Hayi
Help	Nceda
I am sorry	Ndicela uxolo
I love you	Ndiya kuthanda
Internet	i-inthanethi

Numbers

One	Nye
Two	Mbini
Three	Ntathu
Four	Ne
Five	Ntlanu
Six	Ntandathu
Seven	Xhenxe
Eight	Bhozo
Nine	Lithoba
Ten	Lishuymi

Swati (siSwati):

SiSwati is the primary language of Swaziland, and along with English, is an official language of the kingdom. siSwati is for the most part mutually intelligible with isiZulu, but because of historical clashes and more recent projects of standardization, siSwati has developed its own distinct linguistic identity. Apart from inside the kingdom, the siSwati language can also be heard in the eastern regions of Mpumalanga.

Pleasantries

Hello	Sawubona (singular)
	Sanibonani (plural)
How are you?	Unjani?
I am fine	Ngikhona
Goodbye	Sala kahle
Have a safe journey	Ube neluhambo loluphephile (singular)
	Nibe neluhambo loluphephile (plural)

Timing

Sunday	LiSontfo
Monday	uMsombuluko
Tuesday	Lesibili
Wednesday	Lesitsatfu
Thursday	Lesine
Friday	Lesihlanu
Saturday	uMgcibelo

Necessities

Yes	Yebo
No	Cha
Please	Ngiyacela
Thank you	Ngiyabonga
Internet café	Likhefi le-inthanethi

Numbers

One	Kunye
Two	Kubili
Three	Kutsatfu
Four	Kune
Five	Kusihlanu
Six	Kusitfupha
Seven	Kusikhombisa
Eight	Kusiphohlongo
Nine	Kuyimfica
Ten	Kulishumi

The Sotho-Tswana Language Group

The closely related Sotho-Tswana languages of South Africa are the tongues of the Sotho-Tswana peoples who have inhabited the Highveld and northeastern region the country since around the fifth century. The three major branches of the Sotho-Tswana language group – the Southern Sotho (Sesotho), Northern Sotho (Sesotho sa Leboa) and Western Sotho or Tswana (Setswana) – are divided into distinct georgraphic regions. While closely related, each of these three language groupings are heterogeneous and comprised of multiple dialects.

OVERVIEW

Northern Sotho (Sesotho sa Leboa or Sepedi):

Sesotho sa Leboa, literally "Sotho of the North" is mostly spoken in the northern provinces of South Africa, namely Gauteng, Limpopo and Mpumalanga. While often called Sepedi, as in the South African Constitution, Sesotho sa Leboa is in fact a more accurate term, for Sepedi is one of about 30 dialects that make up the Northern Sotho language. Historically speaking, Northern Sotho, particularly in its written form, has centered on the Pedi people and their dialect, hence the erroneous conflation of the two.

There are seven main vowels in Norther Sotho:

a	similar to "i" in "night"		i	similar to "i" in "pick"
e	similar to "ee" in "feet"		o	similar to "o" in "tool"
ê	similar to "e" in "bed"		ô	similar to "oo" in "door"
			u	similar to "u" in "put"

Pleasantries

Hello	Dumela
How are you?	O kae? (singular)
	Le kae? (plural)
I am fine	Ke gona
I am fine, thank you	Le nna ke gona, ke a leboga
Good morning/evening	Dumela (singular)
	Dumelang (plural)
Goodbye	Gabotse
Good luck	Mahlatse
What's your name?	Ke mang lebitso la gago?
My name is ___	Lebitso laka ke ___
I come from ___	Ke bowa kwa ___

Timing

What is the time?	Ke nako mang bjale?
Sunday	Lamorena
Monday	Mošupologo
Tuesday	Labobedi
Wednesday	Laboraro
Thursday	Labone
Friday	Labohlano
Saturday	Mokibelo

Necessities

Yes	Ee
No	Aowa
Please	Hle
Thank you	Ke a leboga
Excuse me	Ntshwarele
I am sorry	Ke maswabi
I love you	Ke a go rata
How much is this?	Ke bokae?
I want ...	Ke nyaka...
What are you doing?	O dira eng?
Where are you going?	O ya kae?

Numbers

One	Tee
Two	Pedi
Three	Tharo
Four	Nne
Five	Hlano
Six	Tshela
Seven	šupa
Eight	Seswai
Nine	Senyane
Ten	Lesome

Southern Sotho (Sesotho):

Sesotho is primarily spoken in Lesotho as a national language. It can also be heard throughout the Free State, the northern part of Eastern Cape and in southern Gauteng.

Pleasantries

Hello	Dumela
How are you?	O kae? (singular)
	Le kae? (plural)
I am fine	Ke teng
Goodbye	Tsamaya hantle (when remaining)
	Sala hantle (when leaving)
What is your name?	Lebitso la hao ke mang?
My name is ___	Lebitso la ka ke ___
Have a safe journey	O tsamaye hantle

Timing

What is the time?	Ke nako mang?
Sunday	Sontaha
Monday	Mantaha
Tuesday	Labobedi
Wednesday	Laboraro
Thursday	Labone
Friday	Labohlano
Saturday	Moqebelo

Necessities

Yes	Ee
No	Tjhee
Please	Hle
Thank you	Ke a leboha
The Sotho way of doing things	Se harona
E-mail address	Poso ya e-maili
Internet café	Khefi ya inthanete

Numbers

One	Nngwe
Two	Pedi
Three	Tharo
Four	Nne
Five	Hlano
Six	Tshelela
Seven	Supa
Eight	Robedi
Nine	Robong
Ten	Leshome

OVERVIEW

Tswana (Setswana):

Setswana is spoken mainly in the North West province, the Free State and Gauteng. It can also be heard in a very similar form in Botswana where it is the majority language. Setswana was the first Sotho language to have a written form. A note on pronunciation: the G is pronounced as an 'h' sound, as in the 'caught you by surprise' expression, 'ah-ha!'

Pleasantries

How are you?	O tsogile jang?
I'm well, Sir/Madam	Ke tsogile sentle, rra/mma
Thank you	Ke a leboga (formal)
	Tanki (slang)
My name is _____	Leina la me ke _____
What's your name?	Leina la gago ke mang?
	O mang? (informal)
Goodbye	Tsamaya sentle (when staying)
	Sala sentle (when leaving)

Timing

Sunday	Latshipi
Monday	Mosupologo
Tuesday	Labobedi
Wednesday	Laboraro
Thursday	Labone
Friday	Labotlhano
Saturday	Lamatlhatso

Necessities

I'm hungry	Ke tshwerwe ke tlala
I want ___	Ke batla ___
This food is good!	Dijo tse di monate!
What is ___ in Setswana?	___ ke eng ka Setswana?

Numbers

One	Nngwe
Two	Pedi
Three	Tharo
Four	Nne
Five	Tlhano
Six	Thataro
Seven	Supa
Eight	Robedi
Nine	Robongwe
Ten	Lesome

OVERVIEW

Tsonga (Xitsonga):

Xitsonga is primarily heard in the northern provinces of Limpopo and Gauteng, but is also spoken in Mpumalanga and North West Province. Besides the clicks, which are not indigenous to the language but are a result of Zulu influence, Xitsonga also incorporates whistling sounds.

Pleasantries

Hello	Avuxeni (morning)
	Inhelekani (afternoon)
	Riperile (evening)
How are you?	Ku njhani?
I am fine	Ndzi kona
I am fine, thank you	Ndzi kona ndza nkhensa
Goodbye	Sala kahle
Good luck	Ndzi ku navelela mikateko
Have a safe journey	Famba hi ku rhula

Timing

Sunday	Sonto
Monday	Musumbunuku
Tuesday	Ravumbirhi
Wednesday	Ravurharhu
Thursday	Ravumune
Friday	Ravunthlanu
Saturday	Muqivela

Necessities

Yes	Ina
No	E-e
Please	Ndza kombela
Thank you very much	Ndzi khense ngopfu
How much is this?	Xana i mali muni?
Internet café	Khefi ya internete

Numbers

One	N'we
Two	Mbirhi
Three	Nharhu
Four	Mune
Five	Ntlhanu
Six	Tsevu
Seven	Nkombo
Eight	Nhungu
Nine	Kaye
Ten	Khume

Venda (Tshivenda):

Tshivenda, the language of the Venda people, is heard mainly in Limpopo in the northeastern region. Tshivenda is considered a language isolate, although there has been some influence from the Nguni languages. The Venda language uses the Latin alphabet with five additional accented letters—there are four consonants with circumflex below the letter (ḓ, ḽ, ṋ, ṱ) and an overdot (ṅ).

Pleasantries

Hello	Lotjhani
How are you?	Unjani?
I am fine	Ngikhona
Fine, thank you	Ngikhona ngiyathokoza
Goodbye	Salakuhle
Good luck	Iba netjhudu
Have a safe journey	Ube nekhambo eliphephileko

Timing

Sunday	uSonto
Monday	uMvulo
Tuesday	uLesibili
Wednesday	uLesithathu
Thursday	uLesine
Friday	uLesihlanu
Saturday	uMgqibelo

Necessities

Yes	Iye
No	Awa
Please	Ngiyabawa
Thank you	Ngiyathokoza
Internet café	Ikefi ye-Internet

Numbers

One	Kunye
Two	Kubili
Three	Kuthathu
Four	Kune
Five	Kuhlanu
Six	Sithandathu
Seven	Likhomba
Eight	Bunane
Nine	Lithoba
Ten	Litjhumi

South African Festivals & Public Holidays

1 JANUARY . . . . New Year's Day (Public Holiday)

1-2 JANUARY . . . . Cape Town - Kaapse Klopse *(www.capetownminstrels.co.za)*

MID-FEBRUARY . . . . Cape Town - Infecting The City *(www.infectingthecity.com)*

LATE FEBRUARY-EARLY MARCH . . . . Cape Town - Cape Town Pride *(www.capetownpride.co.za)*

LATE FEBRUARY-EARLY MARCH . . . . Jo'burg - Dance Umbrella *(www.at.artslink.co.za/~arts/umbrella)*

MID-MARCH . . . . Cape Town - Cape Argus Cycle Tour *(www.cycletour.co.za)*

MID-MARCH . . . . Cape Town - Cape Town Festival *(www.capetownfestival.co.za)*

21 MARCH . . . . Human Rights Day (Public Holiday)

LATE MARCH . . . . Cape Town - Taste of Cape Town *(www.tasteofcapetown.com)*

LATE MARCH-EARLY APRIL . . . . Good Frida (Public Holiday) y

LATE MARCH-EARLY APRIL . . . . Family Day (Public Holiday)

EARLY APRIL . . . . Cape Town - Cape Town Jazz Festival *(www.capetownjazzfest.com)*

EARLY APRIL . . . . Oudtshoorn, Western Cape - Karoo Nasionale Kunstefees *(www.absakknk.co.za)*

27 APRIL . . . . Freedom Day (Public Holiday)

LATE APRIL . . . . Underberg, KwaZulu-Natal - Splashy Fen *(www.splashyfen.co.za)*

LATE APRIL-EARLY MAY . . . . Price Albert, Western Cape - Olive Festival *(www.patourism.co.za)*

LATE APRIL-EARLY MAY . . . . Knysna, Eastern Cape - Pink Loerie Mardi Gras *(www.pinkloerie.com)*

1 MAY . . . . Workers' Day (Public Holiday)

16 JUNE . . . . Youth Day (Public Holiday)

EARLY JULY . . . . Knysna, Eastern Cape - Oyster Festival *(www.oysterfestival.co.za)*

JULY/AUGUST . . . . Cape Town - Encounters *(www.encounters.co.za)*

9 AUGUST . . . . National Women's Day (Public Holiday)

MID-AUGUST . . . . Cape Town - Cape Town Fashion Week *(www.capetownfashionweek.com)*

LATE AUGUST . . . . Johannesburg - Joy of Jazz *(www.joyofjazz.co.za)*

SEPTEMBER . . . . Johannesburg - Arts Alive *(www.artsalive.co.za)*

MID-SEPTEMBER . . . . Cape Town - Cape Town Comedy Festival *(www.comedyfestival.co.za)*

24 SEPTEMBER . . . . Heritage Day (Public Holiday)

LATE SEPTEMBER . . . . Hermanus - Whale Festival *(www.whalefestival.co.za)*

EARLY OCTOBER . . . . Bloemfontein - Macufe *(www.macufe.co.za)*

MID-NOVEMBER . . . . Ficksburg, Free State - Cherry Festival *(www.cherryfestival.co.za)*

LATE NOVEMBER . . . . Harrismith, Free State - Woodstock *(www.woodstock.co.za)*

30 NOVEMBER . . . . Cape Town - Switch On the Festive Lights

EARLY DECEMBER . . . . Cape Town Obz Festival *(www.obzfestival.com)*

EARLY DECEMBER . . . . Franchhoek, Western Cape - Classique and Champagne Festival *(www.franschhoek.org.za)*

MID-DECEMBER . . . . Cape Town - Mother City Queer Project *(www.mcqp.co.za)*

16 DECEMBER . . . . Day of Reconciliation (Public Holiday)

25 DECEMBER . . . . Christmas Day (Public Holiday)

26 DECEMBER . . . . Day of Goodwill (Public Holiday)

OVERVIEW

The townships can be depressing on first glance, as they are made up of rows and rows of makeshift shacks the size of walk-in closets that often house entire families. There are still many residents who have no access to electricity or heat, and in some cases have no running water – they must walk to a communal water source to fetch water and bathe. Social violence, especially rape, is a sad reality, and HIV/AIDS is rampant. Yet there is an unmistakable spirit of hope and sense of community in the townships more inspiring than anything you'll find in the spotless, maximum-security housing developments of the wealthier city suburbs. Grassroots community projects build homes and education from the ground up, and residents reach out to help each other through hardship, exemplifying the classical African concept of "ubuntu": a sense of one's place within the human network. To practice ubuntu is to affirm the existence of others, to offer a helping hand to a neighbor in need or to be happy for a successful friend without envy or resentment. In the townships, where injustice and adversity lurk around every corner, this philosophy thrives and fuels the residents' will to survive.

White South Africans, especially Afrikaners, face an ongoing struggle to come to terms with the recent past, though the focus is now shifting towards finding their place in the new South Africa. Though most are proud of how far their country has come, a large number of whites fear marginalization at the hands of the ANC-led government. ANC Youth League president Julius Malema struck fear in the hearts of whites when he began singing the apartheid-era song "Kill the Boer!" at political functions; his meetings with Zimbabwean president Robert Mugabe to discuss land retrenchment have also stirred controversy. Yet when white supremacist and Afrikaner nationalist Eugene Terre'Blanche was murdered on Easter Sunday 2010, reactions across the race spectrum were encouraging: the vast majority of South Africans weren't riled by his death and backlash on both sides was minimal.

The problem of celebrating culture without the connotation of nationalism is an ongoing discussion. Some Afrikaners have found a unique avenue for expression free of the connotations of the past: music. Afrikaans-language pop, rock, rap, trance and other styles have exploded in recent years, encouraging young Afrikaners to embrace their heritage as their parents continue to adjust to the new South Africa. The Afrikaans-language genre is just one part of a music scene that is one of the most diverse and rich in the world, providing an ideal forum for the expression of ideas, frustrations, and tribute to one's roots. From kwaito (a South African brand of hip-hop fusion) to jazz, gospel to traditional African sounds, South African music is as diverse and exciting as its citizenry, and is an outlet for addressing the social ills and joys of life in the new democracy.

Religion plays a big part in the lives of most South Africans. For many, religion can be intertwined with culture and influential in politics. Over 80 percent of the population identifies as Christian faith, mainly protestant. African Independent Churches are the largest group of Christian churches, with over 10 million adherents. These African-initiated protestant churches are the result of the legacy of European missionaries in the country. Most are a combination of Christian teachings and African traditions and customs. The Zion Christian Church (ZCC) has the largest membership with over 4 million members. Apostolic and Pentecostal churches are also gaining popularity among the African populations.

The Dutch Reform Church is a Calvinist faith that claims almost 10 percent of the population. It has historically been central to Afrikaner life and culture. Many Afrikaans-speaking coloured people are also members of the church. It first came to South Africa with the Dutch East Indian Company in 1652 and was influential with Afrikaner politicians and the apartheid-era National Party. Other Christian churches in the country include the Roman Catholic Church, the Methodist Church, the Anglican Church, and the Lutheran Church.

Roughly 13 percent of South Africans don't ascribe to any organized religion, though many of these people adhere to traditional indigenous religions. Traditional African religion and culture are often inseparable, and therefore take on different forms throughout the country. Generally speaking, ancestors play an important role as an intermediary between humans and deities, and are honored by ritual sacrifices. Rites of passage are still commonly practiced to celebrate birth, coming of age, marriage and death. Male initiation ceremonies and circumcision are important moments in life for young Xhosa men in particular.

A single passion unites most South Africans: sports. Though the two primary sports, soccer and rugby, were once strictly divided along color lines, that is changing. The 2009 film "Invictus" recounts the newly elected president Nelson Mandela's decision to use rugby, traditionally an Afrikaner passion, as a way of uniting the fragile new democratic country when South Africa hosted and won the Rugby World Cup in 1995. More and more white South Africans in turn are following soccer, though the struggling South African team Bafana Bafana leaves much to be desired.

GOVERNMENT

In April 1994, South Africa held its first non-racial democratic elections, after nearly a century of racial discrimination and segregation. The African National Congress (ANC) won 62 percent of the vote and Nelson Mandela was inaugurated as president. Former African "homelands" were reincorporated into South Africa and the country was divided into the nine provinces existing today: Western Cape, Eastern Cape, KwaZulu-Natal, Free State, Gauteng, Mpumalanga, Limpopo, North West and the Northern Cape. Following the election, the new government worked on creating programs that focused on reconciliation, the reconstruction of institutions, the integration of all races and the overhaul of past policy.

ANC-led government was applauded when Mandela signed the new "Constitution of the Republic of South Africa" into effect in 1996, making it the supreme law. South Africa's constitution is one of the most progressive in the world. In stark contrast to the previous government, the constitution prohibits discrimination based on "race, gender, sex, pregnancy, marital status, ethnic or social origin, colour, sexual orientation, age, disability, religion, conscience, belief, culture, language and birth." It also assures that all citizens have a right to housing, property, healthcare, food and water, although the government has yet to make that an on-the-ground reality for much of the population.

South Africa's political system is an inter-connected web of national, provincial, and local levels of government, all of which are governed by the rule of the Constitution. The national government has three capitals, each representing the three different branches of government. The legislative branch, located in Cape Town, is a bicameral parliament composed of the National Assembly and the National Council of Provinces (NCOP). The National Assembly, or lower house, has 350-400 members elected by public majority every five years. The NCOP, or upper house, is composed of delegations nominated by provincial legislatures. Each province sends 10 delegates to the NCOP.

The executive branch, located in Pretoria, consists of a president who is elected from the majority party in the National Assembly and serves as head of state for a term of five years. The President is assisted by a deputy president and ministers chosen from parliament members from other major parties.

The independent judiciary is seated in Bloemfontein. The court system contains Magistrates Courts, High Courts, the Supreme Court of Appeal and the Constitutional Court. Though the judiciary is based in Bloemfontein, the Constitutional Court is located in Johannesburg.

The ANC has maintained a stronghold on South African politics since 1994, earning 65.9 percent of the vote in the most recent 2009 election. The ANC currently rules the National Legislature as well as eight out of nine provinces; the Western Cape is run by the Democratic Alliance (DA). The ANC President, Jacob Zuma, was inaugurated as President of South Africa in 2009, despite charges of corruption, fraud and rape. Eventually the charges were dropped but several prominent political figures have promised to apply for judicial review of the decision. The Democratic Alliance (DA), the main challenger of the ANC, led by Helen Zille, earned 16.7 percent of votes in the 2009 general election. Other parties that received substantial support in the recent election include the ANC-breakaway party Congress of the People (COPE) with 7.4 percent and the largely Zulu-backed Inkatha Freedom Party (IFP) with 4.6 percent.

ECONOMY

South Africa has a larger economy than any other country on the African continent. With a GDP

OVERVIEW

just over $277 billion the country ranks 32nd in the world and has a nominal per capita GDP of $5,600. However the economy is far from healthy with an unemployment rate at over 25 percent and over half of the people in the country living below the poverty line. The country's history of stratification is still strongly felt, and wealth within the country is not shared equally. A majority of the population lives in townships and informal settlements where many people don't have direct access to basics such as running water and flushing toilets. Many of those who live in the townships commute every day to the city for work. Some are employed within the formal economy, but many are employed in the informal economy as unskilled labor or domestic help making just $200 per month.

The country is abundantly rich in natural resources and the top industry is mining. South Africa is the world's largest producer of platinum, gold and chromium, and also exports substantial amounts of diamonds, iron and steel. Other sizeable industries within the country are automobile and machinery manufacturing, textiles, chemical and fertilizer production and commercial ship repair.

South Africa's economy relies heavily on international trade. The country's main export partners are China, the United States, Japan, Germany, U.K., and Switzerland and it imports most of its products from China, Germany, the United States, Saudi Arabia, Japan and Iran. Regionally within southern Africa, South Africa is the economic powerhouse and supplies neighboring countries with food and products. The small landlocked neighboring countries of Lesotho and Swaziland lack their own industry and manufacturing infrastructure and are heavily dependent on imports from South Africa.

NEWS & MEDIA

South Africa currently has the freest press in the continent, with over 20 daily newspapers, as well as a slew of strong and independent smaller private publications and radio stations. Today, it leads the region of southern Africa in tackling governmental failures and human rights concerns head-on. However, not too long ago South Africa's press was just as controlled as that of many of its neighboring countries.

South Africa's apartheid government censored

Do foreigners need an International Driving Permit?

In South Africa, foreigners can legally rent a vehicle and drive a vehicle with their foreign driver's license – as long as it is in English. Some South Africa traffic officers claim to be unaware of this law and insist foreigners are required to have an International Driving Permit.

Below is an explanation of the driver's license requirements for Americans (foreigners) by the South African Consulate General:

"Any valid U.S. (foreign) drivers license is accepted in South Africa, provided: it bears the photograph and signature of the holder; is printed in English; and if the license is issued while the holder thereof was not permanently or ordinarily a resident of South Africa for the period thereof; and, subject to the conditions under which such license was issued."

the newspaper and radio, using them as a pipeline for propaganda. Journalists who fought against government censorship were harassed and jailed. Introduction of television in South Africa was delayed until 1976 and even then only government-run stations were permitted to broadcast. However, this all changed under the new post-apartheid democratic government, where freedom of speech and freedom of the press are protected by the Constitution.

TV
SABC (_www.sabc.co.za_) is the state owned broadcaster that operates three national TV networks.
e.tv (_www.etv.co.za_) is the country's only independent national TV broadcaster.
M-Net (_www.mnet.co.za_) is a multi-channel pay TV, encrypted broadcaster with a pan-African audience.
DStv (_www.DStv.com_) is a multi-channel satellite TV service that offers M-Net, SABC and international programming throughout southern Africa.

Radio
567 Cape Talk (_www.capetalk.co.za_) 567 AM - Cape Town's first talk radio station.

5FM (*www.5fm.co.za*) frequency varies - SABC's youth oriented station with domestic and international music.
702 Talk Radio (*www.702.co.za*) 702 AM - Joburg's main current affairs talk radio station.
94.7 Highveld Stereo - 94.7 FM - contemporary music out of Joburg.
Algoa FM (*www.algoafm.co.za*) 94 to 96.7 FM - news and music broadcast primarily in the Eastern Cape.
East Coast Radio (*www.ecr.co.za*) 94 to 95 FM - news and music broadcast throughout KwaZulu-Natal.
Good Hope FM (*www.goodhopefm.co.za*) 93.9 to 96.7 FM - popular SABC-run contemporary station based out of Cape Town.
Jacaranda FM (*www.jacarandafm.co.za*) 94.2 FM - news and contemporary music in Gauteng.
Kaya FM (*www.kayafm.co.za*) 95.9 FM - African-focused contemporary and jazz music.
Kfm (*www.kfm.co.za*) 94.5 FM - contemporary music, mainly in the Western Cape.
Lotus FM (*www.lotusfm.co.za*) 92.5 to 103.8 FM - talk radio and music targeting the Indian community.
Metro FM (*www.metrofm.co.za*) 96.4 FM - the country's most popular contemporary international music station run by SABC.
OFM (*www.ofm.co.za*) 94 to 97 FM - contemporary music out of the Free State.
Radio Sonder Grense (*www.rsg.co.za*) 100 - 104 FM - SABC's national Afrikaans cultural station.
Yfm (*www.yfm.co.za*) 99.2 FM - targets generation Y and plays mostly local music.

Newspapers

Business Day (*www.businessday.co.za*) is the country's main business and financial daily.
Beeld (*www.beeld.com*) is the largest Afrikaans daily in the country, distributed mostly in the northeast.
Cape Argus (*www.capeargus.co.za*) is a major daily newspaper in Cape Town.
Cape Times (*www.capetimes.co.za*) is a popular Cape Town daily newspaper.
Citizen (*www.citizen.co.za*) is a high-circulation daily distributed mostly in Gauteng.
Die Burger (*www.dieburger.com*) is the Afrikaans daily distributed in the Western Cape.
Daily News (*www.dailynews.co.za*) is distributed mostly throughout KwaZulu-Natal.
Isolezwe (*www.isolezwe.co.za*) is the country's leading isiZulu newspaper.
Mail and Guardian (*www.mg.co.za*) is a major foreign-owned weekly newspaper.
Mercury (*www.themercury.co.za*) is a daily Durban-based newspaper.
The Star (*www.thestar.co.za*) is a major daily newspaper and the oldest newspaper in Johannesburg.
The Times (*www.timeslive.co.za*) is a daily newspaper published in Johannesburg.

@INTERNET

South Africa may be a little behind most other developed countries when it comes to Internet availability, speed and price, but it is much better than what is available in neighboring countries.

Customers in South Africa generally pay by the amount of bandwidth (the amount of data downloaded and uploaded) instead of the length of time users are online, although most Internet cafés charge by the minute. Internet cafés are widely available throughout the country in cities big and small. Most will allow you to plug in your laptop if you are traveling with one.

The majority of Internet users in South Africa connect through cell phone networks using a 3G GSM modem. Connection speeds are generally good, although you have to be within range of cell phone reception in order to connect. For travelers who have a laptop, are going to be in the country for an extended period of time and want the convenience of getting online anytime, cell phone stores throughout the country sell 3G GSM modems for roughly $100.

Another alternative for those with laptops and traveling in larger cities is **Skyrove** (☎086-176-8377, *www.skyrove.com*) and **RedButton** (☎086-128-8866, *www.redbutton.co.za*), two wifi service providers that have hotspots at many hostels/hotels, restaurants and coffee shops. Skyrove has a much larger network of hotspots throughout the country, while RedButton is more localized to the Cape Town area. Users can purchase prepaid credit either online or at any of the establishments where the service is offered.

⚙SLEEPING

One area where South Africa excels is its accommodation options, both in terms of quantity and variety. From its capitals to its remote game and nature reserves, the country is well suited to host a large number of both domestic and international travelers. Many lodges, guesthouses and boutique hotels are independent and operate in a very competitive market. It is generally not very difficult to find places that offer superb accommodation and friendly service at reasonable rates regardless of your price range.

Advanced booking for accommodation is recommended if traveling during peak seasons (mid-summer or around the Christmas holiday) or when in one of the popular traveling areas such as Cape Town, along the coastal Garden Route, or at any of the national parks. Outside of those times and locations, reservations are rarely necessary.

BUDGET

From backpackers and students on their gap year to campers and overlanders looking for self-catering facilities, South Africa's range of budget accommodation options is difficult to beat. There are hostels (commonly referred to as backpackers) in almost every major and medium sized city throughout the country and especially in and around popular tourist destinations. The sleeping options, facilities and cleanliness of backpackers span the entire spectrum but most generally offer a place to camp, multi-bed dorm rooms and shared bathrooms, and private rooms that come with a shared or private bathroom, along with a communal lounge and kitchen open to all. The backpackers are generally filled with foreigners and are great places to plug into the local scene, meet fellow travelers and find activities that are geared toward the budget-conscious traveler.

MID-RANGE

The mid-range options in South Africa hit the sweet spot in terms of quality accommodation and options. Independent and family-run hotels, guesthouses, B&Bs and lodges are dotted

---

South African Cuisine

It won't take very long to get accustomed to South Africa's unique food and their names. These South African staples are worth a try:

Biltong - salty dried meat (similar to jerky)

Bobotie - spiced ground meat topped with a thin layer of egg

Boerewors - a sausage that is traditionally braaied (barbecued)

Braai – to barbecue or grill meat

Bunny chow - curry stuffed into a hollowed-out loaf of bread

Mielie-meal - corn based staple food also called pap that is boiled into a thick porridge

Potjie - traditional Afrikaans stew made with meat and vegetables in a cast-iron pot

Rusks - hard, dry biscuit usually dunked in tea or coffee

Fat cakes - fried bread, similar to doughnuts

throughout the country and generally offer individual attention and an opportunity to meet local proprietors and get a flavor of the area, whether it is in a neighborhood of a larger city or a rural outpost. With very few exceptions (generally due to infrastructure issues in remote locations) you can expect all mid-range options to offer high standards of accommodation and amenities with comfortable private en suite rooms.

TOP END

For those looking to travel first-class, finding suitable accommodation should not be a problem. All of the country's large cities feature 5-star accommodation options consistent with international standards, ranging from newly built hotels, to colonial era stalwarts and exclusive boutiques offering impeccable service. Even outside of the main cities there is a rather wide selection of high-end lodges and boutique hotels. Many private game reserves throughout the country offer luxury private lodges and accompanying service. When it comes to the top end of accommodation in South Africa the prices are generally on par with similar establishments in developed countries.

ⓘ EATING

As a rainbow nation and melting pot of people and cultures, South Africa has a wide mix of regional and ethnic dishes. There doesn't tend to be a specific style of cuisine that could be widely identified as "South African", although many meals in the country center on large quantities of meat. Various ethnic groups and regions throughout the country are known for a certain delectable dish or unique style of cooking, and just about every specialty is worth trying.

The staple food of most of South Africa's traditional meals has long been maize, prepared in a variety of ways and accompanied with meat or vegetables. Most traditional meals today come with a heaping pile of it. Various ethnic groups prepare the maize in a slightly different manner and give it its own name. Mealie is full kernel maize boiled in water or roasted on the grill. Samp is dried and crushed maize kernels that are boiled into a chunky porridge and commonly served as umngqusho, a mix with beans, chopped vegetables, butter and spices. Mielie-meal, or pap, is the most common form of maize and consists of dried kernels finely ground and boiled with water into a thick porridge.

Probably the most popular regional cuisine in South Africa is Cape Malay cuisine, which is featured widely in Cape Town and in the surrounding Western Cape. Its roots date back to the 1700s when the Dutch East India Company imported large numbers of slaves from Malaysia, Indonesia and India. Over time, their traditional meals incorporated new elements to form a distinct cuisine. Although Cape Malay curries are quite popular, the best-known Cape Malay dish is Bobotie – a base of spiced ground meat topped with a thin layer of egg and garnished with raisins, nuts and chutney.

The Karoo region that slices through much of the Northern Cape, Western Cape and Eastern Cape is known for its succulent bone-in Karoo Lamb, which is generally free-range and therefore carries the distinct flavor of the region's grass and herbs. The Karoo is also known for multiple methods of preparing locally raised ostrich - a lean, red meat and a delicacy that many visitors lament leaving when they return home.

The West Coast region that starts around Cape Town and runs north along the western coast is a seafood lover's dream. It boasts some of the freshest oysters, mussels, crayfish, and prawns in the world as well as various special preparations of the catch of the day.

The cuisine in the Durban region is a fusion of international influences but is most heavily influenced by the large Indian population. Authentic curries are easy to come by, both in their traditional form as well as in Durban's signature Bunny Chow, a half loaf of bread hollowed out and filled with a thick curry.

ⓞ DRINKING

South Africa is a wine country. Most of the grape-growing and wine production is located in the Western Cape, with the heart of the wine industry surrounding the town of Stellenbosch. However, there are pockets of vineyards scattered in other regions and quality, reasonably priced wine is widely available throughout the country. Numerous grape varieties are grown throughout the region, although South Africa's signature variety is Pinotage - a red wine grape that was created in South Africa in the early 1900s by crossing the Pinot Noir and Hermitage grapes.

Though South Africa can be a vacation destination for wine lovers, the same cannot be said about the country's beer. The large beer industry is dominated by the century old South African Breweries (now SABMiller and the world's second-largest brewery), which produces and markets dozens of labels in the country. It is tough to beat an ice-cold beer on a hot summer day, but those with a taste for craft brews will not be impressed by the standard offering of South African lagers. There are a handful of quality microbreweries in the country, although their distribution is kept fairly local.

ⓩ TRANSPORTATION

ⓞ Air

South Africa's two main international airports are **Cape Town International Airport - CPT** (*S 33 58.157 E 018 35.793*, ☏021-937-1200, *www. acsa.co.za*) and **Johannesburg's OR Tambo International Airport - JNB** (*S 26 07.907 E 028 13.880*, R24, Kempton Park, ☏011-921-6262, *www. acsa.co.za*). The majority of the major international airlines service both airports with direct flights to major hub cities throughout the world.

For domestic and regional flights check out **South African Airways** (☏086-135-9722, *www. flysaa.com*), **South African Airlink** (☏011-961-1700, *www.saairlink.co.za*) or **South African Express** (☏011-978-5577, *www.saexpress.co.za*). Flights can be booked online, over the phone or directly at the ticket sales counters at the airport.

Medical Checklist

While all of the below are available within South Africa, it is a good idea to consider bringing the following with you and to have readily available while traveling:

Antibiotics (ciprofloxacin)
Antidiarrheal pills
Antihistamines (for allergies)
Antimalaria pills (if in infected area)
Bandages
Insect repellant (DEET)
Painkillers
Sunscreen
Water purification tablets
Feminine hygiene products

Budget airlines that offer primarily domestic flights include: **Mango** (☎086-116-2646, _www. flymango.com_), **Kulula** (☎086-144-4144, _www. kulula.com_), **1time** (☎086-134-5345, _www.1time. co.za_) and **Interlink Airlines** (☎086-110-1135, _www.interlinkairlines.com_).

🚆 Train

The main long distance passenger train service in South Africa is operated by **Shosholoza Meyl** (☎086-000-8888, _www.shosholozameyl.co.za_) with trains between most major cities in the country. Almost all routes offer seats and some routes offer sleeper service. Check online or in the transportation section of this book under a specific city for more detailed information on train routes and prices. Luxury train service is offered through **Premiere Classe** (☎086-000-8888, _www.premierclasse. co.za_), which has service between Cape Town, Johannesburg, Durban and Hoedspruit.

🚗 Car Rental

Around About Cars (☎021-422-4022, _www.around aboutcars.com_) is a budget car agent that can make a booking for you at one of the major national car rental companies. By booking through Around About Cars you get a better price and better insurance coverage than you would if you make a reservation directly with the rental company.

For those looking to drive around and explore the country in a camper, **Wicked Campers** (☎011-083-5184 or ☎021-813-6967, _www.wickedafrica.com_) offers kitted out 2-person and 5-person camper vans for rent.

🚘 Driving

Driving throughout South Africa affords the most flexibility and freedom and can be especially enjoyable within any of the numerous national parks and game reserves. South Africa's road network is far superior to that of any of its neighbors, but still slightly below that of most developed countri es. The roads tend to be narrower and lighting, signage, construction warnings and general safety measures are used more sparingly than many drivers are accustomed to. However, it is erratic drivers who present the biggest safety concern on the road. Drinking and driving is a substantial hazard throughout South Africa, Lesotho and Swaziland. Friday (pay day) night tends to be the worst. One of the most recognizable differences in driving practices for foreigners, besides perhaps driving on the other side of the road, is the custom for passing or overtaking on the highway. When a vehicle approaches from behind the slower driver in front is expected to move over into the emergency lane as the vehicle from behind passes in the primary lane. Be careful when driving in the emergency lane both day and night as many times people use the emergency lane for a walkway.

Enforcement of the rules of the road by traffic officers runs the spectrum from legitimately issued citations to fabricated violations followed by a request to settle the fine for a reduced amount on the spot in cash. It depends on the officer and location, but in many rural areas foreigners

South Africa Safety Tips

IN GENERAL:
Be alert and aware of your surroundings
Don't look like a tourist
Don't wear expensive (or expensive looking) jewelry
If mugged, remain calm, hand over your possessions and leave the area

ON FOOT:
Don't walk around with a camera visible
Carry bags in front of you with a firm grip
Don't carry unnecessary valuables with you
If sitting down for a meal or drink, hold onto your bag or buckle it to your chair
Don't stand around looking at a map or ask for directions (in big cities)
Walk in groups and take taxis at night

AT THE BEACH:
Bring with you only what you need
Do not leave items unattended (including car keys)

ON THE ROAD:
Always keep the doors locked
Roll up windows enough to prevent people outside from sticking their hands inside (especially in cities)
When coming to a stop, always leave at least a cars length of space in front of you so that it is possible to maneuver
   and drive away (it only takes a couple seconds to smash the window and loot the contents of an immobile vehicle)
Never leave anything of value inside an unattended vehicle

USING ATMS:
Be aware of con artists working around ATMs. The tricks are far more sophisticated than grabbing your money from you after you've made a withdrawal. Pay very close attention to your surroundings and do not allow anyone to get close to you. Never engage in any interaction around ATMs - do not ask anyone for help and do not respond to anyone asking for help. If there is a problem, just leave and find another ATM. Do not use any ATM where the card reader looks broken, altered, repaired or in anyway abnormal.

are more likely to be presented with the latter situation – explicit or veiled requests for a bribe from the officer. How you decide to handle such a situation if it arises is up to you, but if you are not in a rush, friendly conversation and repeated apologies may convince the officer that his time is best spent requesting a bribe from the next driver. If you'd rather just pay and be on your way, negotiating down to a small amount of R20-100 is doable.

Speed limits are enforced both by police officers standing on the side of the road with dated radar guns mounted on tripods as well as newer unmanned laser speed detectors that will automatically take a photo of speeding cars and mail a ticket to the address associated with the vehicle registration. It is worth noting that if you are driving a rental car and are captured speeding by one of the camera-equipped laser speed detectors, the municipality will get the address on the passport used to rent the vehicle and a speeding ticket will be mailed to that foreign address.

⊖ Bus

South Africa has a strong network of long distance buses and bus transport is one of the more common ways for visitors to get around the country. Some of the major bus companies with the largest route networks include: **TransLux / City to City** (℡086-

158-9282, *www.translux.co.za*). **Greyhound** (☎ *012-323-1154*, *www.greyhound.co.za*), **Intercape** (☎*086-128-7287*, *www.intercape.co.za*) and **SA Roadlink** (☎*011-333-2223*, *www.saroadlink.co.za*). To view the time schedules and prices of all of the above bus companies for any specific route check out **Computicket** (☎*083-915-8000*, *www. computicket.com/web/bus tickets/*). You can make your booking online or over the phone.

Baz Bus (☎*021-439-2323*, *www.bazbus.com*) is a South Africa bus service that is geared exclusively to the backpacking crowd. It offers a convenient way to get from a backpackers or hostel in one city to a backpackers in another city and is a great way to meet other travelers heading in the same direction. The routes are along the most popular backpacking circuits in the country and the bus stops at the front door of most backpackers in each city along the way. There are a variety of different routes and packages available, and they can be purchased online or through any of the backpackers that the bus stops at.

⊜ Minibus Taxi

Minibus taxis are the most popular method of transportation for the majority of South Africans, both for long distance transportation and for getting around within a city. While they don't offer much in the way of personal space or comfort when everyone is packed into the taxi, they are cheaper and faster than taking a bus and there is no need to book or make any advance reservations. For long distance transportation between cities, minibuses gather at a designated minibus taxi rank and wait to fill up with people. Once they fill up, they depart for the minibus taxi rank in their destination city. Within most cities, local minibus taxis also operate in place of or in addition to local bus routes. They typically drive a set route or back and forth between two destinations. Passengers who want to ride local minibus taxis flag them down as they pass on the street and cram inside. Some people choose to avoid using minibus taxis because of their poor safety record.

HEALTH

South Africa has both a private and a public healthcare system. The private healthcare system is comparable to that of many other developed countries. Its public healthcare system suffers from a lack of resources, mainly funding, staffing and training – although for most of the population this is the only option.

For travelers, South Africa presents relatively minor health risks relative to other African

OVERVIEW

countries. Depending on the area of the country you will be traveling in, the biggest concern is likely to be malaria. It is recommended that travelers consult with a doctor four to six weeks before their planned travel to obtain any needed medication for the duration of the trip and to ensure adequate time to complete any vaccinations.

In addition to being up to date with routine vaccinations such as measles/mumps/rubella (MMR), diphtheria/pertussis/tetanus (DPT), and polio, the **US Centers for Disease Control – CDC** (*wwwnc.cdc.gov/travel/*) recommends that travelers to South Africa receive the following vaccinations: hepatitis A, hepatitis B, typhoid and rabies (for individuals with a high risk of exposure). In addition to the above vaccines it is important that you discuss with your doctor where you intend to travel and the risks of contracting malaria (generally present in parts of Mpumalanga, Limpopo, northeastern KwaZulu-Natal, Kruger National Park and Swaziland) as well as the appropriate antimalarial drug if necessary. Although yellow fever is not a disease risk in South Africa, the government requires travelers arriving from countries where yellow fever is present to show proof of a yellow fever vaccination.

Water

It is safe to drink tap water throughout most of South Africa's cities. Communities where the tap water is not safe generally have clear warnings. Most people will also not have a problem drinking tap water in more rural areas and throughout Swaziland or Lesotho, but chances of contamination are much higher. Bottled water is recommended for travelers with sensitive stomachs or those wanting to be cautious.

Sun Exposure

Exposure to ultraviolet (UV) radiation from the sun's rays is something most visitors to South Africa will get a lot of. Excessive and prolonged UV radiation can cause skin cancer. Immediate symptoms of overexposure to the sun include red or reddish skin that is warm to the touch, general fatigue and mild dizziness. To reduce sun exposure, wear protective clothing and a wide-brim hat, and use sunscreen on exposed skin. A sunscreen rated as SPF 15 is recommended for everyday use. For people with lighter skin and those who experience longer periods of direct sun exposure it is advisable to use sunscreen rated as SPF 30 or above.

It is also important to protect your eyes from excessive sun exposure. UV light can cause long-term permanent eye damage such as macular degeneration. Regular use of sunglasses that block UV light is highly recommended.

Malaria

Malaria is an infectious disease caused by a blood-borne parasite that is transferred from human to human by mosquitoes. The likelihood of contracting malaria through mosquito bites can be greatly reduced by wearing clothes that limit the amount of exposed skin, using insect repellent (DEET) and taking antimalarial medication. Malaria is present in only parts of South Africa (generally in parts of Mpumalanga, Limpopo, northeastern KwaZulu-Natal, Kruger National Park) and Swaziland. The risk of contracting malaria is highest during the summer months of November to April and less so during the cooler winter months. Some strains of malaria are resistant to certain types of antimalarial drugs, so it is important that you discuss with your doctor where you intend to travel and what type of antimalarial medicine should be taken if any is needed.

Suspected exposure to malaria should be taken seriously. Treatment is generally easy and inexpensive, but if left untreated malaria can be deadly. If you suspect you might have malaria, go to the nearest hospital or clinic and get tested. Testing is widely available in large and medium-sized cities. Symptoms of malaria include fever and sweating, sudden coldness and shivering, joint pain and vomiting. In severe cases the disease worsens and can lead to hallucinations, coma, and eventually death.

Schistosomiasis (bilharzia)

Schistosomiasis (also known as bilharzia or snail fever) is a disease caused by a parasite that lives in freshwater lakes, rivers, streams and dams in sub-Saharan Africa. The risk of contracting the disease is increased in bodies of water that contain numerous freshwater snails, which may carry the parasite.

Schistosomiasis is a chronic illness that can damage internal organs, but is generally not fatal. Humans contract the disease by swimming or bathing in contaminated water. The parasite penetrates the skin of humans, develops within the blood vessels and travels throughout the body. Most people do not display symptoms in the early phases of infection, but symptoms can include a rash or itchy skin within a few days of infection as well as fever, chills, and muscle aches in the following months. Because many people do not display symptoms, it is recommended that travelers who suspect they have been exposed to the parasite get tested after returning home. Treatment for those found to be infected is generally done with a single pill.

HIV/AIDS

South Africa, Lesotho and Swaziland make up the worst HIV zone in the world. These three countries rank, respectively, as the #4, #3 and #1 countries with the highest HIV infection rates in the world – with neighboring Botswana filling in the #2 slot. Having unprotected sex in general is not safe, but in this region of the world it could easily be a death sentence. Condoms are freely available throughout most of South Africa and much of Lesotho and Swaziland. If you are going to be sexually active with local residents, it is highly advised to use condoms.

SAFETY & SECURITY

Crime in South Africa is a genuine problem. Almost everyone who lives in South Africa has either been mugged, had a house or car broken into or knows someone who has had such an experience. Police protection and response to such incidences seem to be inadequate. Most business and private residences within metropolitan areas are protected by gates, electric fences and private security companies. Despite these unfortunate realities, most visitors to South Africa enjoy their trip without any hiccups. The chances of having an incident-free trip are greatly improved by being aware of your surroundings, not attracting attention, concealing expensive accessories or technology and avoiding dodgy areas at night. While it is good to exercise caution and use your street smarts, we equally caution against allowing paranoia to interfere with or inhibit your experiences and enjoyment of all that South Africa has to offer.

SPECIALIZED TRAVEL NEEDS

Women

Attitudes toward women are slowly changing but tend to be slightly patriarchal regardless of racial group. Though women enjoy good representation in government, social violence and conservative ideas undermine advancement. Sadly, South Africa has one of the highest rates of reported rape in the world, exacerbating the HIV crisis and scarring the psyches of far too many women. Females travelling solo should be extra cautious; walking alone, hitchhiking and traveling in minibus taxis after dark is not recommended.

Traveling with Disabilities

South Africa offers fewer resources for disabled travelers than most developed countries, but relative to other countries in Africa, it is the most accommodating. People who are mobility impaired will find that most buildings throughout the country, including accommodation, restaurants and sights, can be conveniently accessed from the ground level. A great resource for identifying establishments that cater to people with mobility disabilities is (www. disabledtravel.co.za).

The **South African National Parks** system also caters to people with various disabilities. For more information check out (www.sanparks.org/ groups/disabilities).

Traveling with Children

South Africa is a great traveling destination for families with children. Many establishments are specifically geared toward families with children, offering family oriented activities as well as separate adult and child activities. If heading to a private wildlife reserve, it is a good idea to check ahead to see if there are any age restrictions for children, although SAN Parks accommodate children of all ages.

International brands of baby food, diapers and infant supplies are readily available in large and medium-sized cities, but adequate supplies should be taken when visiting smaller towns or rural areas. Special care should be taken when traveling with children in malaria zones, and swimming in fresh bodies of water that are potentially contaminated with bilharzia should be avoided.

Family Travel SA (www.familytravelsa.co.za) is a good resource for information on family and child friendly accommodation, activities and transportation throughout the country.

OVERVIEW

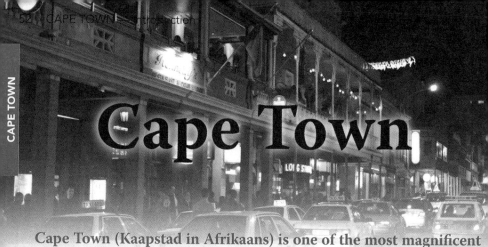

Cape Town

Cape Town (Kaapstad in Afrikaans) is one of the most magnificent cities in the world. Against the iconic silhouette of Table Mountain, the city offers beautiful beaches, incredible natural diversity, renowned restaurants and vineyards, and top-notch accomodation. Travelers who let the easygoing Capetonian pace wash over them find that the longer they stay, the more they love this city.

Cape Town is a cultural melting pot, but its neighborhoods and suburbs have retained distinct characters, and it is worth spending some time in each to get the full flavor of the city. Bo-Kaap, De Waterkant, Green Point, Clifton, Camps Bay, Observatory and the small coastal towns along the peninsula make up the must-see list for most visitors. But too many people spend time in Cape Town without seeing the vibrant townships where much of the population resides. Arrange a township tour or check out the Cape Flats Townships section (p129) to explore Langa, Guguletu and Khayelitsha on your own.

CAPE TOWN

GPS: S 33 55.427 E 018 25.401
pop. 3.5 million | elevation 22 m/72 ft

The vibrant and eclectic city of Cape Town draws people from across the globe. From its stunning natural beauty dominated by Table Mountain, rich cultural history, and top-notch vineyards, to its socialite beach scene and full-throttle nightlife, this multicultural melting pot has something to offer and entertain just about anyone.

Regardless of where you base yourself in the city - and your reflective tastes - it is worth at least checking out some of the more distinct neighborhoods and scenes to get a full taste of the city. Some of the top spots include the come as you are atmosphere of the bustling city center, Long Street lined with budget accommodation, cafes, bars and night clubs, and the see and be seen strip in Camps Bay flanked by bronzed beach goers on one side and swanky cocktail lounges on the other, as well as the bohemian southern neighborhoods of Woodstock and Observatory where you are likely to find some of the city's best hidden gems.

🏛 HISTORY

The "Mother City" of South Africa has long been the focus of the country's cultural evolution. The city's deep roots and complex political history provide a profound foundation for the country's metropolitan epicenter. The stunning and fertile slopes of Table Mountain have attracted settlers for more than 12,000 years. Tools and human remains found in nearby Fish Hoek tell the story of the area's first communities - small bands of San hunter-gatherers and Khoikhoi pastoralists, who were later referred to jointly as the Khoisan.

These Khoikhoi pastoralists migrated from the north and spread their clans across large tracts of land needed for grazing their cattle and sheep, nearly two thousand years before Portuguese explorer Bartolomeu Dias was blown ashore in a storm in 1488. Following in his wake, Vasco da Gama rounded the "Cape of Good Hope" in 1497 to open the trade route to the East Indies. For the next hundred years, the Cape was used sporadically as a midway point for sailors to rest and replenish water and meat supplies through trade with the local Khoisan population before continuing on to the riches of India and Indonesia.

It was not until 1652 that a permanent European settlement came to Table Bay. The Dutch East India Company (VOC), which needed a refueling base for its passing ships, sent a crew headed by Jan van Ribeck to regulate trade with the indigenous Khoisan and plant fruit and vegetables for the merchant sailors. When the Khoisan refused to be subjugated as laborers for their new neighbors, the VOC imported slaves from East Africa and the Indies.

Freeburgher "boers" (Dutch for 'farmers') soon yearned to expand their farms and wineries beyond the confines of the VOC post in Table Bay. They established farms on the grazing land of the Khoisan, which led to conflict and the outbreak of the first Khoi-Boer War in 1659. Temporary Khoisan unity against the invaders was short-lived and they soon lost control of their traditional lands around the Cape. Subsequent wars and a small pox epidemic in 1713 nearly wiped out the entire Khoisan population around Cape Town and ravaged the clans further inland as the Boers continued to expand their settlement.

Cape Town quickly grew from a small port town to a lively and diverse "tavern on the seas." The VOC encouraged immigration to develop the settlement and continued to import slaves to work the Boer farms. Throughout the 1700s, hundreds of slaves were imported each year, and by the end of the century, they had outnumbered the white population. The vast numbers of slaves imported from the Indies are the ancestors of Cape Town's current Cape Malay and Muslim populations.

Meanwhile, in the late 1700s, Napoleon Bonaparte was making great strides across Europe. Fearful that he might gain control of the strategic Dutch colony, the British invaded and temporarily took control of the Cape in 1795. The British returned control to the Dutch when tensions subsided in 1803, but invaded again in 1806. By 1814, the Dutch ceded the Cape Colony to the British Empire. Along with the change in colonial power came a change in culture as the British colonists introduced "liberal" reform to the Cape, which culminated in emancipation of slaves in the Cape Colony in 1834. The Boers did not welcome the change in governance or the loss of their slave labor, and thus began the Boer Great Trek of the 1830s to 1840s as they moved east and north to distance themselves from British control.

The discovery of diamonds in Kimberly in 1866

and vast gold deposits near Johannesburg in 1886 drastically changed Cape Town's identity. Johannesburg quickly replaced Cape Town as the economic and population hub of the region and Cape Town transformed into an important harbor city for the influx of gold prospectors and the export of mineral wealth to Europe. But this was not enough for the British Cape Colony government and Cape Town Prime Minister Cecil Rhodes, who had a keen interest in gold hidden in deep reefs in Boer territory.

Fearing that the British had growing designs for their republic, the Boers launched a preemptive strike in 1899, which commenced the Second Anglo-Boer War, or South African War. Combat was waged in the interior, sparing Cape Town itself from the fighting. The British defeated the Boers in 1902, and in 1910 the Cape Province was united with the Natal, Transvaal and the Orange Free State in the Union of South Africa, with Cape Town established as the seat of its legislature.

By the turn of the century, Cape Town had grown to a population of over 170,000 people. The emerging modern, industrialized city began to see itself as the cultural center of the region; monuments were erected and universities, sports clubs and entertainment venues established. Development also brought urbanization – inner-city working class neighborhoods such as District Six, Bo-Kaap and Woodstock began to flourish. These overcrowded but vibrant neighborhoods were largely home to the city's coloured, black and immigrant populations and were regarded by the white elite as areas of vice and ill repute. The municipal government neglected these neighborhoods and water supply, sanitation and roads were poor. In 1901 an outbreak of bubonic plague was wrongfully blamed on the black working class and, under the pretext of health legislation, used as justification to rid the city center of its "undesirables." People were forcibly removed from the inner city and relocated to areas such as Ndabeni, creating the first black township of the Cape Flats.

In response to these actions and other laws that began to impose stricter racial segregation in the country, the black and coloured educated elite became increasingly politicized. The labor movement was especially strong in Cape Town and unionists organized to protest against the colour-bar that reserved the highest paid and most skilled jobs for whites. In 1919, clerk Clements Kadalie organized Cape Town's dockworkers and founded the Industrial and Commercial Workers' Union (ICU). The union's strike for higher wages was successful and by 1926 it represented over 100,000 members.

However, the rise of the black and coloured upper and middle class was stifled by the rise of Afrikaner nationalism. White Afrikaners struggled to define themselves as superior and demanded policies that reserved better education and employment opportunities for whites. In an effort to maintain a sense of unity among the white population in the Union, British officials placated Afrikaner discontent. Physical segregation increased and in 1923 the Urban Areas Act restricted the black population's movement and access to the city as it expanded the townships in the Cape Flats. In 1936 the white government abolished the right of the land-owning black elite to vote in parliamentary elections in the Cape Province. Despite the series of legislation tightening racial segregation between 1910 and 1940, the black and coloured population in the city continued to grow, peaking during WWII when blacks and coloureds stepped into jobs previously only reserved for the white population.

The post-war backlash against the growing affluence of the non-white population led to the election of the Afrikaner National Party in 1948 and the emergence of the apartheid state. "Separate and unequal" policies of racial segregation solidified restrictions on the movement and aspirations of the black population, and Cape Town further became zoned by race. In reaction to apartheid, the black liberation movement grew in the shantytowns on the outskirts of the city and townships of the Cape Flats. The more militant offshoot of the African National Congress (ANC), the Pan Africanist Congress (PAC), established a stronghold in Langa. Anti-pass demonstrations in Cape Town, which protested the requirement of all black males to carry identification papers at all times, were met with police repression in 1960, and a state of emergency was declared. The following decade witnessed a political clamp down as opposition parties such as the ANC and PAC were banned and the black liberation movement was forced underground. Robben Island Prison, off the coast of Cape Town, soon became a symbol of government oppression as leaders of the ANC and PAC were jailed there.

Under apartheid, the Western Cape was

ALL WHO PASS BY
REMEMBER WITH SHAME THE MANY THOUSANDS
OF PEOPLE WHO LIVED FOR GENERATIONS
IN DISTRICT SIX AND OTHER PARTS OF
THIS CITY AND WERE FORCED BY LAW TO
LEAVE THEIR HOMES BECAUSE OF THE
COLOUR OF THEIR SKINS.
FATHER, FORGIVE US...

deemed a Coloured Labour Preference Area and the coloured population of Cape Town received preferential treatment over blacks. However they too were victims of forced displacement. In 1966, the historically coloured working-class neighborhood of District Six was rezoned as a "white" district and over 60,000 of its residents were displaced as the area was destroyed under the pretext of "slum clearing." Yet Cape Town's coloured population continued to frustrate the apartheid government in Pretoria as efforts to eradicate shantytowns surrounding the city were met with increasing resistance.

Opposition in the 1970s peaked with the 1976 Soweto Uprising and protests broke out across the country. Police repression of black students in Cape Town's townships of Langa, Nyanga and Guguletu led to rioting, and coloured students joined with them in solidarity. During 1976 a total of 128 people were killed and over 400 injured in Cape Town's urban violence, drawing both national and international attention to the situation. Squatter settlements that had emerged during the 1970s on the outskirts of the city became another point of contention between the government and opposition forces. Thousands of people who had come to Cape Town for work and made homes in these shantytowns for lack of other housing were displaced as the government engaged in mass clearings of these areas.

Throughout the 1980s, the government security forces intensified their covert and low-level warfare against the "black menace." Opposition to apartheid became increasingly militant. In response to continued violence, community organizations mobilized and began to demand the dissolution of the apartheid government and an end to repression. Women's movements, students, labor unions and civic organizations banded together to form the United Democratic Front (UDF) in 1983. Facing increased opposition, the government began to repeal some "petty apartheid" measures and institute cosmetic changes, including the creation of a "Tricameral Parliament" which gave token political representation to the coloured and Indian communities in attempts to co-opt their support. However, the need for substantial change was inevitable and the government began to arrange for the release of political prisoners and the dismantling of the apartheid regime.

On February 11, 1990, hours after his release from 27 years of imprisonment in Robben Island, Nelson Mandela addressed his countrymen from the balcony of Cape Town's City Hall. Four years later, he assumed the office of the Presidency in Pretoria. Cape Town has since begun a process of reconciliation and integration, as the city strives to reestablish itself as a vibrant, multicultural hub. Yet the city still struggles. In the midst of an influx of investment and rejuvenation projects to reinvent the city, Cape Town is still host to wide disparities in wealth, racial divisions both in the city center and in the Cape Flats, gang violence and high levels of HIV. This is a city that still carries the heavy weight of its past as its inhabitants strive toward a modern, socially equal and culturally diverse future.

✶ TOURIST INFORMATION

Cape Town Tourism (www.capetown.travel) has three locations that provide information on and make bookings for accommodation, activities, tours and car hire. Its main office is in the **City Center** (S 33 55.272 E 018 25.282, Pinnacle Building, cnr Castle St & Burg St, City Center, ☎021-487-6800, Oct-Mar: 9am-6pm, Apr-Sept: 9am-5pm Mon-Fri, 9am-1pm Sat-Sun). Another office is located at the **Waterfront** (S 33 54.299 E 018 25.163, ☎021-408-7600, 9am-9pm) right outside the mall near Mitchell's Tavern. The third office is at the **Table Mountain Lower Cableway Station** (S 33 56.895 E 018 24.184, 370 Tafelberg Rd, Table Mountain, ☎021-422-1075, 8am-6pm Mon-Fri, 8:30am-2pm Sat, 9am-1pm Sun).
Western Cape Tourist Office (S 33 54.405 E 018 25.354, Clock Tower Centre, Waterfront, ☎021-405-4500, 9am-9pm) has tourist information for the whole Western Cape as well as computers with Internet access available to the public.

✷ MONEY

There are ATMs widely available throughout the city and most branches of major banks can convert common foreign currency.
American Express has a downtown office (S 33 55.176 E 018 25.485, Thibault Square, cnr Adderley St & Hans Stridom Ave, City Center, ☎021-425-7991) as well as at the Waterfront (S 33 54.368 E 018 25.217, Alfred Mall, ☎021-419-3917), both of which offer traveler's check and foreign exchange services.

@ INTERNET

Internet cafés and copy/print shops with Internet service are common throughout the city. For travelers with their own computer, **Skyrove** (☎086-176-8377, www.skyrove.com) and **RedButton** (☎086-128-8866, www.redbutton.co.za) are two wifi service providers that cover much of the Cape Town and surrounding area. You can purchase prepaid credit either online or at many hostels/hotels, restaurants and coffee shops and use your credit anywhere that the service is offered. Some locations offer a limited amount of bandwidth for free. Skyrove has about 500 wifi locations and RedButton has about 300 access points.
Computeria (S 33 55.537 E 018 24.928, 206 Long St, City Center, ☎021-426-5986, open 24hrs, R5/12min) has 12 updated computers and serves coffee and beer. Laptops can connect via Ethernet.
Geek @ Java Internet Café (S 33 55.694 E 018 24.757, 39 Kloof St, Gardens, ☎021-426-0251, 7:30am-11pm Mon-Fri, 8am-11pm Sat, 10am-8pm Sun, R10/30min) has updated computers and wifi for laptops. It is connected to the Java Café next door, which serves drinks and light meals.
Timeline Internet (S 33 54.520 E 018 23.821, 233 Main Rd, Sea Point, ☎021-434-6521, 8am-11pm, R10/30min) has individual cubicles with updated widescreen computers and allows laptops to be connected via Ethernet or wifi. They also provide headsets for Skyping.
Western Cape Tourist Office (S 33 54.405 E 018 25.354, Clock Tower Centre, Waterfront, ☎021-405-4500, 9am-9pm, R15/10min) has an Internet café with 10 computers for public use.
African Access (S 33 56.379 E 018 28.155, 50 Lower Main Rd, Observatory, ☎021-448-7110, 9am-12am, R6/30min) is a large Internet café with about 30 computers. They allow laptops to plug in as well.

⟳ SHOPPING

Greenmarket Square (S 33 55.375 E 018 25.204, Burg St btwn Shortmarket St & Longmarket St, City Center, 9am-5:30pm) is a cobblestone square in the heart of the city that hosts a daily flea market with all kinds of curios, crafts, artwork, sculptures, clothing and tapestries.
Old Biscuit Mill (S 33 55.655 E 018 27.459, 375 Albert Rd, Woodstock, ☎021-462-6361, www.theoldbiscuitmill.co.za) has a handful of design and boutique stores, but really comes alive on the weekends. On Saturday check out the **Saturday's**

Neighbor Goods Market (*021-448-1438*, *www. neighbourgoodsmarket.co.za*, *9am-2pm Sat*). It is bustling gourmet organic food market with biltong (dried meat), cheese, sweets, spreads, fresh vegetables, pizza and most anything else you can imagine. Sip champagne or fresh coconut milk as you stock up on delicacies. On Sundays, check out the **Vintage Fair** (*www.vintagefair. co.za, 10am-3pm Sun*), Cape Town's best kept vintage secret, to sift through collector's items, home furnishings and handmade crafts.

Pan African Market (*S 33 55.328 E 018 25.161, 76 Long St, City Center, 021-426-4478, 9am-5:30pm Mon-Fri, 9am-3pm Sat*) is three stories stocked floor-to-ceiling with African crafts from all over the continent. Whether you are looking for jewelry, carved masks, instruments, 2-meter-tall statues, clothes or curios, if it's African you'll find it here.

Church Street Market (*S 33 55.385 E 018 25.129, cnr of Church St & Long St, City Center, 082-975-3890, 9am-3pm Mon-Fri, 9am-2pm Sat*) is a small antique and secondhand market that can be hit or miss, depending on which vendors show up on a given day. Besides the wares on display, the pedestrian strip of Church Street is lined with galleries, cafés and boutiques, including the cute and creative **Imagenius**

(*S 33 55.383 E 018 25.120*, 117 Long St, City Center, *021-423-7870*, *www.imagenius.co.za*, *9:30am-4:30pm Mon-Fri, 9:30am-1:30pm Sat*), a carefully curated collection of art, oddities and accessories.

IMPACT **Streetwires** (*S 33 55.202 E 018 25.007, 77 Shortmarket St, Bo-Kaap, 021-426-2475, www.streetwires.co.za, 8:30am-5pm Mon-Fri, 9am-1pm Sat*) is a sustainable employment initiative and working studio that provides training and materials to over 100 formerly unemployed men and women, who in turn produce a variety of funky wire art, including functional wire radios, candle holders, earrings and life-sized bead and wire animal sculptures.

IMPACT **African Home** (*S 33 55.675 E 018 25.540, 41 Caledon St, District Six, 021-461-1700, www.africanhome.co.za, 8:30am-5pm*) is a fair-trade initiative that empowers local township crafters and promotes traditional South African arts and environmental awareness. Their products are largely made from recycled materials, including soda tab belts and bottle cap bags.

Galleries

The industrial landscape of Woodstock is home to the most cutting edge and contemporary galleries in Cape Town. Most are relatively close to each other and worth a visit to get a feel for the hip artist scene in the city. New galleries have also emerged in the City Center as investors aim to revive the downtown area.

WhatifTheWorld (S 33 55.629 E 018 27.130, 208 Albert Rd, 2nd Floor, Woodstock, ☎021-448-1438, www.whatiftheworld.com, 10am-5pm Tue-Fri, 10am-2pm Sat, Mon by appointment) is a huge, hipster-run loft that shows the work of young and emerging South African artists, with multimedia installations that aim to challenge traditional art structures.

Michael Stevenson Gallery (S 33 55.664 E 018 26.265, 160 Sir Lowry Rd, Woodstock, ☎021-462-1500, www.michaelstevenson.com, 9am-5pm Mon-Fri, 10am-1pm Sat) offers avant-garde and sometimes shocking multimedia exhibits by South African and African artists that make a political statement, bucking the status quo.

Goodman Gallery (S 33 55.664 E 018 26.287, 176 Sir Lowry Rd, 3rd Floor, Woodstock, ☎021-462-7573, www.goodman-gallery.com, 9:30am-5:30pm Tue-Fri, 10am-4pm Sat) is tucked away in an industrial-building-turned-upmarket-office-space and hosts polished, creative and thought provoking exhibits by South African and African artists who engage with current political and social African contexts.

The Rainbow Experience (S 33 55.424 E 018 25.180, Mandela Rhodes Place, 23 Church St, City Center, ☎021-422-1428, www.therainbowexperience.co.za, 9am-6pm Mon-Fri, 9am-3pm Sat, 10am-2pm Sun) is a vibrant, multilevel venue situated within the urban redevelopment project of the Mandela Rhodes Place, which aims to draw new life and inspiration into the City Center. The gallery displays works from emerging contemporary South African artists and the attached colorful café has light meals, free wifi and creativity in every corner. The Rainbow Room downstairs also hosts live jazz multiple times a week (see the Drinking section or look online for details).

iArt (S 33 55.281 E 018 25.161, 71 Loop St, City Center, ☎021-424-5150, www.iart.co.za, 9am-5pm Mon-Fri, 10am-2pm Sat) is a sleek two-story gallery that features mainly South African artists and has new exhibits every two to three weeks.

Association for Visual Arts (AVA) (S 33 55.392 E 018 25.136, 35 Church St, City Center, ☎021-424-7436, www.ava.co.za, 10am-5pm Mon-Fri, 10am-3pm Sat) is South Africa's oldest nonprofit gallery and shows established, emerging and self-taught artists from the Western Cape. Located off the Church Street Market, it's a nice place to pop in if you are in the area.

⟳ Malls

Victoria Wharf Shopping Centre (S 33 54.235 E 018 25.198 Waterfront, ☎021-408-7600, www.waterfront.co.za, 9am-9pm Mon-Sat, 10am-9pm Sun) is the hub of activity on the Waterfront with over 400 stores including numerous designer brands, cafés, restaurants and two cinemas, all in a large, glitzy building.

Cape Quarter (S 33 54.927 E 018 25.080, cnr Somerset Rd & Dixon St, ☎021-421-1111, www.capequarter.co.za, 10am-6:30pm) is a trendy mall in the heart of the Waterkant, which specializes in high fashion, boutique clothing, interior design, and generally fabulous living. The mall has a grocery store and large courtyard filled with restaurants and cafés.

Canal Walk Shopping Centre (S 33 53.596 E 018 30.684, Century Blvd, Century City, ☎021-529-9799/8, www.canalwalk.co.za, 9am-9pm) is located in the greater Century City community, a commercial city in itself just a 15-minute drive from the center of Cape Town off the N1 highway. It is a massive, modern shopping center with over 400 stores, including designer labels, department stores, restaurants and cafés.

⟳ EMBASSIES / CONSULATES

Australian Consulate (BP Centre, Thibault Square, City Center, ☎021-419-5425).

Canadian Consulate (South African Reserve Bank Building, 60 St George's Mall, City Center, ☎021-423-5240).

Dutch Consulate (100 Strand St, City Center, ☎021-421-5660).

French Consulate (78 Queen Victoria St, Gardens, ☎021-423-1575).

German Consulate (Safmarine House, 22 Riebeek St, City Center, ☎021-405-3000).

Japanese Consulate (Standard Bank Centre, Heerengracht St, City Center, ☎021-425-1695).

Madagascaran Consulate (77 Newlands Ave, Newlands, ☎021-674-7238).

Spanish Consulate (37 Shortmarket St, City Center, ☎021-422-2415).

Swedish Consulate (ABSA Centre, 2 Riebeek St, City Center, ☎021-418-1276).

Swiss Consulate (Thibault Square, cnr Long St & Strijdom St, City Center, ☎021-418-3665).

UK Consulate (Southern Life Centre, 8 Riebeek St, City Center, ☎021-405 2400). **USA Consulate** (2 Reddam Ave, Westlake, ☎021 702-7300).

CAPE TOWN

✪ POLICE & MEDICAL

In the event of a serious medical emergency requiring immediate attention, your best bet is to call the private **Netcare Ambulance Service** (☏082-911). They will bring you to a private Netcare Clinic.

Metro Emergency Rescue Service (☏10177)
Cape Town Central Police Station (S 33 55.650 E 018 25.400, cnr Buitenkant St & Albertus St, City Center, ☏10111, from mobile dial ☏112).
Groote Schuur Hospital (S 33 56.459 E 018 27.832, Main Rd, Observatory, ☏021-404-9111, www.capegateway.gov.za/gsh) is a large public and high quality hospital that offers specialized services.
Netcare Christian Barnard Memorial Hospital (S 33 55.310 E 018 25.095, 181 Longmarket St, City Center, ☏021-480-6111, www.netcare.co.za) is the best private hospital in the Cape Town area.
Netcare Travel Clinic (S 33 55.240 E 018 25.306, Picbal Arcade, 58 Strand St, City Center, ☏021-419-3172, www.travelclinics.co.za, 8am-4pm Mon-Fri) provides vaccinations and other travel related health services.

✪ SIGHTS

Table Mountain (S 33 57.453 E 018 24.189, www.sanparks.org/parks/table_mountain) is part of the Table Mountain National Park, which stretches from the mountain itself all the way south to Cape Point. Table Mountain is Cape Town's most popular tourist destination for its spectacular views of the city, Robben Island and the surrounding expanse of ocean. Most visitors ascend the 1080-meter-high mountain via the **Cableway** (S 33 56.895 E 018 24.184, Lower Cableway Station, 370 Tafelberg Rd, ☏021-424-8181, www.tablemountain.net, Feb-Nov: 8:30am-7pm, Dec-

Jan: 8am-10pm, adult R160, child R80). At the top of the mountain is a café, gift shop and a number of short walking trails where you can take in views from both sides of the mountain. For the more adventurous, the mountain can be ascended on foot via an assortment of trails that vary in length and difficulty (see p96 for more information on hiking the mountain). Note that the top of the mountain is often engulfed in a cloud commonly referred to as the "table cloth," so if it is not sunny and calm outside, it may be worth calling or checking online to make sure the cable car is operating as it frequently closes during windy or cloudy days.
Robben Island (☏021-413-4220, www.robben-island.org.za, ferries depart 9am, 10am, 11am, 1pm, 2pm, & 3pm daily, subject to seasonal changes, adult R200, child R100,) is the infamous island prison off the Cape coast where Nelson Mandela and numerous other political prisoners were held during apartheid.

While the UNESCO World Heritage Site is of undeniable historical and political importance, and a visit can be both emotional and compelling, travelers should be advised that the tour can be a hassle. You should also be prepared for a last-minute change in plans as tours are often cancelled due to weather conditions, but tickets will be refunded or can be rebooked. This does not deter thousands of tourists who make the journey each year, so if you plan to go, make sure to book tickets at least one week in advance and two to three weeks in

Banished & Imprisoned

Robben Island has long been used as a place for imprisonment of political adversaries and isolation of the Cape's "undesirables." Beginning in the late 1600s, the Dutch East India Company (VOC) used the island as a site to banish those who opposed their colonial rule. Many Xhosa leaders and resistance fighters from the Dutch East Indies were held in exile on the island as well as Cape Town's early Muslim leaders, such as Sheikh Matura, who opposed colonialism, slavery and oppression of his people. In addition to housing prisoners, it also served as an isolated leper colony and hospital for the mentally ill throughout the latter part of the 19th century.

But its most notorious role was that as a maximum-security prison for black political prisoners during apartheid. It became a national and international symbol of political oppression as leaders such as Nelson Mandela and PAC founder Robert Sobukwe were sentenced and held here in prolonged detention. Mandela spent most of his 18 years on Robben Island housed in B Section along with many other political prisoners, where he continued his struggle, education and ardent opposition against the apartheid regime until he was released and went on to become the country's first democratically elected president.

With the dissolution of the apartheid state, the last political prisoners were released from Robben Island by May 1991 as the country moved through its transition to democracy. All remaining common-law prisoners, who had been housed separately from the political prisoners, were removed from Robben Island in 1996 and the prison was officially closed. In 1997 it reopened as a museum to remember the abuses of the past and the unwavering resolve of those who fought for democracy in South Africa and in 1999 it was declared a UNESCO World Heritage Site.

advance during peak holiday seasons.

Tours depart from the **Nelson Mandela Gateway** (*S 33 54.387 E 018 25.346, Clock Tower Square, Waterfront*). From there you will be ferried to the island to board a tour bus upon arrival. Many tours of the island are led by former political prisoners who recount their personal stories as you peek into the small cells where they and many others spent years of their lives. However, as the years go on, many new-generation guides have been employed as well. To ensure you get the most authentic experience possible, look out for the older bus drivers and hop on with them. Tours last roughly two hours and include visits to the prison, the isolation hut where PAC leader Robert Subukwe was held, the lime quarry where Nelson Mandela and others were forced into labor, the leper church, and remnants of the island's past history as a strategic war post.

Signal Hill (*S 33 55.057 E 018 24.166*) is also known as Lion's Rump, and the spine or ridge that extends from the "rump" to the pointed lion's head separates the downtown city bowl from Sea Point. Signal Hill is easily accessible via Signal Hill Road, which hugs the ridge and provides impressive views of the city and harbor. There are a handful of scenic lookout points along the road and a park area at the top of Signal Hill that is a popular destination for afternoon picnics and watching sunsets. You can also walk up Signal Hill Road or hike one of the nearby trails to take in the views, but the uphill path can be a workout. Closer to the base of the hill, bordering Bo-Kaap, is the **Noon Gun** (*S 33 54.906 E 018 24.696*), a cannon fired by the South African Navy at noon every day save Sunday. The cannons at the Lion Battery were originally used both to announce the arrival of incoming ships and to set time for residents and passing ships. The most direct access to the Noon Gun is via the extremely steep Longmarket Street, where you can park and take the short walk to the noon gun. You can also drive directly to the site via Military Road.

⚙ City Center & Bo-Kaap

District Six Museum (*S 33 55.663 E 018 25.420, 25A Buitenkant St, City Center, ☎021-466-7200,*

CAPE TOWN

GREATER CAPE TOWN

ℹ TOURIST INFO
Cape Town Tourism.............(see 2)

✳ SIGHTS & ACTIVITIES
Irma Stern Museum.............1   E8
Lower Cableway Station.......2   E4
Rhodes Memorial 3   E8
Upper Cableway Station.......4   F5

🏠 SLEEPING
Les Cascades de Bantry Bay 5   C3

😊 ENTERTAINMENT
Newlands Cricket Stad........6   F8
Newlands Stadium 7   F8

2

3

4

NORTH TO
Robben Island (10km)

Atlantic Ocean

Sea Point (p. 71)

GREEN POINT

M6

M61

THREE ANCHOR BAY

M6

M61

SEA POINT

Signal Hill

M6

M61

FRESNAYE

C

BANTRY BAY 🏠5

TAMBOERS KLOOF

GARDENS

M6

CLIFTON

M61

D

Camps Bay (p. 69)

M6

M62

2

E

M6

CAMPS BAY

Table Mountain Nat'l Park

M62

F

SOUTH TO
Sanctuary Spa (2km)
Llandudno Beach (7km)
Sandy Bay Beach (10km)
Chapman's Peak Drive (12km)

BAKOVEN

M6

1

2

3

4

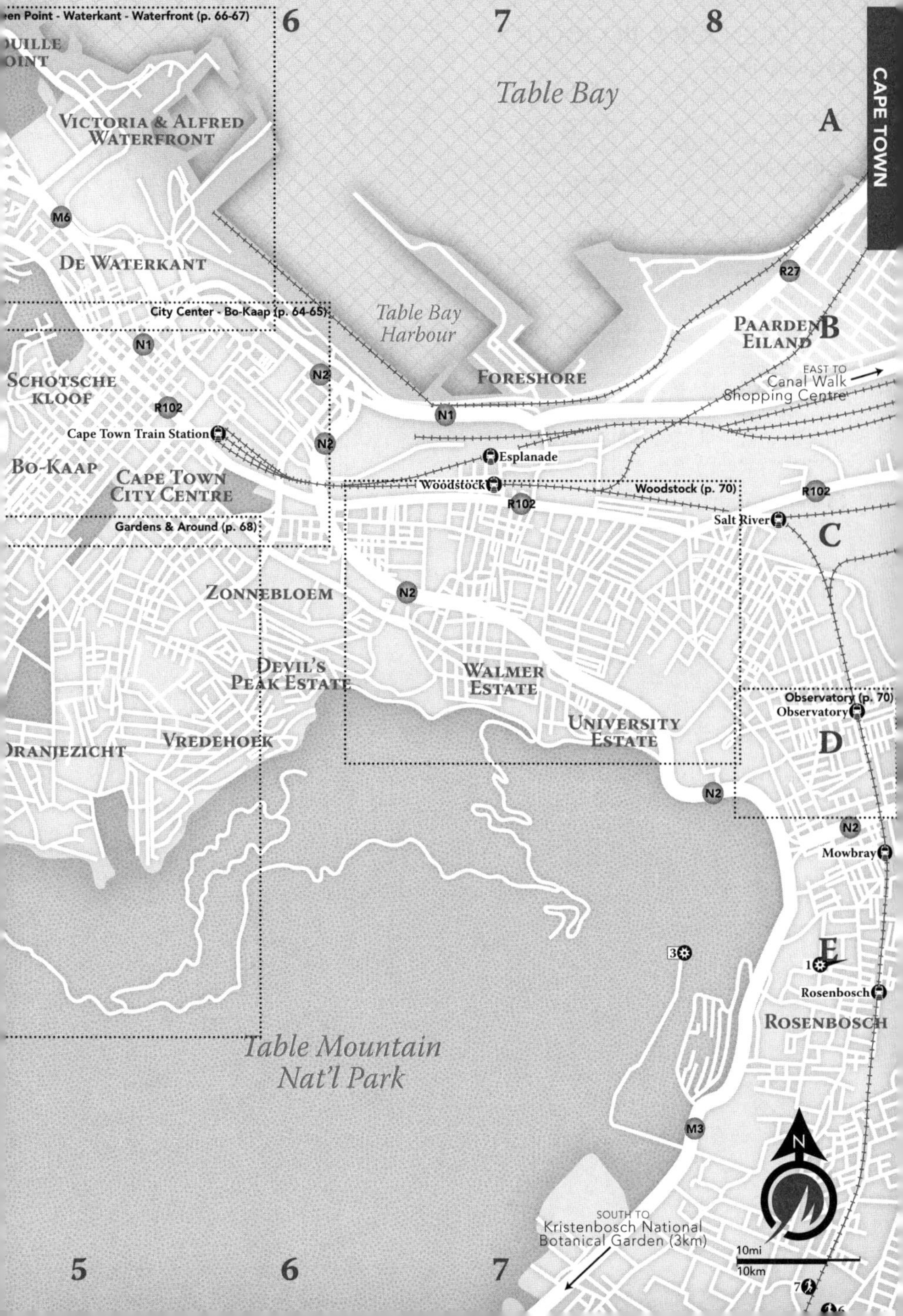

CAPE TOWN

een Point - Waterkant - Waterfront (p. 66-67)   **6**   **7**   **8**

OUILLE
OINT

Table Bay

A

**VICTORIA & ALFRED
WATERFRONT**

M6

DE WATERKANT

City Center - Bo-Kaap (p. 64-65)   *Table Bay
Harbour*

R27

**PAARDEN
EILAND**   **B**

N1

N2   **FORESHORE**

EAST TO
Canal Walk
Shopping Centre

**SCHOTSCHE
KLOOF**

R102

N1

Cape Town Train Station

N2   Esplanade

Woodstock   Woodstock (p. 70)   R102

BO-KAAP   **CAPE TOWN
CITY CENTRE**   R102   Salt River   **C**

Gardens & Around (p. 68)

ZONNEBLOEM   N2

**DEVIL'S
PEAK ESTATE**   **WALMER
ESTATE**   Observatory (p. 70)
Observatory   **D**

ORANJEZICHT   **VREDEHOEK**   **UNIVERSITY
ESTATE**

N2

N2

Mowbray

E

3   1

Rosenbosch

ROSENBOSCH

*Table Mountain
Nat'l Park*

M3

N

SOUTH TO
Kristenbosch National
Botanical Garden (3km)   10mi
10km

5   **6**   **7**

CITY CENTER & BO-KAAP

TOURIST INFO
Cape Town Tourism......... 1   C6

MONEY
American Express............. 2   B7

INTERNET
Computeria 3   E3

POLICE & MEDICAL
Central Police Station 4   F7
Netcare Mem. Hospital ... 5   C4
Netcare Travel Clinic 6   B6

GALLERIES
Assn. for Visual Arts 7   D5
iArt.................................... 8   C5

SHOPPING
African Home.................... 9   F8
Church Street Market...... 10   D5
Greenmarket Square........ (see 22)
Imagenius 11   D5
Pan African Market......... 12   C5
Rainbow Experience......... 13   D5
Streetwires 14   B4

SIGHTS & ACTIVITIES
Abseil Africa 15   E3
Castle of Good Hope....... 16   E8
Company Gardens 17   F4
District Six Museum 18   F7
Evg.Lutheran Church....... 19   A5
Gold of Africa Museum.... 20   A5
Grand Parade................... 21   D6
Greenmarket Square 22   C5
Groote Kerk 23   D6
Houses of Parliament 24   E6
Iziko Bo-Kaap Museum.... 25   C3
Iziko Slave Lodge 26   D6
Old City Hall.................... 27   D7
Old Town House 28   D5
St George's Cathedral 29   D5

SLEEPING
Cape Heritage Hotel......... 30   B5
Cat & Moose
Backpackers 31   F3

Daddy Long Legs Hotel... 32   D4
Grand Daddy 33   B5
Long Street Backpackers. 34   D4
Mandela Rhodes Place..... 35   D5
St Paul's B&B Guest
House 36   D3
Tudor Hotel...................... 37   C5
Urban Chic Hotel............. 38   D4

EATING
Addis in Cape 39   C4
Biesmiellah 40   B3
Birds Boutique Café 41   C4
Caveau.............................. 42   B4
Clay Oven Pizza Café....... 43   D4
Eastern Food Bazaar 44   D6
Gold Restaurant .... (see 20)
95 Keerom 45   E4
Nzolo Brand Café............. 46   D5
Royal Eatery 47   E3
Savoy Cabbage................. 48   B4

DRINKING
&Union 49   C4
Dubliner 50   E3
Fiction 51   E3
Hemisphere....................... 52   B7
Joburg 53   E3
Pink Flamingo.................. (see 32)
Purple Turtle 54   C5
Rainbow Room .... (see 13)
Waiting Room .... (see 47)
Zula Sound Bar................ 55   E4

ENTERTAINMENT
Artscape............................ 56   B8
NewSpace Theatre 57   C5
On Broadway.................... 58   B5

TRANSPORTATION
Cape Town Railway
Station 59   C8
Golden Acre Terminal 60   D8
Long Distance Bus
Terminal 61   B8
Minibus Taxi Rank .... (see 59)

CAPE TOWN
BUITENGRACHT ST
PRESTWICH ST
LONG ST
JETTY ST
HANS STRIJDOM AVE
HEERENGRACHT ST
RIEBEEK ST
LOOP ST
WATERKANT ST
BREE ST
LOWER BUG ST
OLD MARINE DR
R102
CASTLE ST
HOUT ST
ADDERLEY ST
STRAND ST
SHORTMARKET ST
BURG ST
ST GEORGE'S MALL
LONGMARKET ST
CHURCH ST
PARLIAMENT ST
PLEIN ST
WALE ST
DARLING ST
BUREAU ST
PARADE ST
CORPORATION ST
CALEDON ST
ALBERTUS ST
HARRINGTON ST
LONGMKT ST
BARRACK ST
BUITENKANT RD
COMMERCIAL ST
ST JOHNS ST
ROELAND ST
CANTERBURY ST
PRIMROSE ST
N
500ft
200m

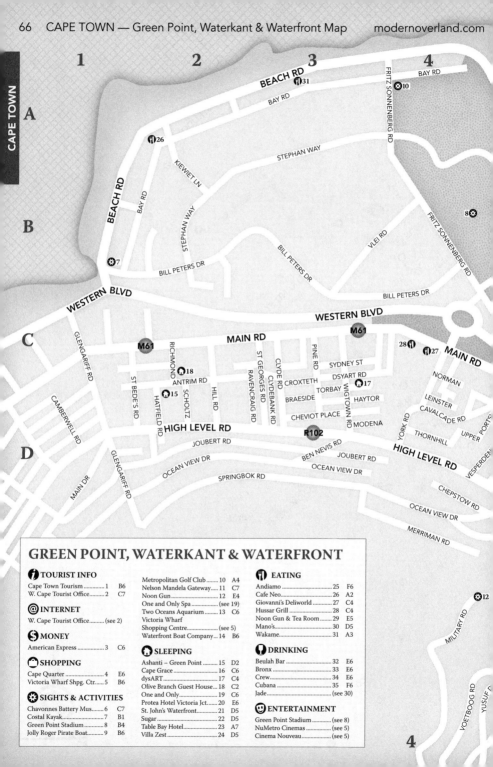

GREEN POINT, WATERKANT & WATERFRONT

TOURIST INFO
Cape Town Tourism 1   B6
W. Cape Tourist Office........ 2   C7

INTERNET
W. Cape Tourist Office.......... (see 2)

MONEY
American Express 3   C6

SHOPPING
Cape Quarter 4   E6
Victoria Wharf Shpg. Ctr...... 5   B6

SIGHTS & ACTIVITIES
Chavonnes Battery Mus........ 6   C7
Costal Kayak........................ 7   B1
Green Point Stadium 8   B4
Jolly Roger Pirate Boat......... 9   B6

Metropolitan Golf Club........ 10   A4
Nelson Mandela Gateway.... 11   C7
Noon Gun 12   E4
One and Only Spa .... (see 19)
Two Oceans Aquarium 13   C6
Victoria Wharf
Shopping Centre..................... (see 5)
Waterfront Boat Company... 14   B6

SLEEPING
Ashanti – Green Point 15   D2
Cape Grace 16   C6
dysART 17   C4
Olive Branch Guest House.... 18   C2
One and Only....................... 19   C6
Protea Hotel Victoria Jct...... 20   E6
St. John's Waterfront............ 21   D5
Sugar 22   D5
Table Bay Hotel.................... 23   A7
Villa Zest 24   D5

EATING
Andiamo 25   F6
Cafe Neo............................... 26   A2
Giovanni's Deliworld 27   C4
Hussar Grill 28   C4
Noon Gun & Tea Room 29   E5
Mano's 30   D5
Wakame................................ 31   A3

DRINKING
Beulah Bar 32   E6
Bronx 33   E6
Crew...................................... 34   E6
Cubana 35   F6
Jade .... (see 30)

ENTERTAINMENT
Green Point Stadium .... (see 8)
NuMetro Cinemas .... (see 5)
Cinema Nouveau..................... (see 5)

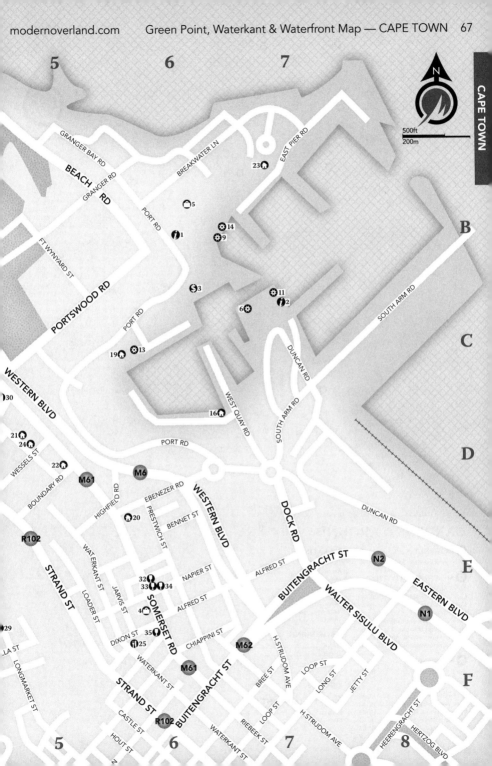

CAPE TOWN

N

500ft
200m

5   6   7

B

C

D

E

F

GRANGER BAY RD

BEACH RD

GRANGER RD

FT WYNARD ST

PORTSWOOD RD

PORT RD

PORT RD

WESTERN BLVD

BREAKWATER LN

EAST PIER RD

SOUTH ARM RD

DUNCAN RD

SOUTH ARM RD

WEST QUAY RD

DOCK RD

DUNCAN RD

PORT RD

WESTERN BLVD

BUITENGRACHT ST

WALTER SISULU BLVD

EASTERN BLVD

BUITENGRACHT ST

STRAND ST

STRAND ST

SOMERSET RD

WATERKANT ST

CHIAPPINI ST

CASTLE ST

HOUT ST

WATERKANT ST

RIEBEEK ST

BREE ST

LOOP ST

H.STRUDOM AVE

LOOP ST

LONG ST

JETTY ST

H.STRUDOM AVE

HEERENGRACHT ST

HERTZOG BLVD

LONGMARKET ST

LA ST

DIXON ST

JARVIS ST

LOADER ST

WAT ERKANT ST

HIGHFIELD RD

PRESTWICH ST

BENNET ST

NAPIER ST

ALFRED ST

ALFRED ST

EBENEZER RD

BOUNDARY RD

WESSELS ST

23

5

1

14

9

3

11

2

6

13

19

16

21

24

22

M61

M6

20

R102

30

29

32

33   34

4

35

25

N2

N1

M62

M61

R102

CAPE TOWN

GARDENS & AROUND

@ INTERNET

Geek @ Java Internet Café..............1 A2

⚙ SIGHTS & ACTIVITIES

🛏 SLEEPING

🍴 EATING

🍷 DRINKING

😊 ENTERTAINMENT

CAPE TOWN

CAMPS BAY

✱ SIGHTS & ACTIVITIES
Camps Bay Beach.....................1   B2
Clifton Beaches.......................2   A1

🏠 SLEEPING
30 Fiskaal Guest House...........3   D3
Bay Hotel................................4   C2
Fullham Lodge 5   F1

🍴 EATING
The Grand...............................6   B2
Paranga..................................7   C2

🍷 DRINKING
Café Caprice...........................8   C2
Dizzy's Pub.............................9   C2
Karma ....(see 7)
La Med...................................10   A1

Table Mountain
Nat'l Park

500ft
200m

CAPE TOWN

WOODSTOCK

GALLERIES
Goodman Gallery	1	A1
Michael Stevenson Gallery	2	A1
WhatifTheWorld	3	A3

SHOPPING
Old Biscuit Mill	4	A4

SLEEPING
Cape Town Deco Lodge	5	B3

EATING
Don Pedro's	6	B3
Jamaica Me Crazy	7	B3

DRINKING & ENT.
Albert Hall	(see 3)	

OBSERVATORY

INTERNET
African Access	1	B2

POLICE & MEDICAL
Groote Schuur Hospital	2	B1

SLEEPING
33 South Backpackers	3	B3
African Heart Backpackers	4	A2
Obviouzly Armchair Bkpkrs	5	A2

EATING
1890 House Sushi and Grill	6	B2
Coco Cha Chi	7	C2
Mango Ginger	8	B2
Mimi's Café	9	B2
Obz Café	10	A2

DRINKING & ENT.
Stones	11	A2
Tagore's	12	B3

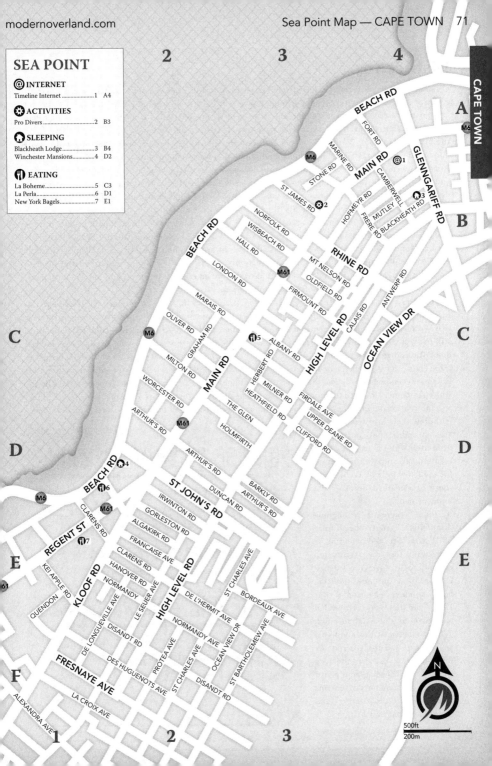

SEA POINT

@ INTERNET
Timeline Internet 1 A4

✷ ACTIVITIES
Pro Divers 2 B3

🏠 SLEEPING
Blackheath Lodge...............3 B4
Winchester Mansions.........4 D2

🍴 EATING
La Boheme..........................5 C3
La Perla..............................6 D1
New York Bagels.................7 E1

CAPE TOWN

District Six

Officially established as the Sixth District of Cape Town in 1867, the area of District Six was historically a working class and migrant neighborhood, however it has gained international fame as a focal point of apartheid's racial zoning laws and the displacement of non-whites from the Cape Town's urban center. It was first developed by former slave-owners turned slumlords as housing for ex-slaves and the black urban poor. By the end of the 19th century District Six had become a bustling and heavily populated working class neighborhood whose population was predominantly coloured, Cape Malay and African intermixed with Indian, Chinese, and European migrants. Living conditions were overcrowded and unsanitary, as the municipal government consistently neglected the area, however District Six developed into a vibrant community famous not only for its night clubs but also for its raucous and colorful New Years parades as residents filled the streets in celebration.

The first forced displacements occurred in 1901 when an outbreak of the bubonic plague in Cape Town was wrongfully blamed on black dockworkers. All black residents of District Six were forcibly removed under the pretext of health legislation to an area in the Cape Flats, establishing the first black township known as Ndabeni. Despite this blow to the neighborhood, District Six continued to flourish throughout the first half of the 20th century and emerged as a central hub for jazz musicians, journalists, writers and intellectuals among the working class.

However after the election of the Nationalist Party in 1948, a series of apartheid laws began to threaten the existence of coloured, African and Indian communities in Cape Town. Despite the fact that Western Cape had been deemed a Coloured Labour Preference Area, the city's coloured population still fell victim to racial zoning laws. In 1966 District Six was rezoned as a "white Group Area" and the demolitions that followed during the next 15 years displaced some 60,000 people from District Six to the Cape Flats. The area was renamed Zonnebloem and District Six homes were destroyed to make room for urban redevelopment projects, the construction of boulevards and freeways and improved housing for white residents. However the housing development plans for District Six were met with fervent local and international opposition as civic and community groups banned together in protest and developers withdrew their investment in the area. Besides the construction of limited white housing and the creation of a new white campus for the University of Technology, the area remained desolate and undeveloped.

Today there are ongoing discussions about the future of District Six and planning is underway for the restitution of land to its former residents. Construction of new housing has commenced and over 1,600 families are scheduled to return to the neighborhood. Tensions between the municipal government and the District Six Beneficiary Trust has delayed some of the redevelopment plans, however the community remains committed to reclaiming and rebuilding what they lost.

FOR USE BY WHITE PERSONS

THESE PUBLIC PREMISES AND THE AMENITIES THEREOF HAVE BEEN RESERVED FOR THE EXCLUSIVE USE OF WHITE PERSONS.

By Order Provincial Secretary

VIR GEBRUIK DEUR BLANKES

HIERDIE OPENBARE PERSEEL EN DIE GERIEWE DAARVAN IS VIR DIE UITSLUITLIKE GEBRUIK VAN BLANKES AANGEWYS.

Op Las Provinsiale Sekretaris

www.districtsix.co.za, 9am-2pm Mon, 9am-4pm Tue-Sat, Sun by appointment, adult R20, child R5) poignantly recalls the demolition of a once-vibrant inner city neighborhood that fell victim to apartheid zoning laws when the area was rezoned as a "white" area in 1966. About 60,000 coloured residents were subsequently displaced. First intended to be a temporary exhibit in 1994, the museum stands as a site of collective memory of the residents of District Six. Across the entire floor of the museum, visitors can walk across a scaled layout that indicates where buildings and homes once stood. Multimedia exhibits tell the story of those displaced and the apartheid regime's effects on them. You can wander on your own or be guided by an ex-resident who can share stories of his or her family's experience. Guided tours of the museum don't have set times, but your best bet to catch one is by coming in the morning. Ex-residents lead walking tours of the neighborhood on Sundays for R50, but you have to book in advance and there is a 10-person minimum.

Grand Parade (S 33 55.489 E 018 25.482, Darling St btwn Buitenkant St & Lower Plein St) is the largest and oldest city square in Cape Town and the site where the Dutch East India Company built its first fort. Though once a commercial center and military parade ground, today it hosts a flea market on Wednesdays and Saturdays. The square is flanked to the east by the Castle of Good Hope and to the south by Old City Hall. It was here in February 1990 that thousands of people gathered to hear Nelson Mandela speak publicly for the first time after his 27 years of imprisonment from the balcony of **Old City Hall** (S 33 55.515 E 018 25.431, cnr Darling St & Corporation St). The large Edwardian structure was built in 1905 and served as the seat of Cape Town local government for the majority of the 20th century, but local government has since relocated to the Cape Town Civic Center and no longer does business here. The old halls are gathering dust, but the auditorium is still used regularly for concerts.

Castle of Good Hope (S 33 55.535 E 018 25.638, cnr Darling St & Buitenkant St, 021-787-1260, www.castleofgoodhope.co.za, 9am-4pm, tours: 11am, 12pm & 2pm, adult R25, child R10) is the oldest standing colonial building in Cape Town. It was built by the Dutch East India Company (and its slaves) between 1666 and 1679, as a stronghold to protect the company's stores of supplies it traded to passing ships. The squat,

pentagonal structure was the Western Cape's military headquarters for the South African Army and today houses the Castle Military Museum and serves as a monument to Cape Town's past. The main house boasts the William Fehr Collection of colonial Cape Dutch furnishings and paintings. Guided tours are available daily at 11am, 12pm and 2pm. The Key Ceremony takes place at 10am and 12pm everyday, followed by the firing of Signal Cannon, both of which are incorporated into the 12pm guided tour. If you show yourself around, make sure to walk the upper level perimeter for a 360-degree view of the city. Horse and carriage rides also are available at 10:30am, 12:45pm, 2:45pm or 6pm daily for a scenic ride through Cape Town and the Company's Gardens (082-575-5669, www.ctcco.co.za, R150).

Company's Gardens (S 33 55.616 E 018 25.064, Government Ave, cnr of Adderly St & Wale St), the green center of Cape Town, is what remains of the original gardens first planted by the Dutch East India Company (VOC) in 1652 to supply passing ships with fresh fruits and vegetables. As the Cape settlement expanded and larger farms were established in the interior, the garden transformed into a botanical experiment for the rising colonial elite. It is a beautiful setting for a picnic or for a quiet stroll and is surrounded by several other important Cape Town landmarks including the National Library, the Tuynhus (or Presidential Residence), Houses of Parliament and the National Gallery. The main path through the Gardens is Government Avenue, which you can access via entrances at the corner of Adderly Street & Wale Street, along Queen Victoria Street and on Museum Street near the South African Museum and Planetarium. Self-guided tours and maps of the gardens are available online at: www.capetown.gov.za/en/parks/facilities/pages/capetowngardens.aspx, but advance study is not necessary to enjoy the scenery.

Iziko Slave Lodge (S 33 55.501 E 018 25.222, cnr Adderley St & Wale St, 021-460 8240, www.iziko.org.za/slavelodge, 10am-5pm Mon-Sat, adult R15, child free) was built in 1679 to house Dutch East India Company slaves imported from Madagascar, Indonesia, India, Ceylon and elsewhere. At its peak, it housed over 1,000 slaves in inhumane conditions. The fortress-like structure later housed various government offices and served as the Supreme Court for the Cape Colony between 1815 and 1914. The museum's touching, thoughtful exhibits serve as a memorial to communities affected by slavery and examine the effects of apartheid and racial discrimination on the country. Your museum experience is best ended with the maze-like Nelson Mandela exhibit, which includes an exclusive documentary on the statesman and his life's struggle for equality. The Mandela show will be on exhibit through January 2011; check the website for exhibit updates.

Houses of Parliament (*S 33 55.544 E 018 25.182, Parliament St, ☏021-403-2266, www. parliament.gov.za, 9am-2pm Mon-Fri, free*) tell the story of South Africa's legislative history. The original legislative chamber and seat of the Cape Colony was built in 1885, and in 1910, Cape Town was christened as the legislative capital of the Union. This arrangement stood until 1984, when constitutional reform gave token representation to the country's Indian and coloured populations in an attempt to quell rising opposition to apartheid. The previously all-white parliament became a "Tricameral Parliament," and met in the Tricameral Chamber. Today, the National Assembly is housed in the old Tricameral Chamber and the Council of Provinces occupies the old Houses of Parliament. Tours are available every hour (from 9am-2pm Mon-Fri) and must be arranged at least one week in advance. The entrance for tours is at the Visitor's Center on 100 Plein Street, at the corner of Lelie Street.

Groote Kerk (*S 33 55.486 E 018 25.253, 43 Adderley St, ☏021-422-0569, 10am-2pm Mon-Fri, services 10am & 7pm Sun, free*) or "Great Church" is the mother church of the Dutch Reformed Church in South Africa and the oldest existing church in southern Africa. The Dutch East India Company did not allow religious freedom in the Cape and the Dutch Reformed Church was the only recognized religion until 1779. The bell tower dates from 1704 and is the only remaining piece of the original construction of the church. Once inside, be sure to check out the enormous pulpit, as well as the massive organ - the largest in southern Africa. Entrance is in the back on Parliament Street and guided tours are available on request at no additional charge, but you'll have to pay for the historical pamphlet.

St George's Cathedral (*S 33 55.483 E 018 25.163, 1 Wale St, ☏021-424-7360, www. stgeorgescathedral.com, 8am-5pm, services 7:15am & 1:15pm Mon-Fri, 8am Sat, 7am, 8am, 10am & 7pm Sun, free*) or "The People's Cathedral," was the pulpit from which Archbishop Desmond Tutu, the first black Anglican Archbishop of Cape Town, called for the end of apartheid. In September 1989, 30,000 people left from the steps of the cathedral to start the famous Cape Town peace march. They defied the state of emergency in peaceful protest through the streets of Cape Town in a march to City Hall, where they demanded an end to racial segregation. The church remains central to Cape Town religious life and boasts a magnificently preserved organ as well as the largest stained glass window in the country.

Greenmarket Square *(S 33 55.375 E 018 25.204, Burg St btwn Shortmarket St & Longmarket St, City Center)* is a cobblestone square that has long been at the center of Cape Town daily life. Flanked to the south by the Old Town House, which served as a city hall for the latter part of the 19th century, the square was a forum for municipal government and later a vegetable market. Today it is one of Cape Town's flea markets, with crafts, drums, statues, tapestries and other curios for sale daily.

Old Town House *(S 33 55.385 E 018 25.195, Greenmarket Square, City Center,* ☎*021-481-3933, www.iziko.org. za/michaelis, 10am-5pm Mon-Sat, donation suggested)* is a stately town house bordering the Greenmarket Square, built in 1755 in the Cape Rococo style. It has served a variety of municipal functions, including a lengthy reign as Cape Town's City Hall from 1840-1905. Today it houses the Michaelis Collection of 17th century Dutch paintings donated by Sir Max Michaelis in 1914.

Long Street *(S 33 55.536 E 018 24.940, cnr Long St & Bloem St, City Center)* is the backpackers and nightlife mecca of Cape Town. The Victorian-style buildings with balconies that extend over the sidewalks are filled with independent cafés, boutiques, backpackers, and travel and tour agents. By night, numerous restaurants, budget accommodations and bars encourage a hedonistic party scene, flocked to by tourists, locals, students and beggars.

Iziko Bo-Kaap Museum *(S 33 55.288 E 018 24.902, 71 Wale St, Bo-Kaap,* ☎*021-481-3939, www.iziko.org.za/bokaap, 10am-5pm Mon-Sat, adult R10, child free)* is a small but worthwhile culture and history museum set in the home of Abu Bakr Effendi, a prominent Muslim leader in Cape Town during the mid 1800s. The exhibits provide insight into the colorful streets of Bo-Kaap as an inner city, working class neighborhood and the historical center of Cape Town's Muslim and Cape Malay community. The museum is dedicated to all those who helped build Cape Town but were not allowed to enjoy the fruits of their labor. Guided tours of the museum and walking tours of the Bo-Kaap neighborhood are available for R150 if you'd like to get a full understanding of the area's rich history. If you wander the colorful streets on your own, make sure to stop by the spice-filled Atlas Trading Company across the street and visit the Owal Mosque, the oldest Mosque in South Africa and the religious hub of the Cape's Muslim community, just one block away.

Gold of Africa Museum *(S 33 55.150 E 018 25.178, 96 Strand St, City Center,* ☎*021-405-1540, www.goldofafrica.com, 9:30am-5pm Mon-Sat, adult R25, child R15)* is a well-designed gallery established for the preservation and promotion of African goldsmithing and jewelry. It traces Africa's gold routes, the role of gold in the great empires of the world and displays stunning pieces from all over Africa. For a more opulent experience, book in advance for a Pangolin Night Tour (R40), when you can view the gallery by torchlight while sipping on wine sprinkled with gold leaf. Your evening would be well culminated with an extravagant dinner at the adjoining **Gold Restaurant** *(*☎*021-421-4653, www.goldrestaurant.co.za)*, where you can enjoy a fixed-price menu of Cape Malay and African food while participating in the drum circle and lively entertainment.

Evangelical Lutheran Church *(S 33 55.141 E 018 25.168, 98 Strand St, City Center* ☎*021-421-5854, 10am-2pm Mon-Fri, free)* was converted from a barn in 1785 to establish the first Lutheran church in South Africa. For more than a century, the Dutch East India Company had banned any religious practice besides the Dutch Reformed Church.

So it was only after years of petitioning that the mainly German Lutheran population in the colony were finally granted the freedom to practice their religion in 1779. Today services are still offered every Sunday from the ornately carved pulpit.

✪ Gardens & Around

Iziko South African National Gallery (S 33 55.738 E 018 25.033, Government Ave, Gardens, ☎021-467-4660, www.iziko.org.za/sang, 10am-5pm Tue-Sun, adult R15, child free) is South Africa's premier art gallery, featuring inspirational, innovative and often controversial exhibits. As far as art galleries go, this one is exceptional. The gallery showcases South African, African and international artists with a renewed emphasis on celebrating the expression of contemporary South African communities long silenced during the country's apartheid past. The exhibits change roughly every three to four months, so check online for updated information. Public tours are available Tue-Fri at 11am, 12pm and 1pm at no additional charge.

South African Jewish Museum (S 33 55.795 E 018 25.017, 88 Hatfield St, Gardens, ☎021-465-1546, www.sajewishmuseum.co.za, 10am-5pm Sun-Thu, 10am-2pm Fri, adult R50, child R20) is acclaimed as South Africa's most high-tech museum. Housed in the Old Synagogue, the museum takes you on an interactive tour through immigrant Jewish life in South Africa and into a 19th-century Lithuanian village, tracing a common Jewish South African family history. Documentary film, family trees, artifacts and tributes by Nelson Mandela make this a truly dynamic museum experience. Audio tours on headset are available for R10.

Cape Town Holocaust Centre (S 33 55.808 E 018 24.995, 88 Hatfield St, Gardens, ☎021-462-5553, www.ctholocaust.co.za, 10am-5pm Sun-Thu, 10am-1pm Fri, free) is just across from the courtyard of the Jewish Museum. It is a small yet stoic memorial to the victims of the Holocaust and all those who have suffered racial discrimination and violations of human rights. Poignant sound and imagery connect the history of anti-Semitism with apartheid and appeal for further education on human rights and an end to racial prejudices and religious intolerance.

Iziko South African Museum (S 33 55.720 E 018 24.915, 25 Queen Victoria St, Gardens, ☎021-481-3330, www.iziko.org.za/sam, 10am-5pm, adult R15, child free) is a multilevel maze of natural history that contains land and sea exhibits, whale skeletons, dinosaur fossils, meteorites and other natural gems. A social history exhibit explores the cultures of South Africa's earliest inhabitants, including an impressive display of San rock art and culture developed in consultation with today's San community. This is South Africa's oldest museum, but unfortunately its age is beginning to show.

Iziko Planetarium (S 33 55.708 E 018 24.897, 25 Queen Victoria St, Gardens, ☎021-481-3900, www.iziko.org.za/planetarium, adult R20, child R6) is attached to the South African Museum and has daily shows at 2pm as well as a variety of special programs, many of which are specifically geared toward children. Call or check online for current programming.

✪ Green Point, Waterfront & Waterkant

Victoria & Alfred Waterfront, or plainly, the "Waterfront" is an enormous shopping area on the harbor. While it boasts great views of Table Mountain and bustling harbor activity, everything here is overpriced and the area isn't authentically Cape Town, so be sure to venture beyond to get a taste for the real city.

Victoria Wharf Shopping Centre (S 33 54.235 E 018 25.198, Waterfront, ☎021-408-7600, www.waterfront.co.za, 9am-9pm Mon-Sat, 10am-9pm Sun) is the main event on the waterfront and all the shopping mall that you could ever need, with over 400 stores encased in a large, glitzy building. There are numerous designer stores, cafés and restaurants, as well as two cinemas: **NuMetro Cinemas** (☎021-419-9700, www.numetro.co.za) that screens a mix of mainstream and independent movies on their 11 screens, and **Ster Kinekor** (☎021-425-8223, www.sterkinekor.com), which has a more independent, art-cinema bent.

Two Oceans Aquarium (S 33 54.463 E 018 25.060, Dock Rd, Waterfront, ☎021-418-3823, www.aquarium.co.za, 9am-6pm, adult R88, child R42-R68) is a state-of-the-art aquarium that focuses on education and appreciation of the diverse marine life from the Atlantic and Indian oceans along South Africa's coast. The interactive exhibits and Alpha Activity Center are great for kids. Try to coordinate your visit with one of the feeding times, especially the predators' feeding at 3pm or African penguin feedings at 11:45am and 2:30pm daily. If you are a certified scuba diver, you can dive with sharks and stingrays in the I&J

Predator Exhibit or feed the hundreds of fish in the Kelp Forest. Call to book your dive in advance. **Nelson Mandela Gateway** (*S 33 54.387 E 018 25.346, Clock Tower Square, Waterfront,* ☎*021-413-4220,* *www.robben-island.org.za*, *7am-5pm, free*) is not only the departing site for ferries to Robben Island, but also houses an emotional exhibit remembering apartheid's political prisoners, abuses and the struggle for human rights in South Africa. Original advocacy posters and international resistance media articles are preserved in the 3rd floor exhibit room and the Political Prisoner and Detainee Message Center hosts a video mural with the heartfelt messages of former prisoners who lost years of their lives in the struggle for equality.

Chavonnes Battery Museum (*S 33 54.414 E 018 25.305, Clock Tower Square, Waterfront,* ☎*021-416-6230,* *www.chavonnes-museum.co.za*, *9am-4pm Wed-Sun, adult R25, child R10*) houses the excavated ruins of one of Cape Town's oldest waterfront cannon batteries. The Battery was built in 1726 by the Dutch East India Company to protect the port against possible attacks by the French and English East India Companies and bellicose pirates. It was demolished and covered during the construction of the waterfront in the mid 1800s and excavated in 1999. Wander the ruins on your own or join one of the costumed tour guides for a by-demand tour anytime after 12pm. Call in advance to ensure that a tour guide will be available.

Green Point Stadium (*S 33 54.196 E 018 24.664, Fritz Sonneberg Rd*) was a mammoth architectural undertaking in preparation for the 2010 World Cup. The R4.5 billion stadium sports a translucent mesh façade, a roof ringed by glass panels and some 68,000

seats. Though its construction has been met with controversy, the completed venue promises to be central to Cape Town's sporting future. After hosting the World Cup, the stadium is now used for other large sporting events, concerts and other "mega-events." Big plans are also in the works for expanding the surrounding urban park around the golf course and biodiversity garden.

✪ Atlantic Coast (Sea Point, Clifton & Camps Bay)

Clifton Beaches (*S 33 56.454 E 018 22.512, Victoria Rd, Clifton*) is the see-and-be-seen spot for scantily clad sunbathers. The water here is freezing, but if you can brave it, it's a relatively safe area for swimming. The impressive houses that cling to the cliffs are some of the most desired and expensive real estate in South Africa. The trendy beaches are known by their numbers and each has its own scene. Beaches 1 and 2 are for the "beautiful people" or those who wish they were, Beach 3 has a prominent gay scene and Beach 4 is touted as a family beach and is also the most easily accessible. Make sure to pack whatever you need because there is not much else available next to the water besides umbrella and chair rentals for R25 each.

Camps Bay Beach (*S 33 57.044 E 018 22.672, Victoria Rd, Camps Bay*) is the most popular beach for tourists and locals to sunbathe and frequent the trendy restaurants, bars and cafés that line Victoria Road. The 12 Apostles of Table Mountain provides a dramatic backdrop for the long stretch of beach. The water is generally too cold to swim in for very long and the wind can be particularly fierce at times, but shelter and a cool drink are never too far away. Umbrellas and chairs can also be rented for the day for R25 each.

Llandudno Beach (*S 34 00.486 E 018 20.483, Llandudno Rd, Llandudno*) is just a 10-minute drive from the more crowded Camps Bay but has a more relaxed local vibe, as well as good surfing. Follow Victoria Rd/M6 south from Camps Bay and watch for the signed turnoff for a winding road down to the beach. Public transportation doesn't reach the beach, but you can ask buses headed to Hout Bay if they can drop you off on the highway and then just walk or hitch a ride down to the beach.

Sandy Bay (*S 34 01.381 E 018 19.903, Sunset Ave, Sandy Bay*) is Cape Town's secluded nude beach. Under apartheid, the police often raided the beach, chasing sunbathers into the hills. Today, the beach is very relaxed, gay friendly, and clothing optional, but there's no pressure to get more naked than you are comfortable with. To get there, take the Llandudno turnoff from Victoria Rd/M6 and keep left at the fork, following the sign to Sandy Bay. Take a left at Sandy Bay Road and continue to follow signs to the car park. Follow the footpath for 10 minutes until you reach your hidden destination.

Chapman's Peak Drive (*S 34 02.919 E 018 21.674, Chapman's Peak Rd/M6, ☎021-791-8222, toll R28*) is an exhilarating 10 km scenic drive stretching from Hout Bay to Noordhoek on a road literally carved into the side of the mountain. It offers spectacular ocean cliff views of Hout Bay and The Sentinel, with a couple of lookout points along the way. It is the preferred way to travel down the peninsula, but occasional falling rocks cause temporary closures, so you may want to call to check conditions before you head out.

✪Southern Suburbs

Kirstenbosch National Botanical Garden (*S 33 59.379 E 018 26.033, Rhodes Dr/M63, Newlands, ☎021-799-8783, www.sanbi.org, Sept-Mar: 8am-7pm, Apr-Aug: 8am-6pm, adult R35, child R10*) is 36 hectares of lush gardens on the eastern slope of Table Mountain and one of Cape Town's greatest attractions. Originally part of Cecil Rhodes' Groote Schuur estate, the land was bequeathed to the government upon his death, and in 1913 it was set aside for the creation of a botanic garden to preserve South Africa's distinct plant life. Today Kirstenbosch is home to a wide variety of unique Cape flora and over 7,000 species of cultivated plants from the surrounding southern Africa region. In 2004, it was declared an UNESCO World Heritage Site. Beyond the home gardening center, Botanical Society Conservatory, sculpture garden, fragrance garden and arboretum are multiple hiking paths that weave up the side of Table Mountain and through the untouched natural terrain of surrounding protected indigenous fynbos and forest. Women are advised not to take some of the upper paths alone due to recent attacks in the area, so you should check with staff for route suggestions. Free guided tours of the gardens are available Mon-Sat at 10am and MyGuide self-guided audio tours are available at Gate 1 for R35. Golf cart tours are R40 per person and leave every hour from 9am-3pm, weather permitting. Tours for visitors with special needs or interests can be arranged and there are large portions of the gardens that are wheelchair friendly. Live concerts in the gardens are a Cape Town Sunday afternoon institution and are a great occasion for a picnic. Take the N2/Eastern Blvd 4 km and keep to your right to continue onto M3/De Waal Dr/Rhodes Dr towards Muizenberg for 4.3 km. Turn right onto M63/Rhodes Dr and follow the signs for Kirstenbosch.

Rhodes Memorial (*S 33 57.137 E 018 27.539, Rondebosch, ☎021-689-9151, www.rhodesmemorial.co.za/memorial.html, 7am-7pm, free*) is a Greek-inspired memorial built in 1912 to pay tribute to diamond baron and former Prime Minister Cecil John Rhodes. Situated on the slopes of Devil's Peak, it is said to be the exact spot where Rhodes came to sit and think, over panoramic views of Cape Town as well as the Cape Flats. There is also an onsite restaurant that serves breakfast and lunch. Take the M3 to the Princess Anne Avenue exit, turn right and go under the bridge and follow the signs for a left turnoff to Rhodes Memorial.

Irma Stern Museum (*S 33 57.146 E 018 28.170,*

Cape Town Vineyards

While the heart of South African wine country is in nearby Stellenbosch, Paarl and Franschhoek, there are a couple of good vineyards in the southern suburbs, just a short drive from the City Center. Wine first came to the region in 1685 when Cape Governor Simon van der Stel established a wine farm on the lower slopes of Table Mountain. He named it "Constantia," and by the 1700s Constantia wines were coveted throughout Europe. Upon Simon van der Stel's death in 1712, his beloved farm was divided up and sold off as smaller farms, yet the region continued to flourish and produce fine South African wines that you can still enjoy today.

GROOT CONSTANTIA *(S 34 01.635 E 018 25.459, Groot Constantia Rd, High Constantia, 021-794-5128, www. grootconstantia.co.za, tastings: 9am-4:30pm May-Sept, 9am-5:30am Oct-Apr, R80, cellar tours: 10am-4pm, R33)* is Simon van der Stel's original estate and today the vineyard most geared towards tourists. If you are doing a wine tour of the area, this is a must stop, but be prepared for swarms of people when tour buses pass through. The tasting center has a small bar and large seating area with lounging couches and tables surrounded by a rotating art exhibit on the walls. The expansive estate has two restaurants and enough to keep you entertained for the better part of the day. The Cape Dutch Manor House, Van der Stel's original home, and Cloete Cellar have been converted to museums and both are available for touring *(021-795-5140, www.iziko.org.za/grootcon, 10am-5pm, adult R15, child free)*. Tours of the cellar begin every hour.

HIGH CONSTANTIA *(S 34 01.524 E 018 25.605, Groot Constantia Rd, High Constantia, 021-794-7171, www. highconstantia.co.za, 8am-5pm, tasting R60)* is a boutique winery and fairly new addition to the vineyard scene. Built in 2000 on a smaller section of the Groot Constantia estate, they specialize in MCC (Methode Cap Classique). The winery can only accommodate a couple parties at a time but if you can get in it is one of the better environments for a tasting. After entering through the cellar, enjoy your free sampling on the tranquil patio overlooking a small pond.

BUITENVERWACHTING *(S 34 02.485 E 018 24.986, Klein Constantia Rd, 021-794-5190, www.buitenverwacht-ing.co.za, 9am-5pm Mon-Fri, 10am-3pm Sat, tasting free)*, meaning Beyond Expectations, is known for the Buiten Blanc - a 85% sauvignon blanc and 15% chenin blanc blend. The drive there takes you through an arbor of large, leafy trees and brings you to their stylish tasting bar, complimented by outdoor foun-

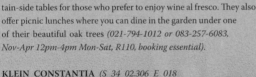

tain-side tables for those who prefer to enjoy wine al fresco. They also offer picnic lunches where you can dine in the garden under one of their beautiful oak trees *(021-794-1012 or 083-257-6083, Nov-Apr 12pm-4pm Mon-Sat, R110, booking essential)*.

KLEIN CONSTANTIA *(S 34 02.306 E 018 24.800, Klein Constantia Rd, 021-794-5188, www.kleinconstantia.com, 9am-5pm Mon-Fri, 9am-1pm Sat, tasting free)* is one of the most scenic of the Cape Town vineyards with sweeping views across the Constantia Valley and over False Bay. The tasting room is surprisingly modern for being one of the oldest vineyards, but their Marlbrook is excellent. Make sure to try the Vin de Constance, their re-creation of the wine that made Constantia famous.

Cecil Rd, Rosebank, ▮021-685-5686; www.irmastern.co.za, 10am-5pm Tue-Sat, R10) is the former home of one of South Africa's most famous 20th-century painters. Irma Stern (1894-1966) became a cultural and artistic icon not only for her fusion of European-inspired expressionist artwork and African subjects, but also for her vast collection of African and ancient artifacts. Her unique portraits and colorful landscapes comprise the museum's excellent permanent collection and are accompanied by a contemporary display of South African artists. After touring the museum, explore the garden.

✪ ACTIVITIES

Ⓐ Abseiling & Kloofing
Abseil Africa (S 33 55.603 E 018 24.880, cnr Long St & Vredenburg Ln, Gardens, ▮021-424-4760, www.abseilafrica.co.za, abseiling R495) arranges all sorts of adrenaline pumping activities. You can rappel off the side of Table Mountain, hike up a river gorge, or try your hand at kloofing in their all-day Kamikaze Kanyon trip. Guides are experienced and safety and fun are their number one priorities.

Ⓑ Bungee Jumping
Bloukrans Bridge is one of the world's highest commercial jumps, and is located 40 km east of Plettenberg Bay along the N2, about a six-hour drive from Cape Town. The Gouritz Bridge is slightly closer and most two-day trips to Bloukrans will stop at Gouritz as well.
Downhill Adventures (S 33 55.650 E 018 24.819, cnr Orange St & Kloof St, Gardens, ▮021-422-0388, www.downhilladventures.com, trip from R2,000) can organize overnight bungee tours to Bloukrans Bridge or day trips to Gouritz Bridge. They also offer combination shark diving and bungee trips.
Bungy Bus (▮079-666-9789, www.bungybus.co.za, trips from R2,500) does overnight trips to Bloukrans Bridge or Gouritz Bridge. Trips include transport, jumps, food and the option to shark cage dive.

Ⓒ Cruises
Waterfront Boat Company (S 33 54.262 E 018 25.256, Quay 5, Waterfront, ▮021-418-5806, www.waterfrontboats.co.za) is the largest cruise operator in the harbor. They offer harbor cruises (1hr, adult R100, child R50), bay cruises (1hr, adult R100, child R50) that tour from the Waterfront to the Green Point lighthouse, and sunset sailboat champagne cruises (1.5hr, adults R200, child R100).
Jolly Roger Pirate Boat (S 33 54.269 E 018 25.249, Quay 5, Waterfront, ▮021-421-0909, www.pirateboat.co.za) has cruises aboard an "authentic" pirate ship with a live theatrical pirate show. Cruises depart from the Waterfront daily (11am and 2pm, R100), or you can opt for an all-you-can-drink sunset booze cruise (R200) in the evening.
Nauticat Charters (S 34 02.905 E 018 20.840, Hout Bay Harbor, ▮021-790-7278, www.nauticatcharters.co.za, adult R50, child R20) offers 40-minute tours on its glass-bottom catamaran to Seal Island, home to over 3,000 cape fur seals. Departure times vary but there are usually one or two departures each morning.

Ⓓ Bicycling
Downhill Adventures (S 33 55.650 E 018 24.819, cnr Orange St & Kloof St, Gardens, ▮021-422-0388, www.downhilladventures.com, 8am-6pm Mon-Fri, 8am-1pm Sat, tours from R495) runs mountain biking trips and scenic cycling tours around Cape Town, Table Mountain, Cape Point and the Cape Winelands. They've got something for everyone, so whether you're an extreme biker or a beginner looking for an easy ride, it's your one-stop shop. They also do combination and multi-day tours.
ByBike (▮021-782-6030, www.bybike.co.za, R120/day) is a cool little bike rental cooperative that operates in Kalk Bay, Fish Hoek, Glencairn, Kommetjie and Simon's Town. You can rent a bike and helmet in one base and drop it off at another. It's an easy alternative way to get around the Cape Peninsula and its network is continually expanding. Check online for the contact info and store hours of their different locations.

Ⓔ Scuba Diving
Cape Peninsula offers excellent, if cold, diving all year round. False Bay has better visibility during the winter months and slightly warmer water than the Atlantic Coast, and is full of wrecks and reefs to explore. The Atlantic Coast is best during the summer and boasts expansive kelp forests, seals and colorful coral.
Pro Divers (S 33 54.624 E 018 23.646, 88B Main

Rd, Sea Point, ☎021-433-0472, www.prodiverssa. co.za, 9am-6pm, 2 dives & equipment R600-R710) offers a wide array of specialty dives, including kelp and reef dives and wreck dives in False Bay. Their professional staff can create customized packages tailored to your interests and certification level. They have a full range of PADI certification and specialty courses and equipment rental for PADI certified divers (R360/day). They can also arrange shark cage diving in Gansbaai's "shark alley."

Scuba Shack (S 34 07.797 E 018 22.859, Lekkerwater Rd, Pinetree Business Park, Sunnydale, Kommetjie, ☎021-785-6742, www.scubashack.co.za, 9am-5pm, dive & equipment from R500) offers shore dives, boat dives, and scuba courses as well as shark cage diving trips. Less intense but equally fun is their "Snorkeling with the Seals" package. They also have a booking center on **Long Street** (S 33 55.547 E 018 24.918, 234 Long St, ☎021-424-1115, 8:30am-5pm Mon-Fri, 9am-12pm Sat).

➤ Shark Cage Diving

Shark cage diving is a highly promoted adventure activity among the backpackers and tour operators in town. The closest shark diving site to Cape Town is 160 km southeast, off the coast of Gansbaai, although the diving operations run daily shuttles that pick up and drop off in Cape Town and the surrounding area.

Shark Diving Unlimited (S 34 36.874 E 019 21.311, 1 Swart St, Kleinbaai, ☎028-384-2787 or ☎082-441-4555, www.sharkdivingunlimited. com, R1,350) is one of the more reputable shark cage diving operators. If you book directly they offer pickup in Cape Town (between 4:30am-6am), breakfast, lunch and three to four hours on the boat for R1,700. However, many of the tour operators and backpackers in Cape Town can book the same trip with Shark Diving Unlimited for roughly R1,300.

➤ Golfing

Metropolitan Golf Club (S 33 54.038 E 018 24.532, Fritz Sonnenberg Rd, Mouille Point,

☎021-430-6011, www.metropolitangolfclub.co.za) is a nine-hole course in the middle of the city. It surrounds the new Green Point Stadium, with views of Table Mountain and Signal Hill.

Milnerton Golf Club (S 33 52.849 E 018 29.265, Bridge Rd, Milnerton, ☎021-552-1351, www. milnertongolf.co.za) is an 18-hole, 72-par PGA-hosting course, located along Table Bay with fairways that run along the beach.

Mowbray Golf Club (S 33 56.798 E 018 29.541, Raapenberg Rd, Mowbray, ☎021-685-3018, www. mowbraygolfclub.co.za) is a flat, 18-hole, 71-par course. It is one of the older courses in the area, dating back to 1910.

Westlake Golf Club (S 34 04.985 E 018 26.641, Westlake Ave, Lakeside, ☎021-788-2020, www. westlakegolfclub.co.za) is a popular old-school, 18-hole, 72-par course closer to Muizenberg beside the Silvermine Mountains.

➤ Hiking & Climbing

Whether you are looking for a scenic walk or a daylong hike, there are hundreds of trails in the Cape Town area. If you're interested in hiking with a guide, check out one of the following listings. You can find descriptions, photos, difficulty grading, maps and GPS tracks of hikes in and around Cape Town at www.mountain-meanders.com.

Table Mountain Walks (☎021-715-6136, www. tablemountainwalks.co.za) is run by avid hiker, Margaret Curran, who has been walking the mountains of Cape Town for over 20 years. She can take you on all the hikes around the area, including Table Mountain and those within the Cape of Good Hope Nature Reserve.

Mountain Club of South Africa - Cape Town (S 33 55.838 E 018 25.013, 97 Hatfield St, Gardens, ☎021-465-3412, www. mcsacapetown.co.za) is a long-established club that organizes hiking and climbing activities for all abilities. They maintain an active calendar of events that generally include a few hikes a week. You can call, check out their website or stop at their office to see what's planned.

                Venture Forth (☎086-110-6548

Hiking Table Mountain

There are more than 50 routes of varying difficulty up Table Mountain. The north-facing Platteklip Gorge route is one of the most common and straightforward paths to the top of the mountain. This route conveniently starts on Table Mountain Road (S 33 57.325 E 018 24.948), 1.5 km east of the lower cableway station and ends about a 10-minute walk from the upper cableway station at the top. It should take the average hiker about 2.5hr to complete each way.

Another common and scenic route is the Skeleton Gorge, which starts from the Kirstenbosch Botanical Gardens. This route requires negotiating some steep ravines, climbing over boulders and up ladders, but has the benefit of being shaded by trees for much of the way. Descending via the Skeleton Gorge route can be difficult because of the steep sections. Once you reach the top, it is possible to hike across the mountain to the upper cableway station or return to the Kirstenbosch Gardens via the Nursery Ravine route. From the Skeleton Gorge route, follow the signs along the Kasteelspoort path for roughly 30 minutes to the head of the Nursery Ravine trail, which will take you back to the Kirstenbosch gardens for a rewarding drink.

DO:

1.) Tell someone the route you are planning to climb

2.) Check the weather forecast.

3.) Leave early enough in order to return before dusk.

4.) Take a jersey or jacket – the weather can change quickly.

5.) Ensure that the cableway is running if you plan to take it down.

6.) Wear proper shoes and a hat or sunscreen to protect again the sun.

7.) Bring enough water.

8.) Take a mobile phone.

DO NOT:

1.) Hike alone.

2.) Leave litter on the mountain.

---

or ☎082-770-7876, www.ventureforth.co.za) offers training courses and guided adventures, from half-day hikes up Table Mountain to high altitude expeditions, as well as canyoneering and rock climbing.

🐴 Horseback Riding

Sleepy Hollow Horse Riding (S 34 06.141 E 018 22.241, Sleepy Hollow Ln, Noordhoek, ☎021-789-2341 or ☎083-261-0104, www.sleepyhollowhorseriding.co.za, 9am, 1pm & 4pm, R350/2hr) offers beach rides with breathtaking views of Chapman's peak. Tours pass through wetlands and over the dunes before you descend to the lovely Noordhoek Beach. It's a beautiful ride for all skill levels.

IMPACT **Oude Molen Eco Village** (S 33 56.428 E 018 29.324, Alexandra Rd, Mowbray, ☎073-199-7395, 8am-6pm, R120/hr) has onsite horse stables and offers lessons as well as guided horse tours through the wetlands and along the river. All levels of experience welcome. There are also pony rides for kids.

🛶 Kayaking

Costal Kayak (S 33 54.337 E 018 23.913, 179 Beach Rd, Three Anchor Bay, ☎021-439-1134, www.kayak.co.za, 9am-5pm Mon-Fri, 9am-1pm Sat, Sun by appointment, tours R250/2hr) can take you on guided tours from Sea Point down to the white sands of Clifton Beach. If you are lucky, seals or dolphins may accompany you as you paddle through pristine blue waters and take in the views of the 12 Apostles rock formation and Table Mountain.

Paddlers Kayaks & Stuff (S 34 11.582 E 018 25.745, 62 St Georges St, Simon's Town, ☎021-786-2626, www.paddlers.co.za, 10am-5pm Mon-Thu, 10am-4pm Fri, 10am-2pm Sat, 12pm-2pm Sun) has kayak rentals as well as two-hour tours of False Bay through the associated **Sea Kayak Simon's Town** (☎082-501-8930, www.kayakcapetown.co.za, R250). Tours work in some time to hang out with the penguins at Boulder Beach.

🪂 Paragliding

Para-Pax (☎082-881-4724, www.parapax.com, tandem jump from R950) is one of Cape Town's longest established paragliding companies. Jumps leave from atop Lion's Head or Signal Hill and offer the best 360-degree views in town. Pilots are professional and committed to having fun. They speak 11 languages and accomodate for disabilities, so anyone can fly with them. Special flights in surrounding towns can also be arranged. **Cape Town Tandem Paragliding** (☎076-892-

CAPE TOWN

2283, www.paraglide.co.za, tandem jump R950) is another reputable tandem paragliding company. They can pick you up and drop you off from anywhere in the City Center.

Skydiving

Skydive Cape Town (082-800-6290, www. skydivecapetown.za.net, tandem skydive R1,450) will take you 20 minutes north of town for an exhilarating aerial experience with amazing views of Table Mountain and the Mother City below. You can tandem skydive or learn to jump solo. Note that they do not accept credit cards, so cash or bank transfer is the only way to fly.

Spas & Relaxation

One and Only Spa (S 33 54.504 E 018 24.986, One and Only Hotel, Dock Rd, Waterfront, 021-431-5810, www.oneandonlycapetown.com, 8am-8pm) is a sleek modern spa built on its own small island within the One and Only hotel grounds. They offer an expansive list of single, half and full-day treatments, as well as luxurious manicures and pedicures.

Angsana Spa (S 33 58.743 E 018 27.518, Vineyard Hotel, Colinton Rd, Newlands, 021-674-5005, www.vineyard.co.za, 10am-8pm) is an award-winning, Asian-influenced spa, where private treatment rooms overlook the Liesbeeck River and lush gardens.

D&D Spa (S 34 00.127 E 018 26.086, The Cellars-Hohenort Hotel, 93 Brommersvlei Rd, Constantia, 021-794-2785, www.cellars-hohenort.com/dd-spa, 9am-7pm Mon-Sat, 10am-6pm Sun) is a luxurious, Euro-chic hideaway on a vineyard estate. Indigenous plant extracts are used in many treatments and D&D offers a list of innovative hydrotherapies.

Sanctuary Spa (S 33 59.008 E 018 21.512, Twelve Apostles Hotel, Victoria Rd, Camps Bay, 021-437-0677, www.12apostleshotel.com/wellness/spa, Oct-May: 8am-8pm, Jun-Sept: 9am-8pm) offers imaginative treatments inside a fanciful stone grotto or private gazebos overlooking the ocean.

Surfing & Sandboarding

Surfing is big on the peninsula, which is host to a number of annual surfing competitions. The majority of breaks are along the Atlantic Ocean side of the peninsula, but the cold Benguela current that runs up the western side of the peninsula keeps water temperatures between 10°C/50°F and 14°C/57°F, so be prepared to suit up with wetsuits and booties. Long Beach near Kommetjie and Noordhoek Beach that runs along Chapman's Peak Drive are two popular surf destinations on the west coast.

The False Bay side of the peninsula also has a number of fantastic spots with slightly warmer waters from the eastern Indian Ocean that average between 15°C/59°F and 18°C/64°F. Muizenberg is the most established surf spot with easy access to a number of surf shops that offer gear rental and lessons.

Check out www.wavescape.co.za for detailed and animated forecasts and live webcam feeds of the surfing beaches.

Surf Shack Surf School (S 34 06.480 E 018 28.142, Surfer's Corner, Beach Rd, Muizenberg, 021-788-9286, www.surfshack.co.za, 8:30am-5pm weather permitting) is run by a handful of hardcore surfers who offer lessons and equipment rentals. Individual lessons run R300 for 1.5hr, two-person lessons are R275/person and three to five people are R200/person. Regular group lessons are R200 and offered at 10:30am and 2:30am. Board rentals are R70 for 1.5hr but cheaper per hour the longer you are out. To set up a lesson just call in advance or stop in.

Downhill Adventures (S 33 55.650 E 018 24.819, cnr Orange St & Kloof St, Gardens, 021-422-0388, www.downhilladventures.com) has surfing, sandboarding, biking and kite surfing gear to rent and offers lessons and day trips (surfing half-day R550, full-day R695).

Windsurfing & Kiteboarding

Beaches north of Cape Town are a paradise for windsurfers and kiteboarders. **Blouberg Beach**, or **Big Bay**, in Bloubergstrand (S 33 49.303 E 018 28.555, Tableview) is Cape Town's most famous spot for wind-propelled water sports. Just south is **Sunset Beach** (S 33 51.261 E 018 29.331, Milnerton), which consistently has comfortable wind in the morning and stronger gusts as the day progresses. Both beaches offer excellent views of Table Mountain across the bay and are less crowded than the southern beaches. Take the N1 north and exit onto R27/Marine Dr toward Milnerton. Sunset Beach is 8.6 km up the R27. Turn left on Ocean Way, right on Beach Bay Ave and take an immediate left on to Forata. For Blouberg continue on the R27/Marine Dr 2.3 km further north and stay left onto M14/Marine Dr until you hit the beach.

Best Kiteboarding Africa *(S 33 49.367 E 018 28.657, cnr Athens Rd & Marine Dr, Tableview, 021-556-2765, www.bestkiteboardingafrica.com, 9am-5pm Mon-Fri, 10am-3pm Sat-Sun, R550/2hr lesson)* offers lessons in Cape Town and beyond, as well as gear rental. Book at least a day in advance because they are in high demand.

Ocean Spirit *(S 33 49.208 E 018 28.563, 14 Beach Blvd, Tableview, 021-556-3305, www.oceanspirit. co.za, 9am-6pm Mon-Fri, 9am-3pm Sat, 9am-2pm Sun, R495/2hr lesson)* offers windsurfing and kiteboarding lessons and gear rental. They also sell secondhand equipment.

Windswept *(082-961-3070, www.windswept. co.za, R495/2hr lesson)* is run by Phil Baker, who rents out gear and gives personalized instruction for any skill level.

✪ TOURS

City Sightseeing Cape Town *(021-511-6000, www.citysightseeing.co.za, 1-day: adult R120, child R60, 2-day: adult R200, child R120)* offers hop-on, hop-off access to all major city sights on a large, double-decker bus. The Red City Tour departs every 20 minutes from the Two Oceans Aquarium and hits 17 stops as it passes the Waterfront, through the city center and the Gardens, up to Table Mountain and loops back past Camps Bay and Sea Point. The Blue Mini Peninsula Tour leaves every 45 minutes and includes the farther destinations such as the Kirstenbosch Gardens and Hout Bay, before returning along the beaches to the Waterfront. It's a cheap means of transport if you want to see a lot of Cape Town in a short time and many backpackers use it as an all-day taxi service.

IMPACT Coffeebeans Routes *(S 33 55.327 E 018 24.991, 70 Wale St, City Center, 021-424 3572, www.coffeebeansroutes.com)* is all about Cape Town's people, its culture, music and the social fabric that formed the city into what it is today. Some of their more popular tours include the Jazz Safari, Reggae Route, Soccer Route, Storytelling Route, township tours and dinner parties of traditional Cape Malay or Xhosa cuisine. They also can create customized tours based on your interests and needs. Run by urban Africans committed to sustainable development, their tours emphasize the economic empowerment of local communities.

Andulela *(021-790-2592, www.andulela.com)* is one of the most polished tour companies in town and offers a wide range of tours in and around Cape Town. Professional guides can take you through the streets of Bo-Kaap and District Six, give you a culinary introduction to diverse Capetonian cuisines and fine wines or take you on a wildlife day safari. They also offer immersive classes and workshops including African drumming, beading in the townships, and Cape Malay cooking classes. Tours are family friendly and customizable to fit your needs.

IMPACT AWOL Cultural Bike Tours *(021-788-1256 or 083-234-6428, www.awol.travel)* offers private, socially responsible bike tours in the township of Masiphumelele. Instead of being confined to an air-conditioned bus, tourists are encouraged to stay low to the ground and interact with the community. Local qualified guides escort you around town and introduce you to township culture and people. AWOL works in partnership with the **Bicycling Empowerment Network**, or **BEN** *(www.benbikes.org.za)*, which imports secondhand bicycles to South Africa, supports trainings and locally-owned bike workshops, and promotes low-cost, non-motorized transport as a tool to alleviate poverty and increase mobility in low-income neighborhoods.

Day Trippers (☏021-511-4766, www.daytrippers. co.za) is an alternative tour company that is becoming pretty mainstream, but only because of its popularity. They organize day tours that get you out of the bus and on your feet, or swimming when possible. Bike the city, hike Table Mountain, tour the winelands or visit a township.

IMPACT **Bikes 'n Wines** (☏074-186-0418, www. bikesnwines.com) offers an alternative way to visit the winelands for the more adventurous connoisseur. Tours vary in intensity, but all come with scenic views and a sampling of local wines, cheeses and cellar tours at up to four vineyards. Choose your tour carefully, because some come with a brandy tasting or a visit to a cheetah sanctuary. It's a great way to taste some of South Africa's finest grapes and see the countryside minus the carbon footprint. A small portion of your payment also goes towards the Lynedoch Eco-Village and the newly established Lynedoch Cycling Club, a mentorship program for disadvantaged youths.

Cape Insights (☏021-424-0018, www.cape insights.com) is a boutique travel company that offers insider access to the finer side of Cape Town's art, architecture, gastronomy, archeology and history. Private tours are customized for the discerning traveler.

IMPACT **Camissa** (☏021-462-6199 or ☏078-657-7788, www.gocamissa.co.za) offers cultural tours of District Six and the townships of Langa and Gugulethu. Over two-thirds of the company is black-owned and operated and through partnerships with local residents, you are given personal invitations into homes, schools and people's lives. Full day tours also include a trip to Robben Island. Camissa takes their commitment to social investment seriously and along with creating a wide network of partnerships to foster employment opportunities, they also sponsor annual school fees for young township students.

IMPACT **Cape Capers Tours** (☏021-448-3117, ☏083-358-0193, www.tourcapers.co.za) is run by Faizal Gangat, an award-winning tour guide based out of Woodstock. Mr. Gangat is well-respected in the townships and has used his tour business as a platform for training and mentorship of community members and young entrepreneurs. He offers township tours, some of which include Robben Island, District Six and Bo-Kaap city tours, and other more general excursions, including Cape Peninsula, whale watching and wineland tours.

⊙ SLEEPING

⊙ City Center & Bo-Kaap
BUDGET
The City Center is densely populated with budget accommodation options but quality, cleanliness and service vary substantially. Long Street is lined

CAPE TOWN WALKING TOUR

Cape Town is full of historical sights and cultural experiences, not to mention, good food. A day is far from enough to experience all its delights, but if you are short on time, a walking tour will help you get a good sense of what the center of the "Mother City" has to offer.

Time: 2-4hr
Distance: 3-5 km

Start your day off with an organic bite at **BIRDS BOUTIQUE CAFÉ (1, p94)**, a trendy and rustic little eatery on the corner of Bree and Church Streets. If you have a car, there is street parking or a large car park just across the street at **VAN RIEBEECK SQUARE (2)**. After you have fortified yourself, walk down Bree Street and turn left on Shortmarket Street, which will take you up into the hills of the Bo-Kaap, Cape Town's historically Muslim neighborhood. On your way up, check out **STREET WIRES (3, p58)**, a community employment initiative that sells all sorts of functional and funky wire art. Continue up Shortmarket and take a left onto Chiappini Street. Make your way back down the cobblestoned Longmarket Street and turn right on Rose Lane, home to Bo-Kaap's iconic colorful houses. Where the road comes to a T-junction, you will find the **BO-KAAP MUSEUM (4, p75)**, the former home of Abu Bakr Effendi, a prominent Muslim leader from the mid 1800s. It's a small museum that will give you a good introduction to the lives of the people who played a large hand in building the Cape Town you see today. After visiting the museum, continue just a few steps up the hill and turn left on Van der Meulen Street and then left down Dorp Street, past the **OWAL MOSQUE**, the first Mosque to be built in Cape Town in the early 1800s.

Continue down Dorp Street to the famous Long Street, the heart of the City Center. Turn right to stroll past the Victorian buildings with wrought iron balconies, independent cafés, boutique shops, backpackers and bars. Turn left on Green Street and then left onto Queen Victoria Road. On the right will be a gate leading into the **COMPANY'S GARDEN (6, p73)**, Cape Town's largest municipal green space. Make your way to Government Avenue, the main thoroughfare of the gardens. If you have the time and interest, veer right and walk to the southern side of the gardens to check out the impressive exhibits at the **SOUTH AFRICAN NATIONAL GALLERY (7, p76)** on Paddock Avenue. Otherwise, continue north on Government Avenue past the red and white **PARLIAMENT BUILDINGS (8, P74)**, the seat of South Africa's legislature.

Upon exiting the gardens, you will find **ST GEORGE'S CATHEDRAL (9, p88)** on your left, from where Bishop Desmond Tutu called for the end of apartheid and national reconciliation. On your right is the **SLAVE LODGE (10, p73)**, a fortress-like structure that used to house the Dutch East India Company's imported slaves. Today it is a poignant museum, which examines the effects of apartheid and racial discrimination in South Africa. Across Bureau Street from the Slave Lodge is the mammoth **GROOTE KERK (11, p74)**, the mothership for the Dutch Reformed Church in Cape Town.

From here, you can continue down Bureau Street to the **DISTRICT SIX MUSEUM (12, p61)**, arguably the most unique museum in Cape Town. It recalls the forced removal of city residents and the memory of a community displaced by apartheid racial zoning. To get there, take Bureau Street down and turn right on Corporation Street. Take an immediate left on Albertus Street down to Buitenkant Road and the District Six Museum is on the southwest corner. It's a sight not to be missed, but if you are crunched for time, continue up Wale Street past St George's Church and turn right to stroll down the pedestrian St George's Mall Street. At Darling Street, turn left to do a little shopping at **GREENMARKET SQUARE (13, p75)**. Once you've had your fill of crafts, head back down Burg Street and take a right on the pedestrian, tree-lined Church Street. If you're lucky, you'll catch some of the more interesting antique vendors, or you can pop into some of the art galleries and stores that line the street. Continue down Church Street to return to your beginning location. If you're hungry after the long walk, head two blocks up Bree Street and grab some tapas and a beverage at the classy **CAVEAU (14, p94)**, to congratulate yourself on a Capetonian day well done.

CALEDON ST
ALBERTUS ST
RRACK ST
BUITENKANT RD
HARRINGTON ST
12

Cape Town Festivals

Cape Town has long been the cultural hub of the country. Festivals, special events and new reasons to have a good time continue to pop up throughout the year. For an updated listing of Cape Town events and festivals check out: http://www.capetown.travel/index.php/whats-on

JANUARY
Kaapse Klopse (Jan 1-2) is Cape Town's historic New Year's Minstrel Carnival when singing and dancing troupes in multi-colored, sequined costumes take to the streets.

FEBRUARY
Infecting the City (*www.infectingthecity.com*, mid-Feb) is a city-wide public arts festival that transforms urban space into performance venues.
Cape Town Pride (*www.capetownpride.co.za*, late Feb-early March) is a celebration of sexuality that rivals any other in the world.

MARCH
Cape Argus Cycle Tour (*www.cycletour.co.za*, mid-Mar) is a race around the Cape Peninsula and one of the world's largest tours.
Cape Town Festival (*www.capetownfestival.co.za*, mid-late Mar) celebrates cultural diversity through music, live performances, lectures and film screenings.
Taste of Cape Town (*www.tasteofcapetown.com*, late Mar) brings together celebrated Capetonian chefs for a culinary tour of the city's best restaurants.

APRIL
Cape Town International Jazz Festival (*www.capetownjazzfest.com*, early Apr) takes over the International Convention Center with international and national artists every year in late March/early April.

JULY/AUGUST
Encounters (*www.encounters.co.za*, Jul or Aug) is South Africa's International Documentary Film Festival showcases international and local talent.
Cape Town Fashion Week (*www.capetownfashionweek.com*, mid-late Aug) draws some of the hottest names in fashion every August.

SEPTEMBER
Cape Town Comedy Festival (*www.comedyfestival.co.za*, mid-Sept) will have you laughing with street performances and comedy showdowns.

NOVEMBER
Switch on the Festive Lights (Nov 30) sparks off the festive season at the end of November with a huge light display on Adderley St and live music accompanied by a laser show.

DECEMBER
Obz Festival (*www.obzfestival.com*, early Dec) transforms Observatory into a bustling weekend street festival filled with music, live acts, and more. There's been talk about it being discontinued, so check online for updated info.

CAPE TOWN

with backpackers and budget accommodation, but many have mixed reputations so investigate a little before handing over your cash. If you are looking for a quiet place within walking distance of Long Street nightlife, check out some of the listings under Gardens - many great places are only a few blocks away.

Long Street Backpackers (*S 33 55.507 E 018 24.984, 209 Long St, City Center,* 021-423-0615, *www.longstreetbackpackers.co.za, dm R120, s R180, d R300, bar, Baz Bus*) was the first backpackers on Long Street and still retains much of its original flavor. If you're looking to experience the Long Street party scene, this is a good place to start. The reception is located behind the bar and the staff, who all know the area well, can point you in the right direction, whatever your interests are.

Cat & Moose Backpackers (*S 33 55.625 E 018 24.854, 305 Long St, City Center,* 021-423-7638, *www.catandmoose.co.za, dm R110, s R300, d R350, Baz Bus, wifi*) is one of the better budget options on Long Street with a sunny central courtyard and splash pool, a balcony overlooking the street, and a comfortable lounge room. They have 24-hour security and can arrange a spot for you in all of the area tours and activities.

St Paul's B&B Guest House (*S 33 55.513 E 018 24.807, 182 Bree St, City Center,* 021-423-4420, *www.stpaulschurch.co.za/theguesthouse.htm, s R300, d R500, breakfast included, secure parking*) was founded by a former priest of St Paul's and is a good city center budget option without the backpacker feel. The rooms are spacious and there is a serene and vine-shaded common courtyard.

MID-RANGE

The Grand Daddy (*38 Long St, City Center,* 021-424-7247, *www.granddaddy.co.za, d R975-1,500, suite R1,500-R2,500, breakfast included, wifi, secure parking*) is a funky and stylish hotel in the heart of Long Street. Their luxury rooms and Daddy Cool Bar are "blingin," but the seven decked-out vintage Airstream caravans in their rooftop trailer park are the real attraction here. Live music and movie screenings also happen on the rooftop during the summer months.

Urban Chic Hotel (*S 33 55.488 E 018 24.978, 172 Long St, City Center* 021-426-6119, *www.urbanchichotel.com, s R1,200-2,000, d R1,400-2,200, wifi*) is a stylish 4-star hotel and one of the more upmarket options on Long Street. Urban Chic is all about setting a modern groove,

especially in the cigar bar and cocktail lounge and the gallery café. The rooms have ceiling to floor windows either overlooking Long Street or with views of Table Mountain, but the wide views may expose you to a little nightlife noise on the weekends.

IMPACT **Daddy Long Legs Hotel** (*S 33 55.425 E 018 25.058, 134 Long St, City Center,* 021-422-3074, *www.daddylonglegs.co.za, s/d R750-1,050, Internet/wifi*) has 13 unique rooms that were each designed by a local artist. Themes vary widely - one room contains a montage of over 3,000 photos of Capetonians, another has a mirrored ceiling with walls covered in pictures of South Africa sunsets. The art continues into the lobby where there is a small art exhibit, with funds from art sales donated to supporting area community projects.

Tudor Hotel (*S 33 55.360 E 018 25.163, 153 Longmarket St, Greenmarket Square, City Center,* 021-424-1335, *www.tudorhotel.co.za, s R590-635, d R765-900, breakfast included, secure parking*) has basic but pleasant value-priced rooms with a superb location overlooking the bustling Greenmarket Square. The hotel is within walking distance of many restaurants and City Center attractions and the friendly staff will go out of their way to make your stay memorable.

TOP END

Mandela Rhodes Place (*S 33 55.427 E 018 25.153, Burg St & Wale St, City Center,* 021-481-4000, *www.mandelarhodesplace.co.za, d R1,300-R2,800, 4-person R1,400-R3,500, breakfast included, Internet/wifi, secure parking, swimming pool*) is a new luxury apartment and hotel complex in the heart of the downtown that is part of an urban renewal project. The complex's spa, gym, rooftop pool and high-end accommodations are luring people back to the City Center, just as the project intended. Downstairs there are fine-dining restaurants and a chic cocktail bar.

IMPACT **Cape Heritage Hotel** (*S 33 55.241 E 018 25.099, 90 Bree St, City Center,* 021-424-4646, *www.capeheritage.co.za, R2,000-4,000/ room, wifi, secure parking*) is one of Cape Town's most luxurious hotels. This lavishly eclectic 17-room establishment consistently gets rave reviews from guests and takes their environment and social responsibility seriously by using solar heating and electricity and natural cleaning products, and by supporting a local NGO that works with homeless children.

CAPE TOWN

⊙ Gardens & Around

BUDGET

The Backpack (*S 33 55.625 E 018 24.627, 74 New Church St, Tamboerskloof, ☎021-423-4530, www.backpackers.co.za, dm R120, s R400, d R550-700, Baz Bus, Internet/wifi, parking, swimming pool*) is widely considered the best backpackers in Cape Town and is also a Fair Trade in Tourism partner. This clean, secure place has a friendly staff who creates a casual welcoming atmosphere and the bar, restaurant, loungy terrace and pool make it a comfortable place to stick around and mingle with fellow backpackers. The in-house African Travel Center is helpful and can book anything from day wine trips to overland excursions. The Backpack tends to be fully booked more often than surrounding hostels, so it's worth reserving your room in advance.

Ashanti Lodge (*S 33 56.005 E 018 24.731, 11 Hof St, Gardens, ☎021-423-8721, www.ashanti.co.za, camping R75, dm R140, s R300, d R420-600, Baz Bus, Internet/wifi, swimming pool*) is generally full of raucous travelers who fill up the bar and restaurant until late, particularly when DJs spin on the weekend. Outside of the bar, guests relax poolside or on the front lawn under the palm trees. Ashanti also has a full-service travel center.

Cape Town Backpackers (*S 33 55.715 E 018 24.571, 81 New Church St, Tamboerskloof, ☎021-426-0200, www.capetownbackpackers.com, dm R120, s R400-450, d R400-550, Baz Bus, Internet/wifi, secure parking*) is a spotless and beautifully styled backpackers in close proximity to the restaurants and bars of Kloof St and Long St. The backpackers is spread over three houses but the central area is the bar, where the friendly staff double as receptionist and bartender.

MID-RANGE

2inn1 Kensington (*S 33 56.375 E 018 24.414, 21 Kensington Crescent, Oranjezicht, ☎021-423-1707, www.2inn1.com, d R1,250-2,000, 4-person: R1,900-2,500, breakfast included, secure parking, swimming pool*) has spacious, uniquely styled en suite rooms with a balcony or private terrace. Guests can unwind in the tranquil garden or soak up the sun beside the 10 m swimming pool with views of Table Mountain, but it is the outstanding staff and attention to detail that attracts many return customers.

TwentyTwo (*S 33 56.469 E 018 24.720, 22 Montrose Ave, Oranjezicht, ☎021-465-8882,* www.capetwentytwo.com, *R1,500-1,900/room, breakfast included, wifi, parking, swimming pool*) is a contemporary 4-bedroom guesthouse on the slopes of Table Mountain with impressive views of both the mountain and the harbor below. The individually designed rooms each have a private terrace or balcony, and hosts Allan and Dominic will go to lengths to make sure your stay is nothing short of the best. With just four rooms and such superb service, TwentyTwo fills up quickly — if a booking is available, we suggest you take it.

Derwent House (*S 33 56.014 E 018 24.327, 14 Derwent Rd, Tamboerskloof, ☎021-422-2763, www.derwenthouse.co.za, d R1,200-2,100, family room R1,750-2,400, breakfast included, wifi, parking, swimming pool*) is one of Cape Town's hidden gems, with its sophisticated style, great location, views and hospitality. The 10 well-appointed rooms come outfitted with extra-long beds, cotton robes and slippers, and a private deck or terrace. Hosts Carol and Jo are excellent at making guests feel at home, starting with delectable breakfasts.

Cape Milner Hotel (*S 33 55.660 E 018 24.547, 2a Milner Road, Tamboerskloof, ☎021-426-1101, www.capemilner.com, Mar-Oct: s/d R1480, Nov-Feb: s R2590 d 5200, wifi, secure parking*) is a fashionable hotel catering to the business crowd. The 40 spacious rooms and 10 luxury suites are within a few blocks of the restaurant-lined Kloof Street and the large terrace, bar and pool overlook Table Mountain.

TOP END

Mount Nelson (*S 33 55.913 E 018 24.703, 76 Orange St, ☎021-483-1737, www.mountnelson.co.za, R3,500-6,200/room, breakfast included, wifi, secure parking, swimming pool*) is Cape Town's luxury stalwart with old-fashioned, 5-star service that will please the most demanding of guests. The classically furnished rooms, expansive lawn, terraced garden, and views of Table Mountain make this urban sanctuary one of the finest establishments in town. Amenities here are appropriately sumptuous, and include a yoga studio, day spa, two restaurants and the city's best high tea.

Kensington Place (*S 33 56.368 E 018 24.307, 38 Kensington Cres, ☎021-424-4744, www.kensingtonplace.co.za, R2,000-4,500, breakfast included, wifi, secure parking, splash pool*) is a chic boutique hotel located at the base of Table

Mountain. Its spacious contemporary suites each have private balconies and are lavishly furnished with anything you might need during your stay, including a laptop and iPod docking station. The concierge service is among the best at arranging activities and will ensure you a spot at the top restaurants and nightlife in town.

Green Pt, Waterkant & Waterfront

BUDGET

Ashanti – Green Point (S 33 54.551 E 018 24.038, 23 Antrim Road, Green Point, 021-433-1619, www.ashanti.co.za, dm R100, s R400, d R550, Baz Bus, Internet, parking, swimming pool) is a new addition to the backpack scene in Green Point but under the same ownership as the successful Ashanti Lodge in the Gardens. This location is quieter and more tame than its sister lodge. The building has been recently remodeled with comfortable new beds, a self-catering kitchen and TV room. The facilities are better than any other backpackers in the city and the staff is friendly.

St. John's Waterfront (S 33 54.638 E 018 24.823, 6 Braemar Rd, Green Point, 021-439-1404, www.stjohns.co.za, dm R120, s R300, d R600, bar, Baz Bus, Internet, parking, swimming pool) is an oldie but goodie that puts you within walking distance of many attractions. St. John's has been operating as a backpackers and lodge for over 15 years and any shortcomings in the dated buildings are made up for with its character. Each house has its own self-catering kitchen and swimming pool and there is a bar, lounge area and deck at the main house.

MID-RANGE

dysART (S 33 54.534 E 018 24.432, 17 Dysart Rd, Green Point, 021-439-2832, www.dysart.de, d R1,000-2,400, breakfast included, wifi, secure parking, swimming pool) is a six-room guest house near the foot of Signal Hill with personable staff. Rooms are generous and have modern bathrooms, TV, AC and minibars; a few have views of Robben Island and the stadium. Downstairs is a narrow infinity pool and a breezy sun deck.

Sugar (S 33 54.681 E 018 24.919, 1 Main Rd, Green Point, 021-430-3780, www.sugarhotel.co.za, s R1,445, d R1,930, swimming pool, wifi, secure parking) is an uber-modern, seven-room hotel with a private restaurant, bar and swimming pool. Each of the strikingly monochromatic rooms has a flat screen TV, sound system, minibar, glass closet and a large floor-lit bathroom. A few rooms have a fireplace, and a private deck with a splash pool. There is also an onsite spa and message center.

Villa Zest (S 33 54.640 E 018 24.835, 2 Braemar Rd, Green Point, 021-433-1246, www.villazest.co.za, s R1,500-2,200, d R1,650-3,000, breakfast included, wifi, swimming pool) is a seven-room upmarket guest house with retro '70s decor. Pass through a gallery of old Panasonic radios and Polaroid cameras to reach the rooms, which sport shag carpets and tasteful open showers. You can relax poolside, in the mid-level lounge, or atop the roof deck while enjoying an evening cocktail.

Protea Hotel Victoria Junction (S 33 54.770 E 018 25.044, cnr Somerset Rd & Ebenezer Rd, 021-418-1234, www.proteahotels.com, R1,200/room, wifi, secure parking, swimming pool) has been recently remodeled and is located in the heart of Waterkant. Rooms have flat screen TVs and AC. The hotel also has a bar and restaurant, but unless you're looking for a quaint meal, you'd be advised to venture out to one of the numerous restaurants, bars, or clubs within a three block radius.

Olive Branch Guest House (S 33 54.535 E 018 24.054, 9 Richmond Rd, Green Point, 021-434-9189, www.olivebranch.co.za, s R650-750, d R850-950, breakfast included, Internet/wifi, parking, swimming pool) is a romantic, owner-managed guesthouse with a friendly staff. Rooms are cozy with plush bedding and bathrooms are large and well appointed. The house has a small courtyard and a splash pool outside.

TOP END

IMPACT Cape Grace (S 33 54.594 E 018 25.232, West Quay Rd, Waterfront, 021-410-7100, www.capegrace.com, d from R5,600, breakfast included, Internet/wifi, secure parking, swimming pool) is one of Cape Town's best in terms of service, style and dining and is superbly situated on the Waterfront beside the harbor. The hotel has recently been redesigned - each room has a unique décor and art. The hotel has a 56-foot yacht available for charter and offers complimentary car service within the city. They also excel in terms of responsible tourism. Their Employee Wellbeing Program aims to address social and economic issues facing their staff and they financially support Salt, a nonprofit community outreach program that works in the suburbs of Cape Town.

Table Bay Hotel (*S 33 54.164 E 018 25.343, Breakwater Blvd, Quay 6, Waterfront,* ☎*021-406-5000, www.tablebayhotel.com, d from R5,600, breakfast included, Internet/wifi, secure parking, swimming pool*) gets consistent rave reviews from guests for its beautiful views and courteous staff. The spacious rooms have marble bathrooms and overlook either Robben Island or Table Mountain. The hotel has world-class amenities, a restaurant and lounge overlooking the harbor and a heated saltwater pool.

One and Only (*S 33 54.504 E 018 24.986, Dock Rd, Waterfront,* ☎*021-431-5888, www.oneandonlycapetown.com, d from R6,000, breakfast included, Internet/wifi, secure parking, swimming pool*) is a relatively new addition to the luxury hotel market in Cape Town having opened in April 2009. The large modern rooms are located in the main waterfront building or on the newly built island. They have great views of Table Mountain and come with a dedicated butler. The hotel includes two high-end restaurants, each featuring a Michelin-starred chef, a bar and wine loft, spa, and clothing boutique.

❂Atlantic Coast (Sea Point, Clifton, Camps Bay & Beyond)
MID-RANGE

Blackheath Lodge (*S 33 54.616 E 018 23.861, 6 Blackheath Rd, Sea Point,* ☎*021-439-4541, www.blackheathlodge.co.za, d R1,000-1,400, breakfast included, wifi, swimming pool, secure parking*) is a warm and homey, 4-star Victorian guesthouse. From plush bedding to detailed advice on area activities, hosts Antony and John go out of their way to ensure guests a pleasant and comfortable stay. There is a courtyard swimming pool with an upper level verandah, from which you can enjoy morning coffee or evening cocktails.

Fullham Lodge (*S 33 57.966 E 018 22.471, 22 Fulham Rd, Camps Bay,* ☎*021-438-1293, www.fullhamlodge.com, s R975, d R1,550, t R1,725, 4-person R2,300, breakfast included, swimming pool*) is a quiet B&B located at the end of a road beside the Table Mountain Nature Reserve, which makes for stunning views of both the mountain and ocean. The B&B has two en suite rooms with private balconies and two fully equipped, self-catering cottages and the ocean-facing pool and sundeck are a beautiful spot to enjoy a sundowner.

30 Fiskaal Guest House (*S 33 57.556 E 018 23.115, 30 Fiskaal Rd, Camps Bay,* ☎*021-438-1206, www.30fiskaal.com, d R1,300-2,500, wifi, swimming pool*) is a Mediterranean-style guesthouse located on the foothills of Table Mountain. It is a perennial favorite with travelers for its panoramic views of the mountain, Lions Head and the ocean. Each of the seven rooms is elegantly and uniquely decorated and welcoming hosts make this a popular repeat destination.

TOP END

IMPACT **Winchester Mansions Hotel** (*S 33 55.075 E 018 23.175, 221 Beach Rd, Sea Point,* ☎*021-434-2351, www.winchester.co.za, s R1,650-2,500, d R2,150-3,000, breakfast included, Internet/wifi, swimming pool*) is a classic Cape Dutch hotel across the street from a rock-strewn beach and the Sea Point swimming pools. Inside the lush courtyard is Harveys, a delicious restaurant that hosts a popular jazz brunch on Sundays. The hotel has a heated swimming pool, sun deck and a spa. The hotel is a good value and is a socially and environmentally responsible business that is active in supporting community projects.

Les Cascades de Bantry Bay (*S 33 55.777 E 018 22.793, 48 De Wet Rd, Bantry Bay,* ☎*021-434-5209, www.lescascades.co.za, d R2,250-3,250, breakfast included, wifi, parking, swimming pool*) is a luxury, multilevel guesthouse built high into the slopes of Signal Hill with a beautiful ocean view. Attention to detail here is noticeable in both decor and level of service, and the secluded lounge areas and two infinity pools are divine. The sister boutique hotel, Cascades on 52, looks and feels completely different, but is just as pleasant.

Bay Hotel (*S 33 57.153 E 018 22.683, 69 Victoria Rd, Camps Bay,* ☎*021-438-4444, www.thebay.co.za, d from R2,400, breakfast included, Internet, secure parking, swimming pool*) is a posh 5-star hotel located on the main strip in Camps Bay just across the street from the beach and surrounded by restaurants and bars. It has true Camps Bay style with four swimming pools, enough sun deck real estate for all 78 rooms, poolside cocktail bars, a spa and a hair salon.

❂Southern Suburbs
BUDGET

IMPACT **African Heart Backpackers** (*S 33 56.329 E 018 28.011, 27 Station Rd, Observatory,* ☎*021-447-3125, www.africanheartbackpackers.com, dm R120, s/d R350-400, breakfast included,*

Internet/wifi) is a backpackers recently launched by a young South African couple who also started a successful backpackers in Jeffreys Bay. It has a friendly eco-conscious atmosphere, a large comfortable kitchen and lounge on the top floor, frequented by Mogley the dog. The owners live there and care about making your stay a good experience - they make great recommendations for things to check out in the area.

33 South Backpackers (S 33 56.342 E 018 28.205, 48 Trill Rd, Observatory, ☎021-447-2423, www.33southbackpackers.com, dm R130, s/d R390-450, bar, Baz Bus, breakfast included, Internet) has younger owners and staff that are plugged into the area. Each of the rooms has its own Cape Town-inspired theme. There is a large kitchen, braai area out back and a bar for local friends and guests located in what used to be the parking lot.

Obviouzly Armchair Backpackers (S 33 56.312 E 018 28.125, 135 Lower Main Rd, Observatory, ☎021-460-0458, www.obviouzlyarmchair.com, dm R125, d R440, secure parking R150) is a more recent addition to the Observatory backpacker scene. The building tells its own story - formerly a Barclays Bank (the vault door forms part of the current bar) then a BP filling station (old pumps still in the back) and finally a theater, before its present state. This place gets kudos for having the best bar in a backpackers - or maybe we should say it's a bar with a backpackers upstairs. There is no real self-catering kitchen, but it is in the middle of Observatory, surrounded by options galore.

Cape Town Deco Lodge (S 33 55.908 E 018 27.159, 22 Roodebloem Rd, Woodstock, ☎021-447-4216, www.capetowndeco.com, dm R140, d R350, Baz Bus, secure parking, swimming pool) is an off-the-wall artsy backpackers in the comfortable neighborhood of Woodstock. The purple house has a covered outdoor deck in front of a swimming pool, an upstairs glass-wall shower room with a view, and a small bar with a purple felt pool table to match.

IMPACT Lighthouse Farm Lodge (S 33 56.250 E 018 29.285, Oude Molen Eco Village, Alexandria Rd, Mowbray, ☎021-447-9165, www.lighthousefarm.co.za, camping R100, dm R100, d R220, Internet, parking) is situated within the Oude Molen Eco Village, an organic farm and community micro-enterprise initiative in the suburbs of Cape Town. The lodge is true to its mission - what isn't broke doesn't consume any resources on being fixed or updated. While a few

of the general backpacker crowd do pass through, the lodge is geared toward longer-term guests who pay their way by working on the farm. Also on site are horse stables and the Millstone Café, a delicious little restaurant stocked with fresh ingredients from surrounding gardens.

MID-RANGE

IMPACT Vineyard Hotel & Spa (S 33 58.743 E 018 27.518, Colinton Rd, Newlands, ☎021-657-4500, www.vineyard.co.za, courtyard d R1,460-1,795, mountain d R2,235-3,365, Internet/wifi, secure parking, swimming pool) was originally built for Lady Anne Barnard in 1799. Today it is a 200-room hotel with two restaurants, a bar and swimming pool tucked away on six acres of gardens full of birds and giant tortoises. The hotel has received professional recognition for its social development program and efforts at environmental conservation.

TOP END

The Palm House (S 34 00.003 E 018 27.920, 10 Oxford St, Wynberg, ☎021-761-5009, www.palmhouse.co.za, s R935-1,200, d R1,390-1,850, family cottage R1,595-1,995, breakfast included, secure parking, swimming pool) is an expansive, 10-room guest house built in the 1920s and designed by a protégé of architect Sir Herbert Baker. The estate has two private cottages, a lovely pool and is dotted with massive palm trees. There is an in-house bar and restaurant that can serve lunch and dinner.

⑪ EATING

⑪ City Center & Bo-Kaap

Addis in Cape (S 33 55.372 E 018 25.106, 41 Church St, City Center, ☎021-424-5722, www.addisincape.co.za, 12pm-2:30pm & 6pm-10:30pm Mon-Sat, mains R75-95) serves authentic Ethiopian food in an authentically Ethiopian space by friendly Ethiopian hosts. You can select your favorite dish from the large menu or order one of the set meals (R150 & R200) to sample a selection of Ethiopia's finest cuisine over huge spreads of injera, a pancake-like bread. Either way you will not leave hungry.

Royal Eatery (S 33 55.584 E 018 24.897, 273 Long St, City Center, ☎021-422-4563, www.royaleeatery.com, 12pm-11pm Mon-Sat, mains

CAPE TOWN

R45-65) serves up excellent burgers with sweet potato fries but you don't have to stick with beef - they offer veal, pork and ostrich burgers as well. The restaurant opens its second floor and outdoor balcony for dinner. In addition to burgers, the menu has a selection of pizza, salads, desserts and a large selection of wine and beer.

Biesmiellah (S 33 55.214 E 018 24.837, cnr Wale St & Pentz St, Bo-Kaap, ☎021-423-0850, 12pm-11pm Mon-Fri, 8am-12am Sat, mains R70-80) is a small restaurant in the heart of the Bo-Kaap district with traditional Cape Malay meals and friendly personable service. They have a very good bobotie but it is also worth asking what is cooking in back or for a recommendation on one of their tasty curries. No alcohol is served here.

Clay Oven Pizza Café (S 33 55.484 E 018 24.987, 166 Long St, City Center, ☎021-426-4792, 12pm-late, mains R35-50) is the only pizzeria on Long Street, and does the trick if you're looking for an inexpensive and decent pie any time of the day or night. If you're interested in better pizza and don't mind walking a few more blocks, head to Da Vinci's on Kloof Street.

Nzolo Brand Cafe (S 33 55.391 E 018 25.145, 48 Church St, City Center, ☎021-426-1857, 8am-5pm Mon-Tue, 8am-9pm Wed-Fri, 8am-2:30pm Sat, mains R30-50) is a cozy neighborhood café on a pedestrian section of Church Street that serves breakfast, salads and sandwiches in shaded outdoor seating or at a few tables with comfortable pillow chairs inside.

Eastern Food Bazaar (S 33 55.473 E 018 25.340, The Wellington, 96 Longmarket St, City Center, ☎021-461-2458, www.easternfoodbazaar. co.za, 11am-10:30pm, mains R25-35) is a chaotic collection of Indian, central Asian, and Chinese food stalls that serve up large portions of tasty food at prices that are tough to beat in the City Center. You can get your food as a take away or there is a large communal sitting area. You must prepay at the central register and then take your ticket to the food counter of your choice to collect your dish.

Caveau (S 33 55.251 E 018 25.091, 92 Bree St, City Center, ☎021-422-1367, www.caveau.co.za, 7am-10:30pm, bar open late, mains R80-120) is a stylish bistro, wine bar and specialty foods deli with seating outside or in the antique cellars of the famous Heritage Square building. The proprietors know how to pair ambiance, delicious food and the best wines of the country. Whether it's for a light meal, a glass of wine in the sun or to spend an evening over fine food and wine, your experience at Caveau will be nothing less than top-notch.

IMPACT **Birds Boutique Café** (S 33 55.327 E 018 25.041, 127 Bree St, City Center, ☎021-426-2534, 7am-6pm Mon-Fri, 8am-2pm Sat, mains R35-70) is a friendly family-owned café that serves up fresh concoctions, such as fruit-filled crepes and chicken pie, made exclusively from locally grown organic ingredients. The emphasis here is on quality food, not speed or decor, so come ready to hunker down on a milk crate and wait for a great meal in the making. Restaurant leftovers go to local street vendors who teach healthy recipes to township students.

Noon Gun & Tea Room (S 33 54.962 E 018 24.767, 273 Longmarket St, Bo-Kaap, ☎021-424-0529, 10am-12:15pm, 2pm-4pm & 7pm-late Mon-Sat, mains R75-95) dishes out mouthwatering traditional Cape Malay dishes such as bobotie, roti and curry from the owners' family home. From its vantage point at the top of Signal Hill, the restaurant has panoramic views of the city and harbor. To find it, walk up to the top of the steep Longmarket St. If driving, head up Wale St as the lower part of Longmarket St is a one-way down.

Gold Restaurant (S 33 55.150 E 018 25.178, 96 Strand St, City Center, ☎021-421-4653, www. gold restaurant.co.za, 7pm-10pm, R235/person) is attached to the Gold of Africa Museum and is an experience in itself. Sit down to an extravagant fixed-price, 14-course dinner of traditional Cape Malay and African dishes and live entertainment by singers, dancers and large, graceful Mali puppets. Arrive by 6:30pm to take part in the interactive drumming circle (R85), but get there no later than 8pm if you don't want to miss the opening performance. Reservations required.

Savoy Cabbage (S 33 55.209 E 018 25.094, 101 Hout St,

City Center, ☎021-424-2626, www.savoycabbage. co.za, 12pm-2:30pm & 7pm-10:30pm Mon-Fri, 7pm-10:30pm Sat, mains R110-175) has been internationally acclaimed for its locally sourced food and menu that changes daily. Deliciously fresh dishes are complimented by the innovative dining room – a funky architectural mélange housed in a former warehouse.

🍴 Gardens & Around

95 Keerom (S 33 55.589 E 018 24.952, 95 Keerom St, Gardens, ☎021-422-0765, www.95keerom.com, 12pm-3pm & 7pm-11pm Mon-Fri, 7pm-11pm Sat, mains R60-100, free secured parking) is an elegant Italian restaurant where the owner greets you at the door. The Milanese carpaccio, fish, pasta and meats are a great value and service is impeccable - your glass will never be empty. Advance booking is recommended.

Aubergine (S 33 55.930 E 018 24.968, 39 Barnet St, Gardens, ☎021-465-4909, www.aubergine.co.za, 5pm-10pm Mon-Tue, 12pm-2pm & 5pm-10pm Wed-Fri, 7pm-10pm Sat, mains R100-190) is an intimate, upscale restaurant that offers a polished twist on South African specialties. Chef and owner Harold Bresselschmidt puts his heart and soul into the short, carefully crafted menu. It's one of the more expensive restaurants in Cape Town and a great place for a quiet, formal dinner. Advance booking is recommended.

Arnolds (S 33 55.852 E 018 24.580, 60 Kloof St, Gardens, ☎021-424-4344, www.arnolds.co.za, 6:45am-late Mon-Fri, 8:45am-late Sat-Sun, mains R50-110) is a

homey eatery with a good selection of wild game including springbok, crocodile, warthog, ostrich and gemsbok. Enjoy these dishes, as well as excellently executed, more conventional fare, on the shaded front patio.

Yindee's (S 33 55.970 E 018 24.507, cnr Kloof St & Camps St, Gardens, ☎021-422-1012, www. yindees.com, 6pm-10:30pm, mains R60-90) offers tasty, authentic Thai food with a good selection of soups, stir fries and excellent spicy curries. Adventurous epicureans can lose their shoes and enjoy their meal while sitting on a pillow at a floor table.

Beleza (S 33 55.787 E 018 24.464, cnr Kloof Nek Rd & Upper Buitengracht St, Tamboerskloof, ☎021-426-0795, www.belezarestaurant.co.za, 8:30am-11pm, mains R50-90) is popular with locals as a leisurely brunch spot for their Portuguese "bloody Marias," but can just as easily dish out mouthwatering seafood, burgers and pasta. Vintage treasure hunters can peruse the small clothing shop inside while they wait for their orders.

Da Vinci's (S 33 55.953 E 018 24.496, 70 Kloof St, Gardens, ☎021-424-7504, www.davincis.co.za, 11:30am-11pm, mains R40-80) is best known for their mouthwatering, wood-fired, thin crust pizza. But this Italian restaurant also has an array of salads, burgers and pastas that are worth a try. Your meal is best enjoyed outside, where staff will wait on you attentively.

Green (S 33 55.736 E 018 24.649, 5 Park Rd, Gardens, ☎021-422-4415, 9am-11pm, mains R50-90) is all about the "urban-chic" with decent standard fare served on a shaded terrace. Breakfast is available all day, as well as sandwiches, light meals, more substantial dishes and handmade pizza.

Hudson's (S 33 55.803 E 018 24.655, 69 Kloof St, Gardens, ☎021-426-5974, 12pm-late, mains R35-65) is an upmarket burger joint that sticks to what they know best. Pick from a mouthwatering menu that includes free-range chicken, ostrich and vegetarian patties. If you order one of their burgers with a tall beer, you'll surely leave with a smile.

🍴 Green Pt, Waterkant & Waterfront

Wakame (S 33 54.014 E 018 24.319, cnr Beach Rd & Surrey Pl, Mouille Point, ☎021-433-2377, 12pm-11pm, mains R70-100) is a trendy, Asian fusion restaurant that is flocked to by sushi lovers who want their raw fish and cocktails with a view. Adventuring away from the sushi menu will make your meal more revelatory; afterwards, head upstairs to Wafu, where wide, loungy balconies overlooking the harbor invite you to settle in and watch the sunset. Advanced booking on the weekends is recommended.

Mano's *(S 33 54.565 E 018 24.788, 39 Main Rd, Green Point,* ☏*021-434-1090, 12pm-late Mon-Sat, mains R70-110)* is a chic restaurant that keeps its menu short and flavorful. Continental fare includes seafood, chicken, steak and pasta, which is complemented by an equally brief but well curated wine list and full cocktail bar. The reasonable prices and quality service keep this place busy over the lunch hour when reservations are suggested and in the evening, when reservations aren't accepted.

Caffe Neo *(S 33 54.109 E 018 23.998, 129 Beach Rd, Mouille Point,* ☏*021-433-0849, 6:30am-7pm, mains R40-60, free wifi)* is a trendy eatery located directly across the street from the Green Point Lighthouse. It serves up fresh and healthy dishes that satisfy, but more are drawn here for the ocean view seating and the free wifi, which make for a delightful mobile office.

Giovanni's Deliworld *(S 33 54.478 E 018 24.578, 103 Main Rd, Green Point,* ☏*021-434-6983, 7:30am-9pm, mains R20-40)* is a small but bustling sidewalk café that proves a quick bite can still be memorable. The deli makes great sandwiches with fresh bread and a large selection of imported cheese and meats, as well as prepared meals you can eat there or on the go. It also has good selection of specialty foods, which you can pop in to peruse any time of the day.

Hussar Grill *(S 33 54.466 E 018 24.553, 107a Main Rd, Green Point,* ☏*021-433-2081, www.hussargrill. com, 12pm-11pm Mon-Fri, 6pm-11pm Sat, 12pm-10:00 Sun, mains R70-150)* boasts great food and service and reasonable prices. While the menu has something for everyone, Hussar is known for their in-house aged steaks. They are particularly known for their Carpetbagger: a sirloin steak stuffed with smoked oysters and a mix of melted cheeses.

Andiamo *(S 33 54.988 E 018 25.050, 72 Waterkant St, Cape Quarter Center, Waterkant,* ☏*021-421-3687, www.andiamo.co.za, 8am-11pm, mains R50-90)* is a courtyard Italian restaurant, deli and bar in the popular Cape Quarter. Italian favorites are straightforward, traditional and delectable. The deli, full of more than 2,000 local and imported goods, is superb.

⑪ Atlantic Coast (Sea Point, Clifton & Camps Bay)

La Perla *(S 33 55.117 E 018 23.141, cnr Beach Rd & Church Rd, Sea Point,* ☏*021-434-2471, www. laperla.co.za, 1:30pm-late, mains R85-130)* is a stalwart Sea Point restaurant and cocktail bar with formal indoor dining and a deck overlooking the

ocean. A recent revamp means the Italian-style fish, seafood, veal and homemade pastas are consistently delicious, but service by the primly clad waiters is still a toss up.

La Boheme Wine Bar & Bistro (S 33 54.853 E 018 23.477, 341 Main Rd, Sea Point, ☎021-434-8797, www.labohemebistro.co.za, 7am-11pm Mon-Sat, mains R70-90) has one downside - you can never order "the usual" because the delectable menu changes so often. Locally sourced ingredients shape the tapas and bistro fare, and the cozy sidewalk seating, cordoned off by wine casks, is a popular spot to enjoy a drink while you deliberate on what dish to try next.

New York Bagels (S 33 55.213 E 018 23.087, 51 Regent St, Sea Point, ☎021-439-7523, 7am-4pm, mains R20-50) is a café and small deli stuffed with homemade foods and is a mecca for those hankering for a good roll-with-a-hole. There are 13 kinds of bagels to choose from, as well as a breakfast menu and a selection of feel-good deli favorites, including chopped liver and chicken noodle soup.

The Grand Café (S 33 57.025 E 018 22.731, 35 Victoria Rd, Camps Bay, ☎021-438-4253, www.thegrand.co.za, 12pm-late Tue-Sat, 10am-late Sun, mains R80-200) offers fine bistro food, upmarket French flair and a rare quiet spot to overlook Camps Bay Beach, but at an inflated price.

Paranga (S 33 57.184 E 018 22.641, The Promenade, Victoria Rd, Camps Bay, ☎021-438-0404, www.paranga.co.za, 9am-11pm, mains R100-180) is the ultimate see-and-be-seen restaurant on The Promenade. The menu serves primarily seafood (with a complement of classic meat and pasta dishes) in a sophisticated space flanked by stone and marble. If you can't get a table at Paranga, the two restaurants next door, Bungalow and The Kove, are by the same owner and have similar menus at a better value.

⑪ Southern Suburbs

A Tavola (S 33 59.141 E 018 28.060, Library Square, Wilderness Rd, Claremont, ☎021-671-1763, www.atavola.co.za, 12pm-3pm & 4pm-10pm Mon-Fri, 4pm-10pm Sat, mains R70-100) is a modern, open kitchen Italian restaurant by former Joburg chef Giancarlo Pironi. The selection of wine and hearty Italian meals of fresh creamy pasta and delicious veal are tough to beat. It is a relatively recent addition to the southern suburb restaurant scene but already popular with locals.

1890 House Sushi and Grill (S 33 56.350 E 018 28.160, 40 Trill Rd, Observatory, ☎021-447-1450, 12am-3pm & 5pm-10:30pm Mon-Sat, 5pm-10pm Sun, mains R25-50) may not get five stars for ambiance, but this authentic and unpretentious Observatory staple serves up fantastic sushi and steak in large portions at a price that can't be beat.

Jamaica Me Crazy (S 33 56.058 E 018 27.094, 74 Roodebloem Rd, Woodstock, ☎021-448-0691, www.jamaicamecrazy.co.za, 10am-11pm Mon-Sat, mains R55-85) is a little bit of Jamaica in Woodstock, in both fare and bar. Jerk chicken, fancy burgers and Trinidad roti fill out the menu; head over on a Monday night to rub elbows with locals for the popular and cheap Monday Madness menu. Upstairs, the balcony has a view and a big screen TV for sports games.

Don Pedro's (S 33 56.107 E 018 27.103, 113 Roodebloem Rd, Woodstock, ☎021-447-4493, www.donpedros.co.za, 9am-late, mains R40-80) is a no-frills restaurant serving traditional Cape Flats and Cape Malay curries and stews. Don Pedro's was known as a Woodstock cultural hub and anti-apartheid institution in the early '90s before the system collapsed. Not much has changed in this place over the past few years - come as you are and enjoy the good food.

Mimi's Café (S 33 56.346 E 018 28.138, cnr Lower Main Rd & Trill Rd, Observatory, ☎021-447-3316, 7:30am-5:30pm Mon-Sat, 8:30am-5pm Sun, mains R30-60) is an Observatory staple - a homey corner café filled with well-worn tables and a quirky collection of old books and magazines lining the shelves. They have a large breakfast menu with fresh crumpets and croissants, light meals and gourmet filled breads and wraps.

Mango Ginger (S 33 56.355 E 018 28.137, 105 Lower Main Rd, Observatory, ☎021-448-2500, 7:30am-5pm Mon-Fri, 8am-3pm Sat, mains R30-60) is a welcoming, owner-run café that serves up healthy, hearty and inventive fare. Indulgences include fresh-pressed juice, piping hot bread and pastries from their onsite bakery, organic meals, free-range chicken pies, vegetarian quiches and gluten-free designer desserts.

Coco Cha Chi (S 33 56.518 E 018 28.135, 20 Lower Main Rd, Observatory, ☎021-448-3637, 7am-11pm Mon-Sat, 9am-5pm Sun, mains R30-70, wifi) is a café and pizzeria that offers yummy fare at a great value. Just as much of a treat are the friendly staff and the free wifi with any purchase. Dine in the back garden

Cape Town Nightlife Seven Days a Week

There is never a lack of party in Cape Town, but if you want to party like a local, follow these seven simple rules:

Monday ....Mercury Lounge (p114)
Tuesday..............................Dizzy's (p115)
Wednesday ....Karma (p115) & Assembly (p114)
Thursday .... Jade (p114)
Friday ....Hemisphere (p114)
Saturday....... Anywhere - everyone is out partying
Sunday ....La Med (p115)
followed by Café Caprice (p115)

and try one of their delicious smoothies.
Obz Café (*S 33 56.337 E 018 28.137, 115 Lower Main Rd, Observatory,* ☎*021-448-5555, www. obzcafe.co.za, 7am-10:30pm, mains R40-R70)* is a café by day and bar by night that offers all the standards and particularly tasty burgers in an airy lounge. Thursday is open mic night and there are usually live gigs on weekends.

♪ DRINKING & ENTERTAINMENT

♪ City Center & Bo-Kaap

Zula Sound Bar (*S 33 55.515 E 018 24.955, 196 Long St, City Center,* ☎*021-424-2442, www. zulabar.co.za, 4pm-late Mon, 12pm-late Tue-Sat, cover)* is one of Cape Town's more popular weekend spots and has live acts most nights.

The bar pulls in a range of entertainers that include some of South Africa's best, with occasional amateur and comedy nights thrown in. No matter the talent on tap, a night here is guaranteed to be loud and packed.

Waiting Room (*S 33 55.587 E 018 24.896, 273 Long St, City Center,* ☎*021-422-4536, 7pm-2am Mon-Sat, cover Fri-Sat)* draws an eclectic mix of locals and newcomers with a diverse DJ lineup on the weekends. Grab a drink on the main level, then head up to the rooftop deck for a great view of Long St. To get there, enter the unmarked doorway between Royal Eatery and Ado Grocery and take the fire escape stairs between the two buildings.

Fiction (*S 33 55.559 E 018 24.907, 226 Long St, City Center,* ☎*021-424-5709, www.fictionbar. com, 9:30pm-4am Tue & Thu-Sat, cover for entertainment)* is the university crowd's go-to bar and dance club on the weekends. The second-story bar and balcony overlooks Long Street and Tuesdays are designated student nights, with R10 bottles of beer and shots of Jagermeister.

The Dubliner (*S 33 55.562 E 018 24.924, 251 Long St, City Center,* ☎*021-424-1212, www.thedubliner. co.za, 11am-4am)* is that Irish pub that all the expats flock to. The Guinness, pub grub and live entertainment ensures a full bar almost every night of the week.

Pink Flamingo (*S 33 55.264 E 018 25.226, 38 Long St, Grand Daddy Hotel, City Center,* ☎*021-424-7247, www.pinkflamingo.co.za, 12pm-8:30pm, movies: 7:30pm)* is an open-air rooftop bar, stage and cinema that hosts occasional live music in the evenings and screens classics from Casa Blanca to Wayne's World between September and March. Patrons are encouraged to snuggle up on a lounge chair and make liberal use of the bar. Blankets are available and the movie ticket price (R50) includes popcorn and a welcome

drink. Check the website for current listings.

Rainbow Room *(S 33 55.424 E 018 25.180, Mandela Rhodes Place, 23 Church St, City Center,* ☎*021-422-1428,* www.therainbowexperience.co.za*, cover R50)* is a downstairs jazz club situated in the upmarket Mandela Rhodes Place that hosts live jazz by local and international talents as well as up-and-coming performers multiple times a week. Book your table in advance and while you're at it, order your drinks and eats so they are ready for you upon arrival. Show times and days vary so call or check online for current listings. Parking lot is off Burg Street with direct access to Mandela Rhodes Place.

Joburg *(S 33 55.548 E 018 24.919, 218 Long St, City Center,* ☎*021-422-0142 or* ☎*074-192-8177, 5pm-late Mon-Thu, 3pm-late Fri-Sat, 6pm-late Sun)* is a loud, urban, DJ-driven bar that packs in a diverse crowd. The scene may be too gritty for some, but it is certainly worth checking out if you're interested in partying, dancing, and more partying. Many consider it among the best bars on Long Street.

The Purple Turtle *(S 33 55.330 E 018 25.182, cnr Long St & Shortmarket St, City Center,* ☎*021-424-0811,* www.thepurpleturtle.co.za*, 10am-4am)* is a large, recently renovated downtown venue. It now hosts a comedy night on Tuesday and karaoke on

Gay Friendly Cape Town

Cape Town is the most gay-friendly city in Africa and has a robust nightlife scene. Unlike elsewhere in the country, and indeed the continent, sexual diversity is celebrated in Cape Town and it's quickly becoming an international gay-destination. The Waterkant area in Green Point, dubbed the "gaybourhood," is Cape Town's gay village and is packed with bars, clubs and men-only saunas that are popular with locals and tourists alike.

The annual **Cape Town Pride** (*www.capetownpride.co.za*) takes over the city late-February and early May with parties, live performances and film festivals, culminating in a Pride Parade which rivals any other in the world. The 10-day **Out In Africa Gay & Lesbian Film Festival** (*www.oia.co.za*) in late October showcases films from around the world and promotes a home-grown LGBT film industry. In December there is also a fabulous annual themed costume party hosted by **Mother City Queer Projects** (*www.mcqp.co.za*), the biggest party of the year with multiple dance floors and live music. Check out their website for this year's theme and come dressed to impress.

There are multiple websites and publications to help you orient yourself in the city and steer you towards the hottest places in town. **The Pink Map (021-685-4260**, *www.capeinfo.com*) is your guide to gay-friendly and gay-owned places to eat, sleep, shop and drink in Cape Town and around. You can pick one up at the tourism offices either at the Waterfront or in the City Center and at many hotels. For an online guide to what's on in town check out *www.gaycapetown4u.com*.

SAUNAS

The Hot House (S 33 54.892 E 018 25.018, 18 Jarvis St, Waterkant, **021-418-3888**, *www.hothouse.co.za*, 12pm-2am Mon-Thu, wkend 24hrs, R80-100) is one of the more popular upmarket saunas with two jacuzzis, a steam room, maze, full bar and restaurant, and a rooftop sun deck which affords great views of the city. It's open 24hrs/day on weekends.

DRINKING

Bronx (S 33 54.888 E 018 25.090, cnr Somerset Rd & Napier St, Waterkant, *www.bronx.co.za*, 8pm-late) is one of Cape Town's flagship gay bars and is usually packed, sweaty and shirtless. DJs spin six nights a week and Monday night is karaoke. The upstairs **Navigaytion (083-626-4615**, *www.navigaytion.co.za*) is a more exclusive dance club where men go to dance and lose all their inhibitions.

Beulah Bar (S 33 54.880 E 018 25.085, cnr of Somerset Rd & Coburn St, Waterkant, **021-421-6798**, *www.beulahbar.co.za*, 5pm-2am Tue-Thu, 5pm-4pm Fri-Sat) is a laid-back, lesbian-owned bar and lounge where girls, boys and hipsters come to play. It's a cool place to hang out all week long, but the small dance floor gets packed on weekends when DJs spin Top 40 hits.

Crew (S 33 54.884 E 018 25.103, 30 Napier, Waterkant, **021-418-0118**, *www.crewbar.co.za*) is a packed and popular gay dance club with hot bartenders in colorful little boxer briefs. If table dancing and grinding is your thing, you'll be right at home.

Thursday, but live rock, electro, glam and hip-hop still packs the place with young punks and old rockers alike on the weekends.

Hemisphere *(S 33 55.210 E 018 25.470, 31st Floor, ABSA Building, 2 Riebeck St, City Center,* ☎*021-421-0581,* www.hemisphere.org.za, *10pm-4am Thu & Sat, 4:30pm-4am Fri, cover R50-R70)* is a sky-high bar with 360 degree views of the city, a glass-walled VIP area and an air of general fabulousness. Open only Thursday through Saturday, it enforces a strict dress code and glamour is highly recommended.

&Union *(S 33 55.295 E 018 25.041, 110 Bree St, City Center,* ☎*021-422-2770,* www.andunion.com, *7am-11pm Mon-Thu, 7am-12am Fri-Sat, R55-85, wifi)* is a microbrewery and restaurant that serves up fine, high-octane artisan brews as well as specialty natural foods. They have live music on weekends and jazz on Wednesdays.

☯ Gardens & Around

Asoka *(S 33 55.940 E 018 24.501, 68 Kloof St, Gardens,* ☎*021-422-0909,* www.asokabar.co.za, *5pm-2am)* is a chic cocktail bar and lounge where the bartenders actually pour you a healthy cocktail instead of measuring it out in a shot glass. The intimate dance floor and outdoor deck is a playground for Cape Town's posh young socialites. Live jazz sets the stage on Tuesdays and DJs spin house and chill beats through the weekend.

Ginja *(S 33 55.616 E 018 24.661, 70 New Church St, Gardens,* ☎*021-426-2368, 11am-3pm & 6:30pm-11pm Mon-Sat, 6:30pm-11pm Sun)* is a restaurant and cocktail lounge that recently relocated. Their new third-story balcony has a great view of the City Bowl, Table Mountain and Lion's Head. Though better known for their tony restaurant (popular with the business crowd), the lounge has a good tapas menu and makes

dynamite martinis.

Rafiki's *(S 33 55.798 E 018 24.488, cnr Kloof Nek Rd & Upper Buitengrach St, Tamboerskloof,* ☎*021-426-4731, 11am-2am, mains R45-75)* is a second-floor bar and veranda where tall drinks flow both day and night. They have a full food menu but stick to the drinks and bar fare or pizza. Guest DJs pack in the crowds on weekends.

Kink *(S 33 55.744 E 018 24.661, 3 Park Rd, Gardens,* ☎*021-424-0757,* www.kink.co.za, *12pm-3pm & 6pm-2am Tue-Fri, 7pm-3am Sat)* attracts an alternative and goth crowd, perhaps for its drink menu, which includes the Pearl Necklace, Ben Dover, S&M, and Spank the Skank, or for the sex toyshop upstairs. If you stay late enough you might catch a bit of a show.

The Assembly *(S 33 55.706 E 018 25.446, 61 Harrington St, District Six,* ☎*021-465-7286,* www.theassembly.co.za, *8pm-late, cover R40-R110)* is a trendy hipster hideout, popular for its alternative and electro live concerts. The large dance floor is often a hot mess, but the beats are from some of the newest names in the biz. Wednesdays and Saturdays are most popular; buy tickets in advance for a discount.

The Mercury Lounge *(S 33 55.926 E 018 25.547, 43 De Villiers St, District Six,* ☎*021-465-2106,* www.mercuryl.co.za, *8pm-late, cover R15-R60)* is the granddaddy of alternative music in Cape Town and a firm local favorite for live gigs, fresh rock and established indie bands. Manic Mondays are legendary among students, but the best live music happens on the weekends.

☯ Green Point, Waterfront & Waterkant

Jade *(S 33 54.566 E 018 24.787, 39 Main Rd, Green Point,* ☎*021-439-4108,* www.jadelounge.co.za, *8pm-2am Tue-Sat)* is an exclusive, uber-posh

lounge frequented by Cape Town's high society. Located above Manos, French nouveau decor and plush sofas set the mood and the bar gets packed Thursday through Saturday. Be prepared for a strictly enforced dress code and a long line.
Cubana (S 33 54.960 E 018 25.096, Somerset Rd, Waterkant, ☎021-421-1109, www.cubana.co.za, 8am-4am) is a spacious Latin lounge that is open all day and a popular place to either begin or end your night. Sip on cocktails in dark wicker chairs in the open-air lounge or take to the dance floor.

❶ Atlantic Coast (Sea Point, Clifton & Camps Bay)

Café Caprice (S 33 57.039 E 018 22.720, 37 Victoria Rd, Camps Bay, ☎021-438-8315, www. cafecaprice.co.za, 9am-12am Tue-Sun, 12pm-12am Mon) is the pinnacle of the Camps Bay lifestyle - located at the beginning of Camps Bay, it's a good place to grab a drink any time of day or night to watch the Cape Town beach scene go by. At night it's packed with the "beautiful people."
Karma (S 33 57.184 E 018 22.641, 3rd floor, The Promenade, Victoria Rd, Camps Bay, ☎021-438-7773, guest list ☎072-400-9542, www. karmalounge.co.za, 9pm-2am Wed-Sun, cover R50-100) is a trendy Camps Bay beachside lounge where the young, bronzed and occasionally beautiful shake their stuff until the early hours of the morning. Lines can be long and there is often a cover.
La Med (S 33 56.581 E 018 22.480, Glen Country Club, off Victoria Rd, Clifton, ☎021-438-5600, www.lamed.co.za, 12pm-11pm Mon-Fri, 9am-11pm Sat-Sun, cover) is a relaxed restaurant and bar overlooking the ocean and the Twelve Apostles near Clifton Beach 4. The atmosphere changes a bit on Sundays when crowds fill it up for a late afternoon meal and pre-gaming, before hitting the clubs in neighboring Camps Bay.
Dizzy's Pub (S 33 57.252 E 018 22.639, 41 The Dr, Camps Bay, ☎021-438-2686, www.dizzys.co.za, 12pm-4am) is a laid-back pub and party scene opposite Dizzy's restaurant that hosts live music and DJs. Drink specials and Karaoke night draw a large crowd on Tuesdays. Pizza is served until 2am.

❶ Southern Suburbs

Stones (S 33 56.311 E 018 28.143, 84 Lower Main Rd, Observatory, ☎021-448-9461, www.stones. co.za, 12pm-4am) is part of a franchise of pubs throughout South Africa and an Observatory hot spot. The large second-story bar and balcony are generally packed with UCT students squeezed between the dozen pool tables.
Tagore's (S 33 56.349 E 018 28.165, 42 Trill Rd, Observatory, ☎082-711-2051, 5pm-2am) is classic bohemian, with a two-level maze of small rooms inside a converted apartment. Tagore's hosts live music almost every night by incredible artists. The bar usually hits capacity shortly after the music starts. Upstairs there's a bedroom for those interested.
Albert Hall (S 33 55.629 E 018 27.124, 208 Albert Rd, Woodstock, ☎082-336-0314, www.alberthall. co.za) is an eclectic, antique-strewn venue in the heart of Woodstock that hosts live music, dance parties and alternative gigs — but they don't have a regular schedule and are sometimes only open a couple nights a week. They often hold open mic jams on Tuesdays, but the lineup can change often, so call in advance.

🎭 THEATRES

Tickets for theatre, music and festivals throughout South Africa can be purchased through **Computicket** (☎021-918-8910, www.computicket. com).
Artscape (S 33 55.185 E 018 25.816, DF Malan St, Foreshore, ☎021-410-9800, www.artscape.co.za, R75-275) is the state-owned art and performance center. It hosts opera, ballet, contemporary dance, musical theatre, concerts and a variety of other polished theatrical productions within its impressive three venues.
Baxter Theatre Centre (S 33 57.424 E 018 28.241, Main Rd, Rondebosch, ☎021-685-7880, www. baxter.co.za, R60-125) is a vibrant cultural center located on the University of Cape Town campus. Locals, university students and international guests can enjoy theater, comedy, and concerts ranging from jazz and African to contemporary music.
On Broadway (S 33 55.274 E 018 25.123, 88 Shortmarket St, City Center, ☎021-424-1194, www.onbroadway.co.za, shows start 8:30pm, show R70-95, mains R50-90) is an extremely popular dinner theater venue that presents musical ensembles, comedians, and the occasional drag diva while you dine. Tickets must be booked in advance.
NewSpace Theatre (S 33 55.283 E 018 25.208, 44 Long St, City Center, ☎021-462-5269, www. newspacetheatre.co.za) was first established

in 1972, and has long been billed as an anti-establishment venue for plays, one-man shows, musicals and comedy. At the time of research, shows had been suspended as they searched for a new theater director, but we hope that this Long Street establishment will be open again soon. Call for updated information.

◉ CINEMAS

Labia Theatre (S 33 55.789 E 018 24.753, 68 Orange St, Gardens, ☎021-424-5927, www.labia. co.za, adult R30, child R25) was originally the Italian embassy ballroom and today is a small, independent theater that screens a variety of artsy and classic films as well as new releases. Enjoy a snack or libation with your screening from their fully licensed bar and café. Their second location, **Labia on Kloof** (S 33 55.773 E 018 24.654, Lifestyles Centre, 50 Kloof St, Gardens) is an upmarket boutique theater with two screens and daily specials.

NuMetro Cinemas (S 33 54.235 E 018 25.198, Shop 223, Victoria Wharf Shopping Centre, Waterfront, ☎021-419-9700, www.numetro.co.za, R40) screens mostly mainstream movies and blockbuster hits on 11 screens.

Ster Kinekor (S 33 54.268 E 018 25.150, Red Shed, Victoria Wharf Shopping Centre, Waterfront, ☎082-16789, www.sterkinekor.com, R48) has a more independent art-cinema bent and multiple screens.

◉ SPORTS

Tickets for most sporting events can be purchased through **Computicket** (☎021-918-8910, www.computicket.com).

◉ Football

Catching a football game in Cape Town is a deal, with tickets to almost all games starting at R20. The football season runs from August to May. Two of Cape Town's home teams are **Ajax** (www.ajaxct.com) and **Santos** (www.santosfc.co.za).

Green Point (Cape Town) Stadium (S 33 54.196 E 018 24.664, Fritz Sonneberg Rd, Green Point) was built for the 2010 World Cup with capacity for 69,000 people. The stadium is now used for football, rugby and non-sporting events.

Athlone Stadium (S 33 57.708 E 018 31.041, Klipfontein Rd, Athlone) is an older stadium built in 1972 with capacity for 30,000 and is primarily used for football.

Newlands Stadium (S 33 58.226 E 018 28.116, Boundary Rd, Newlands) holds 52,000 people and hosts both football and rugby games.

◉ Rugby

Cape Town's home rugby team is the **Stormers** (www.iamastormer.com).

Newlands Stadium (S 33 58.226 E 018 28.116, Boundary Rd, Newlands, ☎021-685-3333, www.clubnewlands.co.za) hosts both football and rugby games and is the home base of the Stormers.

◉ Cricket

The Cape Cobras (www.capecobras.co.za) are headquartered in Cape Town at the Newlands Cricket Stadium. The cricket season runs from September to March.

Newlands Cricket Stadium (S 33 58.416 E 018 28.128, Boundary Rd, Newlands, ☎021-657-3300) is the big cricket stadium in Cape Town located beside the Newlands Stadium.

⊘ TRANSPORTATION

◉ Air

Cape Town International Airport - CPT (S 33 58.157 E 018 35.793, 021-937-1200, automated flight information ☎086-727-7888, www.acsa.co.za) services domestic and international flights. For domestic and regional flights check out **South African Airways** (☎086-135-9722 or ☎011-978-5313, www.flysaa.com), **South African Airlink** (☎011-961-1700, www.saairlink.co.za) or **South African Express** (☎011-978-5577, www.saexpress.co.za). Flights can be booked online, over the phone or directly at the ticket sales counter at the airport.

Some budget airlines that offer primarily domestic flights include: **Mango** (☎086-116-2646 or ☎021-936-2848, www.flymango.com), **Kulula** (☎086-144-4144 or ☎011-921-0111, www.kulula.com), **1time** (☎086-134-5345, www.1time.co.za) and **Interlink Airlines** (☎086-110-1135, www.interlinkairlines.com).

◉ Train

Cape Town Railway Station (S 33 55.324 E 018 25.509, cnr Strand St & Adderley St, City Center)

offers regional and long distance transport.
The Metrorail (☎080-065-6463, _www.capemetro rail.co.za_) offers regular regional service, which includes the red line to Wynberg-Simon's Town, blue line to Langa-Bellville-Kapteinslip-Khayelitsha, and green line to Bellville-Wellington-Stellenbosch-Strand. Call or check online for exact schedule and rates. To access nearby beaches on the Cape peninsula, the **Southern Line Tourism Route Ticket** (☎021-449-2366, _www.capemetrorail. co.za/Marketing/Product Definition/Tourism/Info. htm_, one-day R25, two-day R45) offers unlimited hop on, hop off transport between Cape Town, Observatory, Newlands, Muizenberg, Kalk Bay and Simon's Town from 8:30am to 4:30pm daily.
Shosholoza Meyl (☎086-000-8888, _www. shosholozameyl.co.za_) offers passenger train service from Cape Town to most major cities and other smaller cities that fall in between, including East London, Johannesburg, Kimberly, Bloemfontein, and Durban. Trains depart for Joburg every day, but other lines leave only once a week. Some routes offer sleeper service. Luxury train service is offered through **Premiere Classe** (☎086-000-8888, _www.premierclasse.co.za_) and has service from Cape Town to Johannesburg, Durban, Kimberly, Oudtshoorn, George and Port Elizabeth.

🚗 Car Rental

Around About Cars (☎021-422-4022 or ☎086-0422-4022, _www.aroundaboutcars.com_) is a budget car agent that can make a booking for you at one of the major national car rental companies. By booking through Around About Cars you get a better price and better insurance coverage than you would if you make a reservation directly with the rental company.
Avis (☎086-102-1111, _www.avis.co.za_)
Budget (☎086-101-6622, _www.budget. co.za_)
Europcar (☎021-421-5190, _www. europcar.co.za_)
Tempest (☎021-481-9860, _www. tempestcarhire.co.za_)

🚌 Bus

Long distance buses have ticket sales offices at, and depart from, the northeast corner of the railway station in **City Center** (S 33 55.241 E 018 25.507, cnr Adderley St &

Riebeek St, City Center). Some of the major bus companies with the largest route networks include:
Translux/City to City (☎086-158-9282 or ☎021-449-6209, _www.translux.co.za_), **Greyhound** (☎021-418-4326, _www.greyhound.co.za_), **Intercape** (☎086-128-7287, _www.intercape.co.za_) and **SA Roadlink** (☎011-333-2223, _www.saroadlink.co.za_).
To view the time schedules and prices of all of the above bus companies for any specific route check out **Computicket** (☎083-915-8000, _www. computicket.com/web/bus tickets_), where you can also make your booking online or over the phone.
Baz Bus (☎021-439-2323, _www.bazbus.com_) is a popular and convenient way to get around for those doing the South African circuit and stops at most backpackers in town. From Cape Town, the Baz Bus heads to Stellenbosch, Hermanus, Swellendam, Mossel Bay, Oudtshoorn and Knysna, and continues all the way along the coast to Durban, Swaziland and Johannesburg. All the backpackers in Cape Town who are Baz Bus stops will have a current timetable and be able to make a booking for you.

🚐 Minibus Taxi

Minibus taxis are a popular way to get to and from

CAPE TOWN

CAPE TOWN

Cape Town and surrounding cities. While they don't offer much in the way of personal space or comfort, they are faster and frequently a little cheaper than taking a bus.

Minibus Taxi Rank *(S 33 55.374 E 018 25.612, Cape Town Railway Station, cnr Strand St & Adderley St, City Center)* is on the upper deck of the railway station in the City Center. Here you can get a minibus taxi to the Cape Flats and to most of the major and medium-sized cities in the country. This is also the main rank for local Minibus taxis in the city.

⮐GETTING AROUND

⮐ To / From OR Tambo Airport

Taxis are the easiest way to get to and from the airport (one-way to City Center is about R240). If there aren't any taxis waiting when you arrive, you can call any of the Cape Town taxi companies listed below under Metered Taxis.

There is also an airport shuttle service operated by **Noble Tours** (☎*021-934-1510 or* ☎*076-135-0049)* that provides shared transport from the airport to destinations around the city *(1 person R170, 2 people R200)*. They have a desk just before you exit the international arrivals terminal.

🚌 Bus

City Sightseeing Cape Town (☎*021-511-6000, www.citysightseeing.co.za, 1 day: adult R120, child R60, 2 day: adult R200, child R120)* offers unlimited hop-on, hop-off access to all major city sights on two routes. The red line hits the City Center, the beaches and the Waterfront. The blue line does a wider loop that includes the Kirstenbosch Botanical Gardens and Hout Bay. Both depart from the Waterfront, but can be boarded at any stop along the line. Tickets can

be bought onboard, online or from a Cape Town Tourism office.

🚕 Metered Taxis

Cape Town has plenty of taxis and they can frequently be found waiting outside of restaurants, bars and some hotels. Many of the taxis do not have or do not use meters, so it's a good practice to agree on a price before setting out.

Rikkis (☎*086-174-5547, www.rikkis.co.za, 6:30am-2am Mon-Thu, 24hrs Fri-Mon)* is a popular shared-ride taxi company that services the city bowl and surrounding areas. They are slightly less expensive than a standard taxi but may take a bit longer. Rikkis has free phones located throughout the city that you can use to call for a ride.

Other established metered taxi companies include **Grab a Cab** (☎*021-556-6344, www.grab-a-cab.co.za)*, **Marine Taxis** (☎*021-434-0434, www.marinetaxis.co.za)*, **EBR** (☎*021-424-9418)* and **Sea Point Radio Taxis** (☎*021-434-4444)*.

🚐 Minibus Taxi

Minibus taxis are one of the cheapest ways to get around and are a standard form of transport for many people in Cape Town. Most drive on informal routes around the city and a guy will be yelling out the window where they are headed as they whiz by. They can get very crowded and stop often to pack more passengers in. The main local minibus taxi rank is above the train station, but it's more common to just flag them down on the street. To avoid confusion and the risk of getting lost, stick to the simplest routes: Adderly St - Kloof St - Long St patrols up and down the city center; Strand St - Main Rd - Sea Point takes you out of the city center and towards Sea Point along the Main Road. During the summer months, the route is often extended to Clinton and Camps Bay

AROUND CAPE TOWN

The small towns that dot the coastline of the Cape Peninsula make for superb day trips or longer jaunts if you're in need of a break from the big city. Muizenberg, Kalk Bay, St James and Simon's Town are all a short train ride from Cape Town, but having your own wheels will afford you more freedom and access to the area's delights. Head down the east coast from Cape Town to leisurely explore the quaint beach towns en route to Cape Point. On the way, you may encounter baboons sitting in the road and can stop and see the colony of jackass penguins in Simon's Town.

MUIZENBERG
& KALK BAY
GPS: S 25 05.366 E 030 27.228
pop. 20,000 | elevation 1,403 m/4,603 ft

Muizenberg is considered the birthplace of surfing in South Africa and its surfer vibe is still vibrant today. It initially developed as a holiday resort for gold and diamond magnates in the late 1800s, including the former Prime Minister Cecil Rhodes, who built a small holiday cottage on the seafront. Further down the False Bay coast is St James, with its iconic colorful beach huts and the old fishing village of Kalk Bay. Once home to a large Filipino fisherman population, Kalk Bay is now a relaxed strip of town with antique stores, boutiques and restaurants lining the main drag opposite the harbor.

❶ TOURIST INFORMATION

Cape Town Tourism Muizenberg (S 34 06.428 E 018 28.300, The Pavilion, Beach Rd, Muizenberg, ☎021-787-9140, 8:30am-5:30pm Mon-Fri, 9am-1pm Sat-Sun) has free Muizenberg area maps and information on area accommodation and activities. They are familiar with the places to stay around town and are more than willing to call and make a booking for you.

❸ MONEY

In Muizenberg there is a **Standard Bank** (S 34 06.381 E 018 28.118, Checkers Shopping Center, cnr Main Rd/M4 & Atlantic Rd) with an ATM as well as a **Nedbank ATM**.

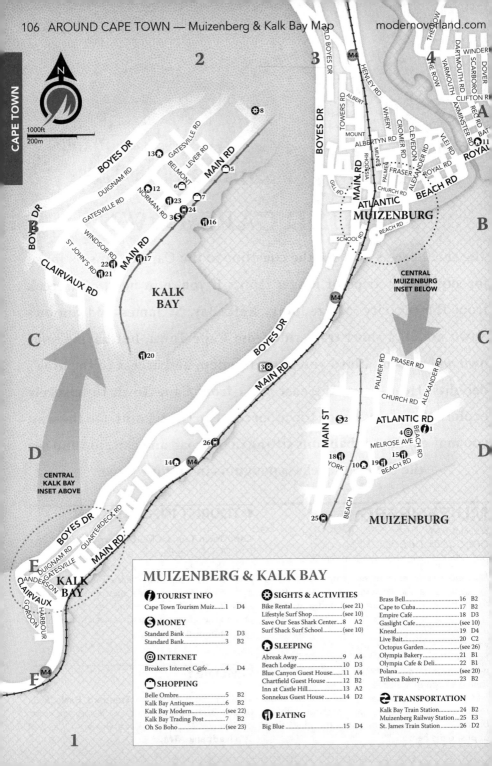

MUIZENBERG & KALK BAY

TOURIST INFO
Cape Town Tourism Muiz.......1   D4

MONEY
Standard Bank 2   D3
Standard Bank 3   B2

@ INTERNET
Breakers Internet C@fe............4   D4

SHOPPING
Belle Ombre....................................5   B2
Kalk Bay Antiques.......................6   B2
Kalk Bay Modern....................(see 22)
Kalk Bay Trading Post................7   B2
Oh So Boho ....(see 23)

SIGHTS & ACTIVITIES
Bike Rental.................................(see 21)
Lifestyle Surf Shop ....(see 10)
Save Our Seas Shark Center....8   A2
Surf Shack Surf School............(see 10)

SLEEPING
Abreak Away 9   A4
Beach Lodge 10   D3
Blue Canyon Guest House.......11   A4
Chartfield Guest House 12   B2
Inn at Castle Hill........................13   A2
Sonnekus Guest House 14   D2

EATING
Big Blue 15   D4

Brass Bell....................................16   B2
Cape to Cuba.............................17   B2
Empire Café...............................18   D3
Gaslight Cafe........................(see 10)
Knead 19   D4
Live Bait.....................................20   C2
Octopus Garden ....(see 26)
Olympia Bakery.........................21   B1
Olympia Cafe & Deli.................22   B1
Polana ....(see 20)
Tribeca Bakery..........................23   B2

TRANSPORTATION
Kalk Bay Train Station.............24   B2
Muizenberg Railway Station ...25   E3
St. James Train Station...........26   D2

In Kalk Bay there is a **Standard Bank** (S 34 07.566 E 018 27.007, Kalk Bay Station, Main Rd) ATM just outside Kalk Bay Train Station.

@INTERNET

Breakers Internet C@fe (S 34 06.431 E 018 28.266, 48 Beach Rd, Muizenberg 021-788-8076 or 021-788-4103, 9am-7pm Mon-Sat, 11am-5:30pm Sun, R20/hr wkday, R15/hr wkend) has 12 computers for Internet use and LAN and wireless connections for your laptop. They also offer faxing, photocopying and international calls.

At the time of research there weren't any public Internet cafés in Kalk Bay.

SHOPPING

Main Street in Kalk Bay has a bohemian flair and is lined with art galleries, antique stores and clothing stores. There's a lot to look at, so we suggest you start with the following places:

Kalk Bay Modern (S 34 07.658 E 018 26.881, 136 Main Rd, Kalk Bay, 021-788-6571, www.kalkbaymodern.com, 9:30am-5pm) is by far the best art gallery in Kalk Bay. Its tasteful and contemporary collection of photography, paintings, jewelry and sculpture herald not only from South Africa, but also feature African artists representing the Sudan, Congo, and Ethiopia, as well as San communities from southern Africa.

Oh So Boho (S 34 07.566 E 018 26.980, 96 Main Rd, Kalk Bay, 021-788-2443, 9am-5pm) has a huge selection of silver jewelry and classic Kalk Bay bohemian apparel and accessories.

Kalk Bay Trading Post (S 34 07.547 E 018 27.014, 71 Main Rd, Kalk Bay, 021-788-9571, 9am-5pm Mon-Fri, 9:30am-5pm Sat-Sun) is an inviting collection of antiques, old coins, maps and rusted home furnishings that begs to be rummaged through. If rummaging isn't your style, check out **Kalk Bay Antiques** (S 34 07.542 E 018 27.012, 76 Main Rd, Kalk Bay, 021-788-8882, 9:30am-5pm) for a more refined selection. For African artifacts visit **Belle Ombre** (S 34 07.518 E 018 27.052, 19 Main Rd, Kalk Bay, 021-788-9802, 9am-5:30pm Mon-Fri, 9:30am-5pm Sat-Sun), where you'll find exquisite woven baskets and wood carvings.

SIGHTS & ACTIVITIES

The main attraction to Muizenberg is the surf. There are a handful of local surfing stores along Surfer's Corner that offer surf lessons and equipment rentals.

Surf Shack Surf School (S 34 06.480 E 018

28.142, Surfer's Corner, Beach Rd, Muizenberg, ☎021-788-9286, www.surfshack.co.za, 8:30am-5pm weather dependent) is run by a handful of true surfer dudes who offer lessons and equipment rental. Individual lessons run R300 for 1.5hr, 2-person lessons are R275/person and 3-5 people are R200/person. Regular group lessons are R200 and offered at 10:30am and 2:30am. Board rentals are R70 for 1.5hr but cheaper per hour the longer you are out. To set up a lesson just call in advance or stop in. Prices may be negotiable, so it doesn't hurt to ask.

Lifestyle Surf Shop (S 34 06.480 E 018 28.147, Surfer's Corner, Beach Rd, Muizenberg, ☎021-788-8218, 8am-6pm Mon-Sat, 9am-5pm Sun or days when weather is bad) is a fully stocked store that sells anything a surfer needs. Individual surf lessons run R275 for 1.5hr, 2-person lessons are R200/person and 3+ person lessons are R170/person and lower. Group lessons are R100 and offered at 10am and 12pm on Sat and 10:30am on Sun. Board rentals are R60/hr. Special packages and rates can be arranged.

Bike Rental (S 34 07.664 E 018 26.868, Olympia Bakery, 134 Main Rd, Kalk Bay, ☎021-788-6396, www.bybike.co.za, R120/day) is available through Olympia Bakery whose entrance is off of the alley just south of the Olympia Café. You can pick up your bike and drop it back off here or at any ByBike location in a neighboring town.

IMPACT Save Our Seas Shark Center (S 34 07.436 E 018 27.135, 28 Main Rd, Kalk Bay, ☎021-788-6694, www.saveourseas.com, 10am-4pm Mon-Sat, admission free) is an educational center that promotes shark awareness and responsibility. A large fish tank displays a number of local fish species and the friendly staff is happy to share information about their research and conservation efforts.

⊙SLEEPING

⊙ Muizenberg

Beach Lodge (S 34 06.480 E 018 28.145, Surfer's Corner, Muizenberg, ☎021-788-1771, www.thebeachlodge.co.za, dm R130, s R200, d R300) is tough to beat in terms of location. It's steps from the water and has a beach house feel with sand-worn steps, an open kitchen and TV lounge, as well as a large balcony to hang out on that overlooks the beach.

Abreak Away (S 34 05.940 E 018 28.645, 24A Hastings Rd, Muizenberg, ☎021-788-8839 or

☎079-138-6116, surfabreak@yahoo.com, dm R100, s/d R300) is essentially a surfer-home-turned-backpackers located in a residential part of town within walking distance to the waves. The staff and surfers are friendly and they also run a program to teach disadvantaged children how to surf. Other than that, it feels like staying over at a friend's house.

Blue Canyon Guest House (S 34 06.202 E 018 28.561, ☎021-788-3418 or ☎082-719-0737, www.bluecanyon.co.za, s R370, d R625, breakfast included) is in a historic house with smart minimalist en suite rooms and polished old hard wood floors throughout. It's located just across the street from the beach and right beside the lagoon and also has two fully equipped, self-catering cottages beside a heated pool and braai area.

Admiralty (S 34 05.687 E 018 28.530, 6 Admirals Walk, Cannon Island, Muizenberg, ☎021-788-1028 or ☎076-194-2173, www.admiraltybb.co.za, s R400, d R700, breakfast included) is located on Cannon Island with a deck and braai area that extends over the calm water of the Zandvliei estuary. There are five uniquely designed rooms, a large common area with plenty of space to lounge both inside and out, a swimming pool, deck and braai area, as well as a canoe if you're up for a little paddling. To get there, head east out of town for about 1 km on Beach Rd/R310, which becomes Royal Rd. At the traffic circle head north on Prince George Dr for about 700 m. Take a left on Cannon Island Way and a left on Admirals Walk. The destination will be on your right.

⊙ Kalk Bay

Sonnekus Guest House (S 34 07.227 E 018 27.375, 88 Main Rd, St. James, ☎021-788-2992, www.sonnekus.co.za, s R345-470, d R690-940, breakfast included, wifi) is a well-restored guesthouse built in 1926, with nine rooms of varying size, located just across the street from the ocean. The friendly owner and host will go out of her way to make your stay pleasant, including arranging pickups, dinner reservations, picnic lunches and laundry service.

Chartfield Guest House (S 34 07.540 E 018 26.927, 30 Gatesville Rd, ☎021-788-3793, www.chartfield.co.za, R800-900, breakfast included, Internet/wifi, swimming pool) is a 4-star lodge perched on a hill overlooking the ocean that feels like a boutique hotel. All 13 rooms are spacious with comfortable beds, large bathrooms and a TV. Below the main lodge, which has a small café and bar, is a good-sized swimming pool and grassy lawn for lounging in the sun.

Inn at Castle Hill (S 34 07.497 E 018 26.958, 37 Gatesville Rd, Kalk Bay, 021-788-2554, www.castlehill.co.za, s R460-580 d R800-1,040, breakfast included) has five individually decorated rooms with tall ceilings, wood floors and doors that open up onto a balcony overlooking the ocean. The owner and host's family has lived in the area for generations, and will happily provide recommendations and make arrangements to visit area sights and activities.

🍲 EATING & DRINKING

The best selection of places to eat and drink are along the Main Street in Kalk Bay and St. James, but there are a couple of local favorites in Surfer's Corner in Muizenberg

🍲 Muizenberg

Empire Café (S 34 06.471 E 018 28.107, 11 York Rd, Muizenberg, 021-788-1250, 7am-4pm Mon-Sat, 8am-4pm Sun, mains R50) is a surfer's favorite, serving up large portions and the best breakfast in Muizenberg, which makes it the most popular morning spot in town.

Knead (S 34 06.484 E 018 28.184, Surfer's Corner, Muizenberg, 021-788-2909, 9am-5:30pm Mon, 8am-5:30pm Tue-Sun, mains R30-60) bakes to feed the beach-going masses - bunny chow, sandwiches, bread boards, pizza, you name it. Right in the heart of Surfer's Corner, it's a popular place to grab a slice. Takeaway is also available.

Gaslight Café (S 34 06.480 E 018 28.145, Surfer's Corner, Muizenberg, 021-788-6994, 8am-4:30pm

Mon, 8am-5:30pm Tue-Sun, mains R30-60) is right under the Beach Lodge and is a great place to grab coffee, breakfast or lunch. As you munch on open-faced sandwiches or heartier fare, you can take in the Muizenberg photographic history that lines the walls.

Big Blue (S 34 06.467 E 018 28.235, Surfers Corner, Muizenberg, 021-788-2552, 8am-late, mains R30-60) is a surfer's bar/restaurant that is a quick few steps from the water. It is a laid-back place that serves food and drinks until the crowd heads home.

🍲 Kalk Bay

Olympia Café & Deli (S 34 07.655 E 018 26.881, 134 Main Rd, Kalk Bay, 021-788-6396, 7am-9pm, mains R60-100) is a popular seaside café on the main drag opposite the harbor. They serve up a delicious selection for breakfast and a Mediterranean inspired lunch of hearty salads, saucy pastas and fresh seafood. Their homemade bread is excellent and sourced from the **Olympia Bakery** (S 34 07.664 E 018 26.868, 6:30am-7pm) hidden in the alley just south of the café. It's by far the best smelling place in town (not to mention a site for bike hires.)

Octopus Garden (S 34 07.149 E 018 27.502, St James Train Station, Main Rd, St James, 021-788-5646, mains R50-80) is a tastefully designed love-themed café overlooking St James Station. The hosts enjoy what they do and the restaurant has tapas, full meals, and a sizable whiskey selection. Wacky Wednesdays are parties with half-priced drinks.

Tribeca Bakery (S 34 07.568 E 018 26.978, 106 Main Rd, Kalk Bay, 021-788-3424,

7am-10pm, lunch mains R20-50, dinner mains R60-80) is a sophisticated café that brings the feeling of New York to the harbor of Kalk Bay. Walls are covered with Tribeca building scenery and the bakery serves delicious breakfasts, gourmet sandwiches, salads and savory-topped flatbreads for lunch. For dinner, your best bet is their two or three course set menu that changes monthly.

Live Bait *(S 34 07.777 E 018 26.961, Kalk Bay Harbour, Kalk Bay,* ☎*021-788-4133, www. harbourhouse.co.za, 12pm-10pm, mains R70-110)* is an open-air restaurant right on the harbor. Its nautical atmosphere and delicious selection of Greek-inspired seafood makes it a great place for dinner. They've got some of the freshest and tastiest oysters in town. By the same owner, Harbour House is upstairs and has a similar menu but a more formal feel. Also by the same owner and next door is **Polana** *(S 34 07.785 E 018 26.956, Kalk Bay Harbour, Kalk Bay,* ☎*021-788-7162, www.harbourhouse.co.za kitchen: 12pm-10pm, bar open late)* a sea level restaurant and cocktail lounge with large windows overlooking crashing waves just 10 m away. There is live rock music on Friday and Saturday nights.

Cape to Cuba *(S 34 07.632 E 018 26.913, Main Rd, Kalk Bay, 8am-late, mains R70-110)* is a Cuban-themed restaurant that serves a mix of Cuban and standard fare including tapas, steaks, seafood and pasta. Outside is a sand-floor beach bar with palm branch huts where you can enjoy a Cuba Libre, Mojito or Martini.

Brass Bell *(S 34 07.560 E 018 27.014, Kalk Bay Station, Main Rd, Kalk Bay,* ☎*021-788-5455, www. brassbell.co.za, 11am-10pm, bar open late, mains R50-80)* has a restaurant and bar that protrudes out into the ocean, with the waves crashing on the wall and occasionally spraying the tables close to the edge. The restaurant is divided into five different sections each with a different level of formality and view. The restaurant specializes in seafood but also has good pizza and burgers. Brass Bell has the most active night life scene in town.

⮀ TRANSPORTATION

Train
The Metrorail (☎*080-065-6463, www.capemetro rail.co.za)* runs a Cape Town-Wynberg-Simon's Town route which stops at **Muizenberg Railway Station** *(S 34 06.574 E 018 28.066, Main Rd, Muizenberg)* and **Kalk Bay Train Station** *(S 34*

07.572 E 018 26.992, Main Rd, Kalk Bay) from 5am-8pm Mon-Fri (leaving every 10-30min), 5:30am-7pm Sat (leaving every 20-45min), 6am-7:30pm Sun & public holidays (leaving roughly every 30min). The ride from Cape Town to Muizenberg is about 45min, 50min to Kalk Bay, and costs roughly R10. Call or check online for an exact schedule and rates. You can also buy a **Southern Line Tourism Route Ticket** (☎*02-721-449-2366, www.capemetrorail.co.za/Marketing/ Product_Definition/Tourism/Info.htm, 1-day R25, 2-day R45)* for unlimited hop-on, hop-off transport between Cape Town, Observatory, Newlands, Muizenberg, Kalk Bay and Simon's Town from 8:30am-4:30pm daily.

SIMON'S TOWN
GPS: S 25 05.366 E 030 27.228
pop. 20,000 | elevation 1,403 m/4,603 ft

Simon's Town is a sleepy naval town in False Bay that was first founded by Simon van der Stel in 1687 and established as the official winter anchorage of the Dutch East India Company in 1743. The town was largely built with the use of slave laborers, many of whom were brought from Indonesia, which contributed to the development of a vibrant Muslim community. However, Simon's Town was deemed a "white" area under the Group Areas Act in 1967 and over 7,000 coloured town residents were forcibly removed to an inland settlement that was ironically named Ocean View. Today the city is the official home of the South African Navy and is a great launching point for water activities. But the real attraction here are Jackass Penguins at Boulder Beach, one of the largest colonies of African penguins in South Africa.

❼ TOURIST INFORMATION

Cape Town Tourism - Simon's Town *(S 34 11.597 E 018 26.028, 111 St George's St,* ☎*021-786-8440, 9am-5pm Mon-Fri, 9am-1pm Sat-Sun)* can offer helpful information about lodging and activities in the area. If nothing else, stop by for a free map.

⊖ MONEY

There is an **FNB** *(S 34 11.604 E 018 25.938, 106 St*

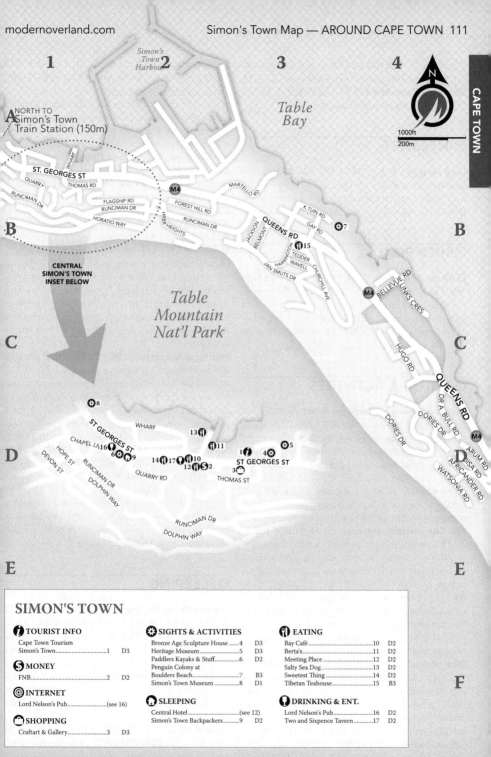

1   **2**   **3**   **4**

CAPE TOWN

Simon's Town Harbour

Table Bay

N

1000ft
200m

A NORTH TO Simon's Town Train Station (150m)

ST. GEORGES ST

WHARF

QUARRY

THOMAS RD

RUNCIMAN DR

FLAGSHIP RD
RUNCIMAN DR

HORATIO WAY

HRBR HEIGHTS

FOREST HILL RD

RUNCIMAN DR

JACKSON

BELMONT

MARTELLO RD

QUEENS RD

K TUIN RD

GAY RD

HARRINGTON
TEDDER
WAVELL

JAN SMUTS DR

CHURCHILL AVE

15

7

M4

M4

BELLEVUE RD

LINKS CRES

B

CENTRAL SIMON'S TOWN INSET BELOW

Table Mountain Nat'l Park

HUGO RD

QUEENS RD

DR A BULL RD

DORIES DR

DORIES DR

C

ARUM RD

DISA RD

AFRICANDER RD

WATSONIA RD

M4

D

8

ST GEORGES ST

WHARF

CHAPEL LA 16

HOPE ST

DEVON ST

RUNCIMAN DR

DOLPHIN WAY

QUARRY RD

6

9

14

17

12

10

13

11

1

4

5

St GEORGES ST

3

THOMAS ST

2

RUNCIMAN DR

DOLPHIN WAY

E

F

SIMON'S TOWN

🛈 TOURIST INFO
Cape Town Tourism
Simon's Town........................1 D3

💲 MONEY
FNB.....................................2 D2

@ INTERNET
Lord Nelson's Pub.............(see 16)

🛍 SHOPPING
Craftart & Gallery..................3 D3

✹ SIGHTS & ACTIVITIES
Bronze Age Sculpture House.......4 D3
Heritage Museum....................5 D3
Paddlers Kayaks & Stuff............6 D2
Penguin Colony at
Boulders Beach....................7 B3
Simon's Town Museum................8 D1

🛏 SLEEPING
Central Hotel....................(see 12)
Simon's Town Backpackers..........9 D2

🍴 EATING
Bay Café..........................10 D2
Berta's...........................11 D2
Meeting Place.....................12 D2
Salty Sea Dog.....................13 D2
Sweetest Thing....................14 D2
Tibetan Teahouse..................15 B3

🍷 DRINKING & ENT.
Lord Nelson's Pub.................16 D2
Two and Sixpence Tavern...........17 D2

George's St, ☎021-784-1140, 9am-3:30pm Mon-Fri, 8:30am-11am Sat) or if you just need an ATM, **Standard Bank ATMs** (S 34 11.597 E 018 25.940, St George's St) are just across the street.

@INTERNET

Lord Nelson's Pub (S 34 11.578 E 018 25.732, 58 St Georges St, ☎021-786-1386, R20/45min) was the only place in town with public Internet access at the time of review and has two computers available.

⊙SHOPPING

Craftart & Gallery (S 34 11.607 E 018 26.022, 128 St George's St, ☎021-786-1997, 9am-5:30pm) is just across the street from the Tourism Information Centre, which is the best of a number of cutesy gift and clothing stores along St George's Street.

⊛SIGHTS & ACTIVITIES

Penguin Colony at Boulders Beach (S 34 11.742 E 018 26.960, Klein Tuin Rd, ☎021-786-2329, www.sanparks.org/parks/table_mountain/tourism/attractions.php#boulders, Dec-Jan: 7am-7:30pm, Feb-May & Sept-Nov: 8am-6:30pm, Jun-Aug: 8am-5pm, adult R30, child R10) is home to a colony of over 3,000 Jackass Penguins. There are two entrances into the South African National Parks managed section of the beach where the penguins are. **The second entrance** (S 34 11.874 E 018 27.181, Bellevue Rd) is generally a little less busy. If you're interested in getting closer to the penguins and avoiding an admission fee, you can head to the entrance off of Bellevue Rd and go directly onto the uncontrolled area across the road to the east, where there are generally hundreds of penguins. You can even put on your swimsuit and jump in the water with them, but remember that these are wild animals and they will bite if they feel threatened.

Bike Rental (S 34 11.325 E 018 25.524, St. George's St, ☎083-595-0588, www.bybike.co.za, 7am-8pm, R120/day) is available through Fluids Place Coffee Shop, which is a cool little coffee shop where the owner serves patrons like friends. You can pick up your bike and drop it off here or at any ByBike location in a neighboring town.

Paddlers Kayaks & Stuff (S 34 11.582 E 018 25.745, 62 St Georges St, Simon's Town, ☎021-786-2626, www.paddlers.co.za, 10am-5pm Mon-Thu, 10am-4pm Fri, 10am-2pm Sat, 12pm-2pm Sun) has rental gear available to head out on your own, or you can book a 2hr sea kayak tour of False Bay, that includes a stop at Boulder Beach to hang with the penguins, through **Sea Kayak Simon's Town** (☎082-501-8930, www.kayakcapetown.co.za, R250).

Bronze Age Sculpture House (S 34 11.577 E 018 26.095, King George Way, Simon's Town, ☎021-786-5090, www.bronzeage.co.za, 8am-4:30pm Mon-Thu, 8am-3pm Fri, admission free) is situated in the historic Albertyn's Stables, which in its day served as slave quarters, horse stables and housing for sick sailors. Today, it's home to a breathtaking display of contemporary bronze-casted sculptures from South African and international artists, as well as a foundry workshop in the back. Its surprising amount of style seems slightly out of place in naval Simon's Town and is well worth a visit.

Heritage Museum (S 34 11.577 E 018 26.108, Almay House, King George Way, ☎021-786-2302, 11am-4pm Tue-Thu & Sun, R5) pays tribute to the history and culture of the Cape Malay Muslim population in Simon's Town and their forced removal from Simon's Town when the city was declared a "white" zone under apartheid in 1967.

Simon's Town Museum (S 34 11.477 E 018 25.660, Court Rd, ☎021-786-3046, www.simonstown.com, 10am-4pm Mon-Fri, 10am-1pm Sat, 11am-3pm Sun, suggested donation adult R5, child R2) provides extensive information about the history of Simon's Town. The building itself was built in 1777 as the winter home for the Governor of the Dutch East India Company.

⊙SLEEPING

Simon's Town Backpackers (S 34 11.588 E 018 25.754, 66 St George's St, ☎021-786-1964, www.capepax.co.za, dm R135, s/d R360-420, Internet) is a tranquil backpackers located on the main drag with a large second-story balcony overlooking Simon's Bay. The rooms are comfortable, there is a well-stocked bar and a computer for Internet use. The backpackers can also assist in arranging area activities and tours.

Central Hotel (S 34 11.597 E 018 25.904, 96 St George's St, ☎021-786-3775, www.centralhotel.

co.za, s R500 d R880, breakfast included) has stood at the center of town since 1828 and operated as a hotel since 1894. It has been restored in Victorian style and converted into a 10-room guesthouse with balcony rooms with a great view of the harbor.

Simonsview Guest House (S 34 10.027 E 018 25.643, 3 Seemeeu St, Dido Valley, Simon's Town, ☎021-786-1962, www.simonsview.co.za, s R450, d R550, 4-person loft R1,000) has three large, airy rooms on two levels of a house on the hillside overlooking the ocean. The friendly host, Eleanor lives at the house and is more than willing to provide advice and arrange area activities. Two of the rooms have a kitchen for self-catering. From Simon's Town, head north on the Main Rd/M4 and turn left on Dido Valley Rd, take the first right onto Penguin Rd and then the third left onto Seemeeu St.

The Winston (S 34 12.713 E 018 27.700, 15 Erica Rd, Murdock Valley South, Simons Town, ☎021-786-1700, www.winston.co.za, s R750, d R1,100, breakfast included, Internet/wifi, swimming pool) has stunning views from each of its large rooms, which all have a TV and small wine fridge, and open to a communal patio. Upstairs there is a comfortable lounge with panoramic views that you can whale watch from between July and October. Outside is a small swimming pool and sunny lounge deck. From Simon's Town, head south on the Main Rd/M4 and turn right onto Rockland Rd. You will see the guesthouse immediately on your right.

⊕EATING

Tibetan Teahouse (S 34 11.815 E 018 26.823, 2 Harrington Rd, Seaforth, Simon's Town, ☎021-786-1544, www.sopheagallery.com, 10am-5pm Tue-Sun, mains R30-55) is a vegetarian gem in Simon's Town with a fabulous view of False Bay that will please vegetarians and meat-eaters alike. The Tibetan restaurant is adjoined to a gallery that displays a wide selection of jewelry, paintings, textiles and glasswork, much of which is for sale. They also have meditation sessions and film screenings. Check their website for details.

Berta's (S 34 11.570 E 018 25.960, 1 Wharf Rd, Simon's Town, ☎021-786-2138, www.berthas.co.za, 7am-10pm, mains R60-100) has one of the better settings in town. You can enjoy seafood, sushi, or the catch of the day within 2 m of the water.

Bay Café (S 34 11.593 E 018 25.879, 90 St George's St, ☎021-786-4529, 11am-late Tue-

Sun, mains R45-75) is trendier than your average Simon's Town café. It serves bruschetta, pizza, pasta, burgers and more substantial daily specials in a carefully aged dining room with rough hardwood floors and peeled paint picture frames. They serve Illy coffee and their playlist is decent.

Black Marlin (S 34 13.779 E 018 28.270, Main Rd, Millers Point, www.blackmarlin.co.za, 12pm-10pm Mon-Fri, 8am-10pm Sat-Sun, mains R70-120) is located in a former whaling station right on the point with panoramic views of the ocean. The menu is long with an emphasis on fresh seafood and includes Cape Rock lobster, oysters and mussels. They also have an extensive wine list and selection of whiskey. It also happens to be the lunch spot for some tour buses making their way to the Cape Point.

The Meeting Place (S 34 11.601 E 018 25.919, 98 St George's St, Simon's Town, ☎021-786-1986, 9am-5pm, mains R40-50) serves a tasty breakfast and lunch among a predominantly white and silver array of home décor for sale, as well as teas, jams and coffee.

The Sweetest Thing (S 34 11.592 E 018 25.823, 82 St George's St, Simon's Town, ☎021-786-4200, 8am-5pm Mon-Fri, 9am-5pm Sat, 9am-4pm Sun, mains R20) is an adorable patisserie with a wide selection of sweet tarts, treats and tortes, as well as a few more savory specialties.

Salty Sea Dog (S 34 11.567 E 018 25.933,

Wharf St, Simon's Town, ☎021-786-1918, 9:30am-9:30pm Mon-Sat, 9:30am-4:30pm Sun, mains R25-40) is your standard seaside fish and chips. Take away or dine in within spitting distance of the docks.

○ DRINKING & ENTERTAINMENT

The Two and Sixpence Tavern *(S 34 11.595 E 018 25.863, 88 St George's St, Simon's Town, ☎021-786-1371, 11am-2am)* has been serving newcomers since 1902. Nowadays it looks more like a sailor's pub but has a selection of drafts and a pool table. **Lord Nelson's Pub** *(S 34 11.578 E 018 25.732, 58 St. Georges St, ☎021-786-1386)* is a small but well-stocked sailors pub that tends to have a steady stream of customers by day and night.

⊜ TRANSPORTATION

○ Train

The Metrorail *(☎080-065-6463, www.capemetrorail.co.za)* runs a Cape Town-Wynberg-Simon's Town route which stops at **Simon's Town Metrorail Station** *(S 34 11.213 E 018 25.520, Main Rd, Simon's Town)* from 5am-8pm Mon-Fri *(leaving every 10-30min)*, 5:30am-7pm Sat *(leaving every 20- 45min)*, 6am-7:30pm Sun & public holidays *(leaving roughly every hour)*. The ride from Cape Town to Simon's Town is just over one hour and costs roughly R12. Call or check online for exact schedule and rates. You can also buy a **Southern Line Tourism**

Route Ticket *(☎021-449-2366, www.capemetrorail.co.za/Marketing/Product Definition/Tourism/Info.htm, 1-day R25, 2-day R45)* for unlimited hop on, hop off transport between Cape Town, Observatory, Newlands, Muizenberg, Kalk Bay and Simon's Town from 8:30am-4:30pm daily.

CAPE POINT
& CAPE OF GOOD HOPE

The Cape of Good Hope Nature Reserve *(☎021-780-9204, www.sanparks.org/parks/table mountain/tourism/attractions.php#goodhope, Oct-Mar: 6am-6pm, Apr-Sept: 7am-5pm, entrance adult R75, child R10)* is a popular day trip for many who visit Cape Town. In addition to Cape Point and the Cape of Good Hope, the nature reserve offers numerous outdoor activities including hiking, fishing, surfing, biking and beaching. On a drive through the park, you'll likely encounter some of the wildlife that lives within the reserve such as eland, red hartebeest, bontebok, zebra and ostrich. **The Cape of Good Hope** *(S 34 21.422 E 018 28.419)* is the southwestern most point of the African Continent. It is often mistakenly referred to as the southern most point of the African continent, however that designation rightfully belongs to Cape Agulhas, situated some 150 km to the southeast. **The Cape Point** *(S 34 21.214 E 018 29.408)* is located 2.3 km/1.4 mi to the east of the Cape of Good Hope, but is slightly higher in elevation. Near the tip of Cape Point is the original lighthouse built in 1860. From the restaurant and information center visitors can either walk or take the Funicular Railway *(adult R43, child R15)* on a 0.6 km trip along the edge of the point to the old lighthouse. Even after the installation of the old lighthouse, ships continued to wreck on the point as fog and low clouds reduced its visibility until 1919, when a new lighthouse was built further out and closer to sea level. The more adventurous can hike down a narrow and winding path to visit it.

CAPE FLATS TOWNSHIPS

The townships on the Cape Flats are home to millions of people, but are an often overlooked part of the city. The area is densely populated by the masses of black and coloured people who made their livings in Cape Town but were restricted to living on the outskirts of town. The townships have long suffered from neglect and misguided restructuring, but have recently benefited from infrastructure investment. Though many still live in poor and overcrowded conditions, there are also affluent and developed neighborhoods.

🏛 HISTORY

The first black townships in Cape Town were created after a 1901 outbreak of the bubonic plague in Cape Town was wrongfully blamed on black dockworkers in the city. As a result, health legislation forced over 5,000 men from their residences at the docks and in District Six and resettled them to an area on the Cape Flats called Uitvlugt. The initial settlement, later renamed Ndabeni, was little more than a collection of makeshift tents for male laborers. There was no infrastructure, sanitation was nonexistent and the men's families were not allowed to live with them in the settlement, which tore many families apart.

In 1923, the Urban Areas Act declared the city of Cape Town the realm of the white population and regulated the movement of black Africans in the cities through the institution of pass laws. Black males were forced to carry identification at all times and hold proof of employment in order to visit the city. Langa was established as a "model" township for the settlement of black men legally working in the city. At the time, the townships were only meant to be residences for male migrant workers and Langa's large single-sex hostel compounds were kept under strict surveillance and control. Women were not allowed to live in the hostels and were restricted to rural "homeland" areas, which were considered the only appropriate permanent home for the African population.

Despite continued efforts by the city government to keep blacks out of Cape Town, the population of Langa swelled as industrialization and manufacturing attracted increasing numbers of people to the city in search of work. This led to the establishment of Nyanga East in 1948 and Nyanga West 1958, which later became known as Gugulethu. In addition, employers began to demand a more stable work force and low-cost family houses began to be built to supplement the residences.

By the late 1950s, Cape Town's townships emerged as a hub for the black liberation movement. The Pan Africanist Congress (PAC) established a presence in Langa and in 1960 mobilized residents to take part in anti-pass demonstrations where men burned their passes or challenged police to arrest them for not having their passes. Workers also staged stay-aways, where they remained at home en-masse during workdays. The protests were met with violent raids and repression by the police, and on March 30, 1960 over 30,000 Langa and Nyanga residents marched through the streets of Cape Town. PAC leader Phillip Kgosana negotiated an end to the march in exchange for a meeting with the Minister of Justice, but was arrested upon arrival. Riots erupted and the military cordoned off the townships and a state of emergency was declared. The subsequent arrests, the banning of the ANC and PAC, and the increased crackdown on political opposition during the 1960s drove the opposition movement underground.

The 1970s saw renewed fervor among township youth and a rise in the student-led Black Consciousness movement. News of the Soweto Uprising in 1976 spread across the country, along with mass uprisings in the townships. Students from Langa, Nyanga and Gugulethu began to riot, engaging in ongoing battles with the police, and students from neighboring coloured schools joined the protest in solidarity against the oppressive white government. Solidarity between emerging community and civic organizations continued throughout the following decade amidst rising levels of violence and insurrection. The United Democratic Front (UDF) was one such alliance of civic,

women's, student's and community organizations that joined together to demand the dissolution of the apartheid state.

As the government tried to control the influx of migrants from the Transkei and Ciskei homelands and eradicate "illegal" settlements, shantytowns on the city outskirts became a point of contention between the government and opposition forces. Unibel, Modderdam and Crossroads became hot spots and the battle to save Crossroads from demolition grew especially violent. Government security forces covertly supported a local-warlord-turned-community-leader from Crossroads, who instigated gang violence and riots that displaced some 60,000 residents, many of whom fled and took shelter further out in the newly established township of Khayelitsha.

Khayelitsha had been established by the government in the mid-1980s to house "legal" residents living in overcrowded townships or displaced during the demolitions of informal squatter settlements. Throughout the 1990s, Khayelitsha's population grew quickly as pass laws were rescinded and thousands of people from the rural homelands flooded to the city in search of work. Today, Khayelitsha is Cape Town's largest township and home to many of the city's new immigrants.

LANGA

GPS: S 33 56.637 E 018 31.609
pop. 250,000 | elevation 15 m/49 ft

Langa, meaning "the sun" in Xhosa, was named after the chief of the Hlubi tribe, Langalibalele, who was imprisoned on Robben Island in 1875 for resisting the local government in Natal. Upon his release, he was confined to an area on the Cape Flats that later became known as "Langalibalele's Location." Langa was created under the terms of the 1923 Urban Areas Act and developed as a "model" township; its layout and design emphasized strict surveillance and control of its tenants. The first residents of Langa were migrant male workers who were housed in single-sex dorms and lived in cramped and unsanitary conditions. These residences still stand today and some are being converted to family-style apartments. Langa is a popular destination for township tours and whether you arrive on your own or with a group, you are likely to see other visitors exploring the township.

TOURIST INFORMATION

Langa Tourism Office *(S 33 56.646 E 018 31.470, Guga S'thebe Center, Washington St, ☎021-695-5098, 8am-4:30pm Mon-Fri, 9am-12pm Sat-Sun)* has brochures and information that is mostly related to the Cape Town area. There is frequently a local guide nearby to the Guga S'thebe Center and the tourism office can connect you with one of them to show you around the township. The tourism office also has four computers with Internet access *(R5/30min)*.

MONEY

There is a Standard Bank ATM and FNB ATM located at the **Minibus Taxi Rank** *(S 33 56.751 E 018 32.174, cnr of Washington St & Olga Noviata St)*.

A **Standard Bank ATM** and FNB ATM are also at the **Caltex Filling Station** *(S 33 56.742 E 018 32.032, Washington St)*.

INTERNET

African Access *(S 33 56.766 E 018 32.111, Washington St, 9am-6pm Mon-Fri, 9am-3pm Sat-Sun, R5/30min)* has a mix of newer and older computers. There is generally a waiting line to get to a computer. It is not well signed but located directly across the street from the front door of the post office.

Langa Tourism Office *(S 33 56.646 E 018 31.470, Guga S'thebe Center, Washington St, ☎021-695-5098, 8am-4:30pm Mon-Fri, 9am-12pm Sat-Sun, R5/30min)* has four computers with Internet access.

SHOPPING

The commercial district of Langa *(S 33 56.751 E 018 32.174, cnr of Washington St & Olga Noviata St)* is located in the area surrounding the Minibus

Taxi Rank. **Shoprite** *(S 33 56.762 E 018 32.046)* is in the largest building and there are a number of smaller shops lining the street.

Eziko Craft *(S 33 56.625 E 018 31.692, cnr Washington St & Jungle Walk, ☎021-694-0434, www.ezikorestaurant.com, 9am-5pm Mon-Sat)* is operated in connection with Eziko Restaurant and sells art, crafts, jewelry, paintings and tablecloths, all made by local Langa residents.

SIGHTS & ACTIVITIES

Guga S'thebe Center *(S 33 56.646 E 018 31.470, Washington St, ☎021-695-3493, 8am-4:30pm Mon-Fri, 9am-12pm Sat-Sun)* houses the Langa Tourism Office as well as a few tables of crafts and pottery made in the center's workshop. In the back of the center, you can observe the artisans at work. There is also a performance stage where children practice and play African marimba music. If you're interested, they are more than willing to play their instruments for you as others dance.

IMPACT **Love Life Center** *(S 33 56.480 E 018 31.612, Rose Innes St, ☎021-695-0003, www.lovelife.org.za, 9am-6pm)* is a community center that focuses on HIV/AIDS prevention, primarily though a variety of youth development programs. They offer debate, acting and dance classes, as well as several sports and a radio station studio. Visitors can come and work with the children in their arts and dance programs or play volleyball or basketball with them. The center is busiest weekdays from 3pm to 5pm and on weekends.

Old Migrant Hostels *(S 33 56.830 E 018 31.662, south of Rhodes St, btwn Mendi Ave & Jungle Walk)* are the male dormitories built in 1969 to house Langa's migrant workers. Some of the hostels have since been renovated into family apartments alongside newer housing projects. From Washington St, head south on Jungle Walk. One block past Rhodes St, take a right on the unnamed road. If you stop at the intersection near the souvenir and craft stalls, you can easily find someone to take you into their house and show you the cramped living conditions of the updated family apartments.

Informal Shebeens *(S 33 57.020 E 018 31.742)* are scattered throughout the township. A good authentic one to visit is in the south of town. Take Jungle Walk south until it becomes Nolwana Way. At the traffic circle, turn right. Continue heading east after the road turns to gravel, where you can park

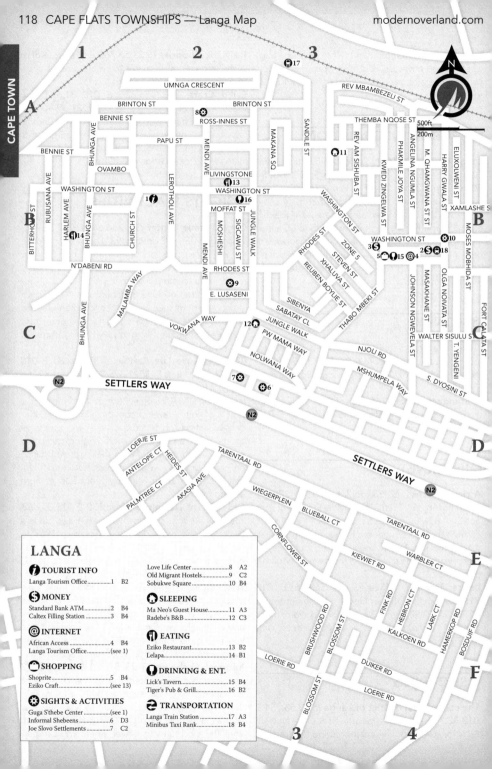

LANGA

TOURIST INFO
Langa Tourism Office 1 B2

MONEY
Standard Bank ATM 2 B4
Caltex Filling Station 3 B4

INTERNET
African Access 4 B4
Langa Tourism Office .... (see 1)

SHOPPING
Shoprite 5 B4
Eziko Craft .... (see 13)

SIGHTS & ACTIVITIES
Guga S'thebe Center .... (see 1)
Informal Shebeens 6 D3
Joe Slovo Settlements 7 C2

Love Life Center 8 A2
Old Migrant Hostels 9 C2
Sobukwe Square 10 B4

SLEEPING
Ma Neo's Guest House 11 A3
Radebe's B&B 12 C3

EATING
Eziko Restaurant 13 B2
Lelapa 14 B1

DRINKING & ENT.
Lick's Tavern 15 B4
Tiger's Pub & Grill 16 B2

TRANSPORTATION
Langa Train Station 17 A3
Minibus Taxi Rank 18 B4

directly across from the line of concrete latrines. Just ask for the shebeen and someone will point the way to a shack where you can enjoy a whole bucket of traditional beer, Umqombothi, for R10.

Joe Slovo Settlements *(S 33 56.980 E 018 31.692, off of Nolwana Way)* line the southern end of town along the N2 highway. Here, you can see evidence of a country in flux as the government tries to build low-cost housing to combat the informal settlements that have sprung up in Langa. The government plans to demolish all shacks and temporarily relocate residents while quality permanent housing is built in their place, but the plans are controversial and not all shack-dwelling residents have bought into the process.

Sobukwe Square *(S 33 56.731 E 018 32.191, roundabout at cnr of Washington St & Olga Noviata St)* was, at the time of research, under construction for a memorial to commemorate the 1960 Langa March, where the PAC led more than 30,000 people in protest of police repression during anti-pass demonstrations.

⊙ SLEEPING

Ma Neo's Guest House *(S 33 56.553 E 018 31.926, 30 Zolile Musie St,* ☎*021-694-2504 or* ☎*073-146-0370,* www.maneos.co.za, *R300/ person, breakfast included)* is the best accommodation in Langa, with four updated rooms with TV. Two rooms are located in the main house, which has a large living room and dining room. Two more rooms are located in a separate building in back.

Radebe's B&B *(S 33 56.902 E 018 31.741, 23 PW Mama Way, Settlers Place,* ☎*021-695-0508,* www. radebes.co.za, *dm R175, s R300, d R500, breakfast included, parking)* has been opening its doors to guests since 2005. There are three bedrooms in the house, which has a comfortable living room with a large flat screen TV. The host family lives in the house next door and can arrange anything from traditional home-cooked meals to a local guide to take you on a tour around the city.

⊕ EATING

Lelapa *(S 33 56.719 E 018 31.268, 49 Harlem Ave,* ☎*021-694-2681, Mon-Sat, meal R120)* isn't a place to just pop in for a meal - you have to book in advance so that fresh food can be purchased and meals prepared. But planning ahead is worth it: Monica and her mother cook up a smorgasbord of delicious and primarily wheat-free dishes – typically a 20-dish buffet, with live music.

Eziko *(S 33 56.615 E 018 31.693, cnr Washington*

St & Jungle Walk, ☎021-694-0434, www.ezikorestaurant.com, 9am-5pm Mon-Sat, mains R50-120) serves traditional African meals of lamb or chicken with veggies, samp and pap, or a full buffet can be prepared for a large enough group. The building is partially constructed out of steel shipping containers and there is a crafts shop with locally made crafts and jewelry next door. The restaurant is supposed to be open all day during the week, but it is probably a good idea to call in advance to let them know you are coming to be sure they'll be open.

♡ DRINKING & ENTERTAINMENT

Tiger's Pub & Grill (S 33 56.650 E 018 31.716, cnr Jungle Walk & Washington St, 9am-9:30pm) is a classy establishment for the township area – a recently remodeled pub and grill where you can order cuts of sirloin, sausage, wings or pig's foot to be grilled while you wait. You can enjoy your meat and drinks inside or out. This is a popular place with both locals and visitors on the weekend, but especially so on Saturdays.

Lick's Tavern (S 33 56.755 E 018 32.060, off Washington St) is a local joint where there are always a few patrons at the picnic tables or shooting pool during the day, and a real crowd in the evening. The bar is behind a steel mesh security gate with a hole for exchanging cash and bottles. On the weekend, going with a local is recommended.

⮂ TRANSPORTATION

Langa Train Station (S 33 56.344 E 018 31.782, Sandile Ave) has regular **Metrorail service** (☎080-065-6463, www.capemetrorail.co.za) to and from Cape Town via Woodstock. City Center to Langa is about 25 minutes. The same train runs to Khayelitsha further east.

Minibus Taxi Rank (S 33 56.751 E 018 32.174, cnr of Washington St & Olga Noviata St) has transport to Cape Town (R7), Joburg (R500), Gugulethu (R6), Khayelitsha (R7) and all of the surrounding townships.

GUGULETHU

GPS: S 33 58.409 E 018 33.692
pop. 340,000 | elevation 20 m/66 ft

Originally named Nyanga West, Gugulethu (or Gugs for short) was established in 1958 to house

the influx of workers to Cape Town from the rural Transkei region. Like neighboring Langa, Gugulethu was a site of mass resistance during apartheid and drew international attention with the murder of the Gugulethu Seven by South African security forces and the killing of American student and activist Amy Biehl in the early 1990s. Monuments now stand in memory of these past abuses and hope for the future. Today, one of Gugulethu's largest attractions is the Sunday braai and street party at Mzoli's, where people from all over the townships and Cape Town gather for an afternoon of eating, drinking and dancing.

⚑ TOURIST INFORMATION

Gugulethu Visitor Information Centre (S 33 58.550 E 018 33.784, College of Cape Town - Gugulethu Campus, cnr NY1 Rd & NY4 Rd, ☎ 021-637-8449, www.capetown.travel/attractions/ entry/Gugulethu, 9am-5:30pm Mon-Fri, 9am-1pm Sat) should be your first stop when visiting Gugulethu. The information center has an impressive photo exhibit on the history of Gugulethu and other surrounding townships and a shop that sells local arts and crafts. The staff are extremely friendly and can point you towards the nearest guesthouse, shebeen or sites in the area. They can also organize a tour.

@ INTERNET

Sakha Isizwe Internet Café (S 33 58.469 E 018 33.817, cnr Klipfontein Rd/NY108 & NY1, ☎021-637-2370 or ☎084-938-4267, 8am-6pm Mon-Sat, R8/30min) has two dated computers and a copy machine and is located inside of a steel shipping container.

⊙ SHOPPING

Gugulethu Visitor Information Centre (S 33 58.550 E 018 33.784, College of Cape Town - Gugulethu Campus, cnr NY1 Rd & NY4 Rd, ☎ 021-637-8449, www.capetown.travel/attractions/ entry/Gugulethu, 9am-5:30pm Mon-Fri, 9am-1pm Sat) doubles as a shop for local artists and crafters to sell their wares.

❂ SIGHTS & ACTIVITIES

Gugulethu Seven Monument (S 33 58.044 E 018 34.074, NY1 Rd) remembers the brutal murder of seven young black activists by South African security forces in 1986. The young men were on their way to what they believed to be a job interview in a minivan driven by an undercover security officer, when they stopped at a roadblock

The Amy Biehl Foundation Trust

On August 25, 1993, Gugulethu entered the international spotlight when a young American activist, Amy Biehl, was attacked and murdered by four young PAC members in the streets of Gugulethu. Amy Biehl was studying in South Africa on a Fulbright Scholarship and had been active in the townships promoting the transition to democracy and the political participation of women from underprivileged areas. But her murderers didn't know her and due to the color of her skin equated her with their oppressor. The event was a wake up call to the country and to the world that meaningful change was imperative to right past wrongs and quell political violence in South Africa.

During the Truth and Reconciliation Commission, the four young men imprisoned for her murder applied for amnesty. In honor of their daughter's commitment to social justice, Amy's parents flew to South Africa to participate in the Commission's hearings. They forgave her murderers and the men were granted amnesty and released from prison. Her family established a foundation in Amy's memory to continue the work that their daughter had started. In the spirit of forgiveness and transformation, the foundation employed two of Amy's murderers to assist in promoting education and reconciliation in Cape Town. The Amy Biehl Foundation Trust has initiated numerous programs focusing on education, health and the development of sports, recreation and the arts throughout the townships. For more information about the foundation's work and to see how you can contribute to continuing Amy's legacy see www.amybiehl.co.za.

and the police opened fire. Security forces covered up the crime, claiming it was an act of terrorism, but the real story was exposed during the Truth and Reconciliation process and a memorial now stands at the sight where they were killed.

Amy Biehl Monument (S 33 58.271 E 018 33.964, NY1 Rd) is a small cross marking the site where Amy Biel, an American student activist living in Cape Town, was killed in 1993 in an act of politically motivated violence by young PAC supporters in Gugulethu.

☉ SLEEPING

Liziwe's Guest House (S 33 58.556 E 018 34.494, 121 NY111 / Johnson Qona St, ☎021-633-7406, www.liziwes-bed-and-breakfast.com, s R350, d R450-500, breakfast included) is a spacious and modern guesthouse with comfortable rooms, each with its own unique African theme. Owners Liziwe and Donald are very welcoming and will go out of their way to make sure you have a memorable stay in Gugulethu. In 2010, they began construction on a new addition and expect to soon have a total of 15 rooms available for guests. They offer satellite TV, a comfortable living area and large dining area where they serve catered African meals.

⊕ EATING

Mzoli's Meat (S 33 58.575 E 018 34.183, NY115, Shop 3, ☎021-638-1355, www.mzolismeat.co.za) is a weekend hot spot where locals from Gugs, university students, Capetonians and visitors meld together for a daylong street party over meat, beer and music. Saturdays are good, but the real party is Sunday afternoon. Bring your drinks or buy six packs there. You can order sausage, wings, ribs or steak, which are grilled up in the back room any way you like it and served to you in a bucket.

☉ DRINKING & ENTERTAINMENT

Gqudu's Place (S 33 58.377 E 018 34.111, 40 NY116 Rd, 7pm-late Thu-Mon, 5pm-8pm Tue-Wed) is a popular lounge and dance club that really gets bumping on the weekends. On Mondays, they also offer a free fish braai when you buy a drink at the bar. **Duma's Falling Leaves** (S 33 58.724 E 018 34.175, NY147 Rd, ☎076-720-7717, 10am-late) is a jovial township shebeen where travelers can mix with locals looking to relax after a day of work. Duma, a former jazz musician who patrols his bar in sleeveless shirts and suspenders, is often entertaining his customers and friends with stories and a nonstop mix of tunes.

⮌ TRANSPORTATION

Minibus Taxis ply Klipfontein Rd/NY108, the main artery through Gugulethu in both directions, with easy transport to Cape Town (R10), Langa (R6) and Khayelitsha (R6).

KHAYELITSHA
GPS: S 34 02.457 E 018 40.093
pop. 500,000 | elevation 22 m/72 ft

Meaning "new home," Khayelistsha was established by the government in the early 1980s to house "legal" black residents who were living in overcrowded townships or evicted from informal squatter settlements on the outskirts of the city. The township quickly expanded as the repeal of pass laws led to rapid urban migration during the 1990s. People formerly restricted to rural "homelands" in the Western and Eastern Cape moved to the city in search of economic opportunities. Today Khayelitsha is Cape Town's biggest township and one of the largest in the country. Infrastructure in some of the areas of Khayelitsha is poor to nonexistent and crime rates are high. But investment into the township has led to rapid development and the construction of many new municipal buildings, including a state-of-the-art tourism center and a new hospital. It can be hard to find your way around on your own and streets are not well marked, so it's best to check out the town with a local.

✆ TOURIST INFORMATION

Khayelitsha Tourism Information Center *(S 34 02.708 E 018 39.401, Lookout Hill, cnr Mew Way/M44 & Spine Rd/M32, ☎021-387-6189 or ☎082-454-7312, 8am-5pm Mon-Fri, 8am-1pm Sat)* is located in the newly constructed Lookout Hill Tourism Facility. They can arrange tours and accommodation and provide you with a map of Khayelitsha, but be warned that the map is only useful for the larger streets in town. The facility also is home to a craft workshop and store and is used as a music practice and performance venue.

💲 MONEY

There are ATMs at most of the filling stations in Khayelitsha. All of the major South African banks have an office and ATMs at the **Khayelitsha Shopping Center** *(S 34 02.818 E 018 40.349, Walter Sisulu Rd)*.

@ INTERNET

Silulo Ulotho IT Center *(S 34 02.818 E 018 40.349 Khayelitsha Shopping Center, Walter Sisulu Rd, ☎021-361-5959, 8:30am-5:30pm Mon-Fri, 8:30am-4pm Sat, 8:30am-2pm Sun, R3/15min)* has five updated computers with small screens. They allow laptops to be connected.

SHOPPING

Khayelitsha Shopping Center (S 34 02.818 E 018 40.349, *Walter Sisulu Rd*) is the biggest shopping complex in Khayelitsha. It has a Shoprite, SuperSpar, a branch of every major bank and an Internet café.
Lookout Hill Tourism Facility (S 34 02.708 E 018 39.401, *Lookout Hill, cnr Mew Way/ M44 & Spine Rd/M32,* 021-387-6189 or 082-454-7312, *8am-5pm Mon-Fri, 8am-1pm Sat*) hosts crafting workshops and sells wares made by local residents.

SIGHTS & ACTIVITIES

Lookout Hill (S 34 02.796 E 018 39.412, *cnr Mew Way/M44 & Spine Rd/M32*) is not much of a hill but the lookout area at the top provides a great view of the expanse of Khayelitsha, the surrounding mountains and False Bay.

SLEEPING

IMPACT **Indlovu Project** (S 34 03.585 E 018 39.724, *off Mew Way, Monwabisi Park,* 073-198-0447 or 021-657-1026, *www.shaster. org.za, dm R200, breakfast included*) offers dorm room accommodation above the Montessori Creche, which cares for children under six. The Shaster Foundation is heavily involved in supporting the Monwabisi Park community and is in the process of building an eco-friendly clinic, youth center and soup kitchen next door. Guests can volunteer with the Indluvo Project during their stay. There is also a guesthouse

that is in the process of being built and is expected to be completed by 2011. Funds from the dorm and guesthouse support the community project.
Ekasie Backpackers (S 34 02.143 E 018 39.216, *Mew Way,* 021-361-7481 or 084-337-8815, *www.ekasie.co.za, dm R100, s R220, d R300, Internet, secure parking*) opened in 2004 as the first backpackers in Khayelitsha, with three dorm rooms and a couple of private rooms that open up onto a second-story balcony. It's a colorful backpackers with a bar, pool table and TV lounge upstairs. Hosts Nome & Luba can prepare meals and take you on a walking tour of the surrounding area. The entrance is in back, on Benyano Crescent.
Vicky's B&B (S 34 00.603 E 018 38.822, *C-685A Kiyane St, Site C,* 021-387-7104, 082-225-2986, *www.vickysbedandbreakfast. com, s R250, d R500, breakfast included*) became the first B&B of all the Cape Town townships when it opened in 1998. It started with two rooms and gradually expanded into a six-room, two-story guesthouse with a couple of en suite rooms and a second story balcony that provides a view of the surrounding area. The guesthouse is located in a vibrant neighborhood and Vicky's three younger children are happy to show you around. There is a popular shebeen just down the road where you can drink with the locals.
Malebo's B&B (S 34 02.514 E 018 40.486, *18 Mississippi Way, Graceland,* 021-361-2391 or 083-475-1125, *www.malebos-bed-and-breakfast.com,* R550/person, breakfast included) is a five-room guesthouse with three en suite rooms on the second level.

The guesthouse was in the middle of getting new hardwood flooring installed when we visited but promises to be freshly finished by 2011. Host Lydia can also prepare traditional Xhosa meals for lunch or dinner. **Majoro's B&B** (*S 34 02.409 E 018 40.527, 69 Helena Cres, Graceland,* 021-361-3412, *www. majoros-bed-and-breakfast.com*, *R450/person, breakfast included*) is a cozily decorated two-bedroom B&B with a living room and TV and one of the oldest of the Khayelitsha guesthouses. It opened in 1998 and is run by host Maria, who lives next door and can cook up an English or pancake breakfast for you in the mornings.

🍴 EATING

Nandi's (*S 34 02.646 E 018 39.579, Spine St*) is a popular braai joint that sells some seriously good meat: sausage, lamb, wings and beef by the kilo. You select your favorite sauce and they grill it up for you while you wait. Seating is outdoors at picnic tables. Note that Nandi's sells only meat and that bread and drinks are sold at the bar next door. **Star Catering** (*S 34 02.371 E 018 40.242, Khayelitsha Training Centre, cnr Spine St & Lwandle Rd,* 021-364-2763 *or* 072-179-4442, *lunch at 1pm Mon-Fri, call to arrange dinners*) is a large restaurant located in the training center. They serve lunch daily and are available upon request for special events and dinners. To find the restaurant, turn off Lwandle Road to Phendula Crescent and follow the signs for 100 m.

🍸 DRINKING & ENTERTAINMENT

Solly's (*S 34 03.203 E 018 40.768, 20062 Helen Khuzwayo St,* 082-483-1909) is easy to pass by, but from Thursday to Sunday, there's usually a crowd in the open courtyard, and around the well-stocked bar. When the DJs are mixing, parking gets tight. Going with a local is recommended. **Ace** (*S 34 02.288 E 018 39.907, E525 Phakamani Rd,* 083-581-3923, *6pm-late*) is where Khayelitshans braai and drink every day of the week. The club itself is modern and always has a flat screen TV on. On Mondays, they braai up a full sheep on a spit, Wednesdays is a fish braai and ladies night and the club is generally packed between Friday and Sunday. Going with a local is recommended. **Kefu's Jazz Pub & Grill** (*S 34 02.634 E 018 39.615, Spine Rd, Ilitha Park,* 021-361-0556 *or* 082-353-9742) is a small pub with big plans for expansion. Next door to the current pub is a two-story brick building that, when finished, will house the new pub, restaurant and a B&B. They are open seven days a week but usually only busy on Friday and Saturday nights. Meals are available if you call in advance.

🚄 TRANSPORTATION

Khayelitsha Train Station (*S 34 02.879 E 018 40.248, behind Khayelitsha Shopping Center, Walter Sisulu Rd*) has regular **Metrorail** (080-065-6463, *www.capemetrorail.co.za*) service to and from Cape Town via Woodstock and Langa. Cape Town City Center to Khayelitsha is about one hour.

Western Cape

Western Cape is best known for the historic Cape Winelands, which have been producing premium wines enjoyed around the world for more than 300 years. But the province is far more than its grape vines. To the east of the winelands, the iconic artery roads of the Garden Route and the interior Route 62 cut through the province to the Eastern Cape. The coastal route is rife with adventure activities such as shark cage diving and bungee jumping, as well as plentiful opportunities to whale watch and unwind on white sand beaches. On the interior route, outlandish pursuits including ostrich racing, squeezing through crevices of underground caves and driving the switchbacks of the 1,583 meter Swartberg Mountain Pass make for memories that last a lifetime. Route 62 is also home to some of South Africa's oldest and most charming country towns.

WINELANDS

Rich history, fertile soil, rolling hills and dramatic mountains make the Cape Winelands one of the world's best wine growing regions and a top destination for wine enthusiasts. The region captivates travelers with its hundreds of top vineyards producing unique wines, 150-year-old cellars with chic, showcase tasting rooms, and estate restaurants that serve some of the country's best food.

WESTERN CAPE

STELLENBOSCH

GPS: S 33 56.231 E 018 51.534
pop. 200,000 | elevation 108 m/354 ft

Stellenbosch is a scenic university town just 45 minutes from Cape Town and smack in the middle of wine country. The town's wide range of accommodation options and top quality restaurants make this an ideal base from which to tour the surrounding vineyards. Quaint downtown streets are lined with cafés and restaurants that invite you to slow your pace and appreciate the scenery. When restaurants start closing up, the area quickly turns into a university watering hole as thousands of students hit the streets to meet and drink. Most city streets do not have signs, so look for the name of the street printed on the curb in a yellow painted block.

🛈 TOURIST INFORMATION

Stellenbosch Tourism *(S 33 56.225 E 018 51.407, 36 Market St,* 📞*021-883-3584, www.*

stellenboschtourism.co.za, Sept-Apr: 8am-6pm Mon-Fri, 9am-4pm Sat, 9am-3pm Sun, May-Aug: 9am-5pm Mon-Fri, 9:30am-2pm Sat, 10am-2pm Sun) can provide you with free maps of downtown Stellenbosch and the surrounding area, brochures about wine tours, hiking and other regional sights. They also run Stellenbosch on Foot (R90/person, minimum 2 people) walking tours of downtown Stellenbosch that depart at 10am & 3pm Mon-Fri. **Stellenbosch Adventure Centre** *(S 33 56.225 E 018 51.407, Stellenbosch Tourism, 36 Market St,* 📞*021-882-8112, www.adventureshop.co.za, 9am-5pm Mon-Fri)* also runs out of the tourism office and can arrange everything from extreme sports, vineyard tours, and car and bike rental, to long-distance tours of Kruger National Park or Namibia.

💲 MONEY

There are a number of banks, money exchanges, and ATMs in downtown Stellenbosch around Die Braak (town square). Most banks close by 3:30pm. **Standard Bank** *(S 33 56.256 E 018 51.596, 20*

Bird St) has full banking services and ATMs open 24 hours.

American Express Foreign Exchange *(S 33 56.181 E 018 51.569, Bird St)* can cash travelers checks and has currency exchange services.

@INTERNET

Java Café *(S 33 56.284 E 018 51.685, cnr Church St & Andringa St, ☎021-887-6261, 8am-10:30pm Mon-Sat, 9am-10:30pm Sun, R30/hr)* is a coffee shop and bar that has an Internet café and wifi. This is one of the larger and better-priced Internet cafés in town.

Netopia Internet Café *(S 33 56.138 E 018 51.656, De Waal Center, Andringa St, ☎021-887-7878, 8am-9pm Mon-Thu, 8am-8pm Fri, 9am-6pm Sat, R3/15mins)* has 16 updated computers with a high-speed connection. No laptops allowed.

Snow Internet Café *(S 33 56.313 E 018 51.584, 12 Meul St, ☎021-887-4828, 8am-10pm Mon-Fri, 8am-5pm Sat-Sun, R10/20mins)* has 12 modern computers and allows laptops to be plugged in.

☼SHOPPING

There are many boutique clothing and art stores centered around Andringa Street and its cross streets, Plein and Church.

Oom Samie se Winkel / Uncle Sammy's Shop *(S 33 56.375 E 018 51.350, 84 Dorp St, ☎021-887-0797, 8:30am-5:30pm Mon-Fri, 9am-5pm Sat-Sun)* was founded in 1904 and since then has acquired every kitschy souvenir you could imagine, as well as an array of spices and jams, medicine bottles from the early 1900s, dried fish, tea sets and more. It's a Stellenbosch institution and worth a stop just to take a look around.

Craft Market *(S 33 56.267 E 018 51.578, cnr of Bird St & Church St, 9am-6pm)* is a small craft market near the town square that sells standard South African souvenirs of paintings, statues, drums and small figurines. It's a quick and pleasant stroll if you are in the city center.

❂SIGHTS & ACTIVITIES

Die Braak *(S 33 56.217 E 018 51.528, cnr Alexander St & Bird St)* is the grassy town square

in the heart of Stellenbosch. On the northern edge of the square you will find the Anglican Saint Mary's Church, built in 1852. Along the east side of the square stands the VOC Kruithuis / Powder House. Built in 1777 to store arms and ammunition for Boer commandos, the armory now serves as a small military museum *(8:30am-4:30pm Mon-Fri, adult R5, child R20)*. The Rhenish Church to the south of Die Braak was built in 1823 by the Missionary Society of Stellenbosch as a missionary school for slaves, and the coloured and black population.

Sasol Art Museum *(S 33 56.116 E 018 51.765, 62 Ryneveld St, ☎021-808-3695, admin.sun.ac.za/usmuseum/sasol.html, 10am-4:30pm Mon, 9am-4:30pm Tue-Sat, adult R5)* is a dramatic two-story building in the heart of the University of Stellenbosch campus. It houses an impressive permanent collection of paintings and sculptures by established international and South African artists, as well an anthropological collection of Xhosa and Zulu art and weaponry. Temporary exhibitions of evocative installations and sculpture change on a regular basis.

Stellenbosch Village Museum *(S 33 56.236 E 018 51.782, 18 Ryneveld St, ☎021-887-2902 or ☎021-887-2948, Sept-Apr: 9am-5pm Mon-Sat, 10am-4pm Sun, May-Aug: 9am-5pm Mon-Sat, 10am-1pm Sun, adult R25, child R5)* makes it easy to imagine how early area residents lived as you wander down garden paths to four houses that represent different eras of the domestic history of colonial Stellenbosch. Costumed greeters welcome you and explain the significance of the design and furnishings in period homes dating from 1709 to 1929.

University of Stellenbosch Art Gallery *(S 33 56.326 E 018 51.602, cnr Bird St & Dorp St, ☎021-808-3489, 9am-5pm Mon-Fri, 9am-1pm Sat, admission free)* displays the work of rising South African artists from the University of Stellenbosch in a 1854 Evangelical Lutheran church. The exhibits usually change every month, but can sometimes change every week.

Toy & Miniature Museum *(S 33 56.233 E 018 51.385, 42 Market St, ☎021-887-9433, 8am-4:30pm Mon-Fri, some Saturday mornings, R15)* has miniature models of old Stellenbosch, antique toys and dolls, boxcars and ornate one-twelfth scale miniatures. The guided tour takes roughly 30 minutes to explore the first house, the lush garden and the second house, which opens up onto Dorp Street. The owner Phillip is very friendly and happy to explain the details of some of the more impressive pieces.

Stellenbosch Golf Club (*S 33 57.516 E 018 51.036, Strand Rd, ☎021-880-0103, www. stellenboschgolfclub.com, R420/18 holes*) is an 18-hole, 72-par scenic course surrounded by the mountains and vineyards. Club rental is R350, carts R250 and caddies are R130.

✪TOURS

IMPACT **Bikes 'n Wines** (☎074-186-0418, www. bikesnwines.com, R450) offers biking wine tours for the more adventurous connoisseur. Tours vary in intensity, but all come with scenic views and a sampling of local wines and cheeses, as well as cellar tours at up to four vineyards. It's a great way to taste some of South Africa's finest grapes and see the countryside without the carbon footprint. A small portion of your payment also goes towards the Lynedoch EcoVillage and the newly established Lynedoch Cycling Club, a mentorship program for disadvantaged youths.

Easy Rider Wine Tours (☎021-886-4651, www.winetour.co.za, R350) is made for those who would rather gulp than sip the local wines. It's run out of Stumble Inn backpackers, but they can pick you up from anywhere in Stellenbosch. Tours leave at 10:30am and hit up four vineyards with a stopover for lunch in Franschhoek. The price includes tastings and lunch.

Vine Hopper (☎021-882-8112/3, www. vinehopper.co.za, R170) is a hop-on/hop-off wine tour bus. On Tuesdays and Thursdays they run a route through six vineyards north of town and Monday, Wednesday and Friday the southern route. Vans leave hourly from Stellenbosch Tourism, where you can also buy tickets. The ticket price covers transportation only; tasting fees and lunch are not included.

Redwood Tours (☎082-443-6480, www. redwoodtours.co.za) specializes in small group and individual excursions and can organize personalized wine tours to suit your interests. They also can arrange day trips to Cape Peninsula or longer jaunts through the Garden route.

Stellenbosch on Foot (☎021-883-3584, 10am-3pm Mon-Fri, R90, minimum 2 people) is a walking tour of downtown Stellenbosch and its historic sights that is run by the Stellenbosch Tourism Office.

WESTERN CAPE

WESTERN CAPE

☺ SLEEPING

BUDGET

Stumble Inn (*S 33 56.334 E 018 51.291*, *12 Market St*, ☏021-887-4049, *camping R40, dm R90, s/d R250, bar, shuttle to Baz Bus, Internet, parking*) is the most popular backpackers in Stellenbosch. As the name suggests, it is an ideal spot for travelers who enjoy a good pub-crawl after a day of wine tasting. There is a TV room and plenty of space to lounge around in back by the pool table or out in the yard.

Banghoek Place (*S 33 55.708 E 018 52.268*, *193 Banghoek Rd*, ☏021-887-0048, *www.banghoek. co.za, dm R100, s/d R400, shuttle to Baz Bus, Internet, secure parking, swimming pool*) is a modern guesthouse by the same owners as Stumble Inn and is substantially more upscale than other budget options in town. It feels more like a boutique hotel and attracts a wide age range for its well-priced en suite rooms. Evenings are cozy as guests return from a day's play to enjoy a bottle of wine beside the pool or courtyard. There is a well-outfitted kitchen and braai facilities, and it is within walking distance to central Stellenbosch restaurants.

Stellenbosch Traveller's Lodge (*S 33 56.400 E 018 50.992*, *8 Stadler St*, ☏021-886-9290, *www. stellenlodge.co.za, dm R100, s/d R340, shuttle to Baz Bus, Internet*) feels more like a highway motel than a backpackers, but has clean budget accommodation, a self-catering kitchen and a pool table. The lodge is best suited for a group traveling together rather than solo travelers looking to socialize.

iKhaya Stellenbosch Backpackers (*S 33 56.191 E 018 51.564*, *56 Bird St*, ☏021-883-8550, *www. stellenboschbackpackers.co.za, dm R110-120, s/d R450-520, bar, shuttle to Baz Bus*) is oddly hobbled together from rooms on the third and fourth floor of an office building, but the location is tough to beat. The kitchens are located inside the dorm rooms and there isn't much communal space apart from the roof deck. A storefront bar serves light meals downstairs.

MID-RANGE

Yellow Lodge (*S 33 56.227 E 018 51.133*, *32 Herold St*, ☏021-887-9660, *www.yellow-lodge. com, s R550, d R700, breakfast included, wifi, splash pool*) was previously a pastor's residence and is now a National Heritage building. The lodge is clean and quiet with eight en suite rooms and a self-catering apartment. The lush lounge area and small splash pool in back are particularly lovely.

De Oude Meul (*S 33 56.319 E 018 51.585*, *10A Mill St*, ☏021-887-7085, *www.deoudemeul.com, s R450, d R700, breakfast included, Internet/wifi*) is a well-kept six-room guesthouse above a coffee shop and antique store by the same owner. Rooms are simple but elegant and open either onto the front balcony or patio in back. There is a common lounge area with a computer available for use, as well as wifi throughout.

Stellenbosch Hotel (*S 33 56.297 E 018 51.688*, *162 Dorp St*, ☏021-887-3644, *www. stellenboschhotel.co.za, s R700, d R1,000, breakfast included*) is a Cape Dutch building with restored facades of two historic 19th-century homes. All rooms have TV and AC and self-catering rooms are available as well. The hotel is centrally located in the middle of town and surrounded by restaurants and shops.

TOP END

D'Ouwe Werf (*S 33 56.265 E 018 51.722*, *30 Church St*, ☏021-887-4608, *www.ouwewerf. com, s R1,085, d R1,320, breakfast included*) is a historic 4-star hotel that was the first lodge in the Stellenbosch area. Today it maintains its bygone character with antiques scattered throughout the lobby and in the Superior rooms. Service is exquisite, as is the restaurant and the courtyard pool area. The hotel is situated in the center of the town's restaurant and bar district.

🍴 EATING

Wijnhuis (*S 33 56.268 E 018 51.659*, *cnr Church St & Andringa St*, ☏021-887-5844, *www. wijnhuis.co.za, 8am-11pm, mains R70-120*) is a Stellenbosch classic for fine dining after a day of touring area vineyards. The Mediterranean menu liberally incorporates local produce and regional game and the wine list is a real stunner, with 350 wines from 40 local vineyards. The restaurant cozily occupies the upper level with slanted eaves and outdoor dining is on the rooftop.

Apprentice @ Institute of Culinary Arts (*S 33 56.268 E 018 51.679*, *Oude Hoek Centre, Andringa St*, ☏021-887-8985, *www.icachef.co.za, 7am-5pm Mon, 7am-9:30pm Tue-Fri, 8am-9:30pm*

WESTERN CAPE

Map labels:

PAUL KRUGER ST
DENNESIG ST
BANGHOEK ST
MERRIMAN ST
BIRD ST
ANDRINGA RD
GEORGE BLAKE
ADAM TAS ST
MERRIMAN ST
NORTH TO
Banghoek Place (500m)
CROZIER DR
VAN RYNEVELD ST
VICTORIA ST
DU TOIT ST
ANDRINGA RD
ALEXANDER
ALEXANDER
BLOEM ST
PLEIN ST
MARKET ST
BIRD ST
CHURCH ST
DORP ST
HERTE ST
DORP ST
HELDERBERG
LOUW
VISSER
NORTHBANK RD
HAMMAN
DORP ST
STELLENTIA AVE
WIEDENHOF
STADLER
HEROLD ST
PAPEGAAI ST
STRAND ST
AAN-DE-WAGEN
S BANK RD
SCHOOL
RAILWAY ST
R44
R310
ROKEWOOD
DOOMBOSCH ST
DOOMBOSCH ST
SAFRAAN AVE
BLENHEIM ST
R44
SANTA ROSA
ELBERTHA AVE
ROKEWOOD ST
KANEEL CRES
FORELLE CRES
VAN REEDE AVE
SULTAN ST
FORMOSA
STRAND ST
RHODES AVE
BARRY ST
LOVELL AVE
SWELLENGREBEL
WOLTEMADE AVE

1000ft
200m

STELLENBOSCH

🛈 TOURIST INFO
Stellenbosch Adv. Centre .... (see 1)
Stellenbosch Tourism 1   B3

💲 MONEY
American Express 2   B3
Standard Bank 3   B3

@ INTERNET
Java Café .... (see 25)
Netopia Internet Café 4   B3
Snow Internet Café 5   C3

🛍 SHOPPING
Craft Market 6   B3
Uncle Sammy's Shop 7   C2

✹ SIGHTS & ACTIVITIES
Die Braak 8   B3
Sasol Art Museum 9   B4
Stellenbosch Village Museum 10   B4
Toy & Miniature Museum 11   B2
Univ. of Stellenbosch Art
Gallery 12   C3

🛏 SLEEPING
D'Ouwe Werf 13   B4
De Oude Meul 14   C3

iKhaya Stellenbosch 15   B3
Stellenbosch Hotel 16   C4
Stellenbosch Traveller's
Lodge 17   C1
Stumble Inn 18   C2
Yellow Lodge 19   B2

🍴 EATING & DRINKING
5 Ryneveld 20   C3
Apprentice @ Institute of
Culinary Arts 21   B4
Basic Bistro 22   C4
Celebrate 23   B3
De Oewer 24   C2
Java Café 25   C4
Wijnhuis 26   B3

🍷 DRINKING & ENT.
Bohemia 27   A3
Hemingway Library
& Cigar Bar 28   B3
Mystic Boer 29   A3
Nu'Bar 30   B4
Rock Room 31   C2
The Trumpet Tree .... (see 7)

⮂ TRANSPORTATION
Minibus Taxi Rank 32   A3
Stellenbosch Railway Station. 33   C1

Sat, 9am-3pm Sun, mains R80-110) presents impressive and artistically prepared dishes from the students of the Institute of Culinary Arts. The sleek restaurant has an open stainless steel kitchen where you can watch the students polish their skills as they create your meal.

De Oewer Riverside Food and Wine Garden (S 33 56.492 E 018 51.168, Aan de Wagen Rd, 021-886-5431, www.volkskombuis.co.za/oewer, mid-Oct–Apr: 12pm-3pm & 6:30pm-9:30pm, mains R70-120) offers Mediterranean inspired lunches and dinners under the shade of large oak trees on the banks of the Eerste River. By the same owner, **De Volkskombuis** (S 33 56.521 E 018 51.167, Aan de Wagen Rd, 021-887-2121, www.volkskombuis.co.za, 12pm-2:30pm & 6:30-9:30pm, mains R60-120) is more formal and has a larger menu featuring seafood, game and regional specialties.

Basic Bistro (S 33 56.282 E 018 51.709, 31 Church St, 021-883-3629, 7am-10pm, mains R40-60) serves a great breakfast, lunch and dinner in a quaint dining room and at sidewalk tables. Some big tastes come out of this little restaurant and kitchen; don't leave without trying a homemade pasta and a scrumptious dessert.

5 Ryneveld (S 33 56.297 E 018 51.776, 5 Ryneveld St, 021-886-4842, 8am-10pm, bar open late, mains R40-80) is all about the gourmet burgers, with a selection that will boggle your taste buds. The dozens of burgers include ostrich, fish and vegetarian patties. The restaurant is in a beautiful old building with a garden courtyard where you can enjoy these delicious monsters and daily dinner specials alfresco.

Java Café (S 33 56.284 E 018 51.685, cnr Church St & Andringa St, 021-887-6261, 8am-10:30pm Mon-Sat, 9am-10:30pm Sun, mains R30-50) is a coffee shop and Internet café with decent, reasonable food available all day long. Java's main attraction, though, is its chic bar and sidewalk seating where you can easily plant yourself for brunch and work away an entire day with a good cup of joe in hand.

Celebrate (S 33 56.115 E 018 51.635, Andringa St, 021-883-8317, 8am-late Mon-Sat, 3pm-11pm Sun, mains R40-70) is a fun and casual eatery that is popular with the student crowd because of their well-priced menu of burgers, pizza and light meals. They also have a daily two-for-one happy hour from 9pm-10pm.

DRINKING & ENTERTAINMENT

Bohemia (S 33 56.075 E 018 51.645, cnr Andringa St & Victoria St, 021-882-8375, www.bohemia.co.za, 10am-2am Mon-Fri, 11am-2am Sat, 12pm-2am Sun) is a beery and mellow bar where patrons kick back with a game of pool or hookah. Come in your flip-flops and leave any dance-club pretentiousness at home.

Mystic Boer (S 33 56.073 E 018 51.654, 3 Victoria St, 021-886-8870, www.diemysticboer.co.za, 11am-2am Mon-Sat, 5pm-2am Sun) is a multilevel bar where the cool-kid contingent of Stellenbosch's student crowd hangs out. There is a pool table on the ground floor and live music or a DJ on Tuesday nights. It's right next door to Bohemia.

The Trumpet Tree (S 33 56.356 E 018 51.359, 84 Dorp St, 021-883-8379, www.thetrumpettree.com, 8am-10pm, bar open late, mains R30-50) is an enchanting vine-covered beer garden situated behind the storefronts on Dorp Street. This is a hot spot with the local crowd for gourmet pizza and beer, and is one of the only places where you can grab a bite to eat after 9pm.

Nu'Bar (S 33 56.228 E 018 51.710, 51 Plein St, 021-886-8998, www.nubar.co.za, 8pm-2am Mon-Sat) is a popular student nightclub with two bars, DJs and a dance floor. In short, this bar is often host to a young wasted mess — it's not an atypical weeknight sight to see a bartender pouring complimentary shots into the mouths of 18-year-olds on the raised dance floor in the back. **Entourage** (083-775-8160) is located upstairs next door and is a similar club scene, but

DJs play a bit more techno.

Hemingway Library & Cigar Bar *(S 33 56.249 E 018 51.663, 13 Andringa St, ☎021-887-3559, www.capetocuba.com, 8am-2am)* offers commie culture and classic Cuban cocktails in the back of the Cape To Cuba restaurant. Order up candelabrum to go with your caipirinha – all the furnishings in the restaurant and bar are for sale. **Rock Room** *(S 33 56.385 E 018 51.275, cnr Dorp St & Market St, ☎021-887-3144, 12pm-2am)* is a small bar that has specials on drinks or food almost every night of the week and gets packed on Saturdays when live bands play.

➋ TRANSPORTATION

➎ Train

Stellenbosch Railway Station *(S 33 56.329 E 018 50.986, Adam Tas St/R310)* is just southwest of town and is serviced nearly every hour by **Cape Town's Metrorail** *(☎080-065-6463, www.capemetrorail.co.za)* on the Cape Town-Bellville-Wellington-Stellenbosch-Strand line. The trip from Cape Town takes about 75 minutes (first class R13).

➎ Bus

Long distance buses stop through the city en route to and from Cape Town. The short Stellenbosch-Cape Town leg is rather pricey (R150) and cannot be booked online, so call if interested. **Greyhound** *(☎083-915-9000, www.greyhound.co.za)* and **Intercape** *(☎086-128-7287, www.intercape.co.za)* stop in the heart of the university **under the footbridge on Merriman Street** *(S 33 55.884 E 018 51.924, Merriman St)*. **TransLux/City-to-City** *(☎086-158-9282 or ☎011-774-3333, www.translux.co.za)* stops at the **Stellenbosch Railway Station** *(S 33 56.329 E 018 50.986, Adam Tas St/R310)*. All of the backpackers in town run shuttle services to the nearest **Baz Bus stop** *(☎021-439-2323, www.bazbus.com)* at the Lord Charles Hotel in Somerset West.

➎ Minibus Taxi

Minibus Taxi Rank *(S 33 55.989 E 018 51.529, Bird St)* has transport to Paarl (R40). To get to Cape Town via minbus you must first go to Bellville (R8) and then from Bellville to Cape Town (R8).

➎ Taxi

Alan Denman *(☎082-854-1541)* runs a taxi service within the city and to nearby surroundings. If he's busy when you call, he can hook you up with other taxis as well.

WESTERN CAPE

WINELANDS

➏ STELLENBOSCH VINEYARDS

Uitkyk *(S 33 51.414 E 018 51.844, off R44 about 10 km north of Stellenbosch, ☎021-884-4416, www.uitkyk.co.za, 9am-5pm Mon-Fri, 10am-4pm Sat-Sun, tasting R15)* is one of the oldest and largest farms in South Africa with 250 of its 650 hectares producing wine grapes. The flagship wine, Carlonet, has been in production at the estate since 1929. After a remodeling in 2004, the tasting room was moved into the former barn building that was erected in 1712 and portions of the fieldstone wall have been purposely left unrestored. Note that there are seven farms in the Stellenbosch area under the name Uitkyk (panoramic view) - this Uitkyk is located beside the Kononkop Wine Estate that is marked with a large canon beside R44.

Muratie *(S 33 52.263 E 018 52.536, Adam Tas St/R44, ☎021-865-2330, www.muratie.co.za, 9am-5pm Mon-Fri, 10am-4pm Sat-Sun, tasting R20)* is another old farm-turned-winery, and the proprietors of the vineyard milk the antique charm by letting thick cobwebs command much of the cellar and tasting room. In 1927, Muratie was the first South African winery to produce Pinot Noir and with four generations of experience it has only improved. In addition to the historic tasting room, antique wine making equipment, and ducks running on the grounds, there is an exhibit room containing paintings by G.P. Canitz and two self-catering guest houses.

Simonsig *(S 33 52.225 E 018 49.496, Kromme Rhee Rd/M23, ☎021-888-4900, www.simonsig.co.za, 8:30am-5pm Mon-Fri, 8:30am-4pm Sat, 11am-3pm Sun, tasting R25)* is one of South Africa's top wineries. Sample 30 different varieties in its informal and cleverly decorated tasting centre. Vineyard and cellar tours are available weekdays at 11am and 3pm, advanced booking required. The estate is also home to

Cuvée (*021-888-4932*, *www.cuveeatsimonsig. co.za*, *11am-3pm Tue-Sat, 7pm-10pm Fri & Sat, 11am-2pm Sun, mains R100-140*) a sleek restaurant serving up fruit and vegetable-infused dishes that are both inventive and delicious.

Jordan (*S 33 56.575 E 018 44.707, Stellenbosch Kloof Rd,* *021-881-3441,* *www.jordanwines.com,* *9:30am-4:30pm, tasting R25*) grows exquisite wines on the rolling hills of its vineyard estate. The panoramic views outside the tasting room let you see from Table Mountain to False Bay. If you like dessert wine, their Mellifera may possibly be one of the best wines you've tasted. Head southwest out of Stellenbosch on the R310 for roughly 5 km until the R310 and M12 split. Continue straight on the M12 for 800 m and turn right onto Stellenbosch Kloof Rd at the Vlottenburg cash store. Continue 6 km to Jordan.

Tokara (*S 33 55.039 E 018 55.200, R310,* *021-808-5900,* *www.tokara.co.za,* *9am-5pm Mon-Fri, 10am-3pm Sat & Sun, tasting free*) is a sleek tasting facility and restaurant perched atop the crest of the Helshoogte Pass. Their high-tech winery produces two quality labels - Tokara and Zondernaam - and the floor-to-ceiling views of the Simonsberg Mountains make it one the best places to end your day. Their reds pack quite the punch, but it's the award-winning Tokara Walker Bay Sauvignon Blanc that you'll want to take home. The Olive Shed also produces superb oils and olive products that are available for tasting at the winery.

IMPACT **Neethlingshof** (*S 33 56.451 E 018 48.120, M12,* *021-883-8988,* *www.neethlingshof. co.za,* *9am-5pm Mon-Fri, 10am-4pm Sat-Sun, tasting R30*) offers an award-winning pinotage among other stunning wines inside a modern tasting room surrounded by a rose garden. The premium Lord Neethling wines come from an area of the estate that implements natural methods to shape the ecosystem. Owl posts are built to attract owls that hunt mice, and caracol (a large wild cat) encourage the natural population control of guinea fowl.

IMPACT **Spier** (*S 33 58.401 E 018 46.961, Baden Powell Dr/Lynedoch Rd/R310,* *021-809-1147,* *www.spier.co.za,* *10am-4:30pm, tasting R10*) is more than just a winery. The complex has walking trails, horseback riding, a golf course, shops and a restaurant that can keep you at the estate all day. During the summer, the amphitheater hosts concerts and events. While the estate is touristy,

it wins points for its Cheetah Outreach Program, which allows you to interact with the big cats in exchange for a donation towards the program's education and conservation efforts. The selection of wines is also excellent.

Van Ryn's (*S 33 57.729 E018 48.113, Baden Powell Dr/R310,* *021-881-3875,* *www.vanryn. co.za,* *10am-4:30pm Mon-Fri, 9am-2pm Sat, 11am-4pm Sun, tasting R30-60, tours: 10am, 11:30am & 3pm Mon-Fri, 10am, 11:30am & 1pm Sat*) takes wines one step further and distills the fermented fruit into award-winning brandies. A visit here is like stepping back in time and into an opulent gentlemen's club. The sophisticated Brand Home perfectly sets the mood for tasting 10-year and 12-year-old vintages. If you are feeling extravagant, go for the brandy, coffee and chocolate tasting which includes the 20-year Collector's Reserve and hand-made Belgian chocolate. Tours allow you to check out the distillery and give you insight into the age-old art of brandy-making and drinking (R35).

❽ PAARL VINEYARDS

Fairview (*S 33 46.338 E 018 55.420, Suid Agter Paarl Rd/R44,* *021-863-2450,* *www.fairview.co.za,* *9am-5pm, wine tasting R25, cheese tasting R12*) produced its first wine in 1699 and today produces some of the finest Shiraz in the region. This is a busy estate with guests that come for wine and cheese tastings, and stay to relax and enjoy a meal in the Mediterranean-style restaurant. If you are lucky you may catch a glimpse of a goat or two climbing up the spiral stairway of the multi-story shed. Inside the large tasting room is also a cheese and specialty food shop with most products made onsite.

IMPACT **Backsberg** (*S 33 49.684 E 018 54.917, Simondium Rd/R45,* *021-875-5141,* *www. backsberg.co.za,* *8am-5pm Mon-Fri, 9:30am-4:30pm Sat, 10:30am-4:30pm Sun, informal tasting R15, guided tasting R35*) is South Africa's first carbon neutral wine estate. In addition to being an environmentally responsible vineyard, the expansive estate is also home to a restaurant, culinary academy, glass-blowing studio and educational Earth Centre. Informal tastings are held in their musty cellar-turned-saleroom and include five wines as well as a sampling of Backsberg's award-winning Sydney Back brandy.

Wine Industry:
Leaders of Sustainable Practices

When you sip on a glass of fantastic South African Chenin blanc or Pinotage, the last thing you want to taste are the chemicals it took to produce that vintage. But vineyards are faced with a tough choice – leave their delicate fruits to the mercy of bugs, fungi and other predators, or risk tainting the highly susceptible grapes with chemicals and enzymes that will keep those little buggers at bay. Luckily, several South African vineyards are leading their local industry towards more sustainable (and delicious) farming practices.

Vineyards, like many businesses in South Africa, are beginning to understand that reducing their carbon footprint makes good environmental and business sense. Using less energy means saving money and time – and makes for some mighty fine grapes, if you're **IMPACT** *Backsberg* (S 33 49.684 E 018 54.917, Suider Paarl, 021-875-5141, *www. backsberg.co.za*, 8am-5pm Mon-Fri, 9:30am-4:30pm Sat, 10:30am-4:30pm Sun). This vineyard is setting industry standards for how to tackle carbon emissions by annually auditing its consumption of fuel and electricity. To reduce its footprint, it has invested in smaller tractors and utility vehicles operated on biodiesel produced from oils from the winery's kitchen. Then there are Backsberg's smart smaller efforts – switching out light bulbs with more energy efficient ones and cooling wines during fermentation with water that is drawn downhill from a dam. With all these efforts combined, the vineyard has managed to become completely carbon neutral. Backsberg believes conservation is equally important, so the vineyard has redesigned their glass bottles to be lighter weight, which saves production materials and decreases the amount of fuel needed to deliver bottles worldwide. You can enjoy a glass of Sauvignon Blanc in Backsberg's garden knowing that the air on this estate is as crisp as the wine.

One of the most effective ways that wineries are establishing sustainable production is by reintroducing indigenous plants and animals to enrich and protect their crops. By reserving a portion of a vineyard to grow indigenous foliage, wineries can reap the benefits of the animals these plants naturally invite. **IMPACT** *Mooiplaas Estate* (S 33 55.254 E 018 44.412, Off M23, 021-903-6273, **www.mooiplaas.co.za**, 9am–4pm Mon-Fri, 10am-2pm Sat) uses cover crops to balance the soil and reduce the need to add nitrogen, phosphates, and potassium chemically. The vineyard also offers nature walks through their 40-hectare reserve.

Biodynamic wineries go a step further by respecting and leveraging all the natural life on a farm to create the best product possible organically. **IMPACT** *Reyneke Wines* (S 33 57.475 E 018 45.137, Polkadraai Road/M12, 021-881-3451, **www.reynekewines.co.za**, 9am-5pm Mon-Thu, 9am-3:30pm Fri) strengthens its crops holistically and naturally. In place of pesticides and fertilizers, the vineyard employs a staff of ducks to eat snails and other parasites. It also has chickens and cows roaming the farm to control weeds, pests, and provide fertilizer. Its wines are made with only grapes and time; no chemicals are added during the process. The result is pure and honest vintages that are well worth taking the time to become acquainted with. Make sure you try the Cornerstone, a half cabernet and half merlot blend - proceeds from this bottle go toward paying the workers' housing deeds.

IMPACT *Avondale Wines* (S 33 45.932 E 019 00.075, Lustigan Road, 021-863-1976, **www.avondalewines.co.za**, 10am-4pm Mon-Sat) is a certified organic farm that also adheres to bio-organic practices. Along with a staff of snail-eating ducks, the estate uses wasps to combat destructive insects. By replanting indigenous plants throughout its farm, Avondale has experienced an increase in the area's bird and owl populations, which in turn protect the crops from unwanted insects and rodents. The winery uses wild yeast fermentation rather than adding chemicals. It also uses farm equipment and tools that are specially designed to eliminate or reduce the farm's dependence on chemicals.

Formal guided tastings and cellar tours must be booked in advance.

Boschendal (S 33 52.459 E 018 58.559, R310, ☎021-870-4210, www.boschendal.com, 10am-6pm, tasting R15) is the second-oldest winery in South Africa, dating back to 1685. While sampling wines in the estate's hydrangea-laden park or touring the expansive grounds, there is no mistaking that the vineyard has had more than 400 years to perfect the wine tasting experience. Boschendal is best known for its Shiraz and Sauvignon Blanc, but be sure to try the vineyard's one-of-a-kind Blanc de Noir, a Rosé-like white wine made from red grapes. Cellar and vineyard tours are available if booked in advance (cellar tour Jan-Dec 10:30am & 3pm, vineyard tour only available on advance booking). The classic Cape Dutch complex has two restaurants and can also pack a picnic for you to enjoy beneath one of their massive oaks. A museum built inside an original 1812 manor house displays the highlights of Cape Dutch daily life (9:30am-5pm, R15).

Seidelberg (S 33 45.830 E 018 55.094, Suid Agter Paarl Rd, ☎021-863-5200, www.seidelberg.co.za, 10am-6pm, tasting R20, tasting w/cellar tour R25) has a distinct resort-like feel. Visitors can enjoy their wine (and a killer vantage point of the valley below) from deck chairs on an expansive lawn or in the arched-brick cellar. The winery also has a piadina stand, guesthouse and a glassblowing studio and gallery. In addition to offering cellar tours, on nice days visitors can also take a tractor ride to neighboring Fairview (adult R20, child R15). **De Leuwenjagt Restaurant** (9am-11am, 12pm-4pm, sunset dinners 6pm-8:30pm Thu-Sat, mains R70-130) offers breathtaking views of the valley below and delectable Cape Malay curries. Book in advance and ask for a spot on the terrace for one of their sunset dinners.

Laborie (S 33 45.971 E 018 57.493, Taillefert St, ☎021-807-3095, www.laboriewines.com, 9am-5pm Mon-Sat, 11am-3pm Sun, tasting R15) is a historic complex of Cape Dutch buildings on the outskirts of Paarl. The tasting room is simple but the window-side tables allow for an idyllic view of the vine-covered valley. Afterwards, stroll through the estate's gardens to the Anglo-Boer War monument or head next door to Laborie Restaurant for some South African country fare. **Laborie Restaurant** (☎021-807-3095, www.laborierestaurant.co.za, 11:30am-3:30pm, 6:30pm-10pm Wed-Sun, mains R70-130) offers continental cuisine, South African country favorites and

homemade preserves and delicacies from its terrace overlooking the Drakenstein Valley. If you stop by on a chilly afternoon or evening, be sure to ask for a spot in the smaller dining room, which is more intimate than the main restaurant and has a large fireplace to keep you toasty.

Rhebokskloof (S 33 41.088 E 018 55.945, off Northern Agter Paarl Rd/R45, ☎021-869-8386, www.rhebokskloof.co.za, 9am-5pm Mon-Fri, 10am-3pm Sat-Sun, tasting R15) has a small tasting center on a beautifully manicured garden oasis surrounded by rolling hills of farmland. But your best bet is to arrange for a luxurious picnic lunch by the lake after you've selected your favorite bottle. **The Victorian Restaurant** (9am-8pm Tue-Sat, 9am-5pm Sun-Mon, dinner after 8pm by reservation only, mains R100, picnic R220/2-person basket) will fill your basket with cheeses, quiche, fresh bread and other delicacies. The restaurant can also wine and dine you on the terrace as you take in the pastoral views. Down the road you can arrange horse or quad bike tours of the countryside.

Nederburg (S 33 42.999 E 019 00.218, Sonstraal Rd, ☎021-862-3104, www.nederburg.co.za, Apr-Oct: 8am-5pm Mon-Fri, 10am-2pm Sat, Nov-Mar: 8am-5pm Mon-Fri, 10am-4pm Sat-Sun, tasting R15-30) is one of South Africa's most acclaimed vineyards. The scenic grounds offer expansive views of the Drakenstein Mountains and are centered around a historic Cape Dutch manor house, built in 1800 and beautifully maintained. It's the kind of place that makes you want to stay all day. The professional staff will graciously welcome you for a tasting, and picnics are available from November through March (by appointment only). In addition to tasting some of their award-winning wines they also offer goats' milk cheese pairings (R30-R40) and brandy tastings (R20). Cellar tours (R25) start with a sparkling wine and include a 90-minute tour and guided tasting.

Glen Carlou (S 33 48.749 E 018 54.197, Simondium Rd/R45, Klapmuts, ☎021-875-5528, www.glencarlou.co.za, 11am-3pm, tasting R25-50) has a state of the art tasting center that offers breathtaking panoramic views of the vineyard and mountains. You can walk over the glass floor and peek down into the cellar or visit their dramatic Hess Art Collection filled with evocative sculptures, paintings and installations by South African and international artists. Tastings here are more generous than most vineyards at R25/10 wines. They also have a restaurant that specializes

WESTERN CAPE

2

3 R44

4 R303

R45

Goedehoop

R45

WELLINGTON

Dagbreek

R44

Hillcrest

Newtown

A

Mbekweni

13 Groenheuwel

R301

Fryheid

R304

R312

PAARL

Charleston Hill

10

R101

Amstelhof

B

14

7

N1

4

1

Fisantkraal

R304

Bennetsville

N1

Paarl Outlying

R45

R301

C

5

R101

R45

R44

2

Simondium

Bloekombos

18

R304

15

9

Devondale

Koelpark

Wemmershoek

R45

Franschhoek North

R44

Pniel

Weltevrede

R304

Cloetesvile

Languedoc

17

Kylemore

Idas Valley

3

R310

D FRANSCHHOEK

8

STELLENBOSCH

6

11

Devon Park

Dalsig

R45

12

19

E

R310

Paradyskloof

16

Webersvallei

Rosedale

Helderberg Estate

R44

N2

Helena Heights

F

Somerset West

1

2

Lwandle

3

N2

in tender meat dishes including venison and pork belly (11am-3pm Tue-Sun, mains R100). The weekends can get quite busy, so book in advance to ensure a table with a view.

FRANSCHHOEK

GPS: S 33 54.703 E 019 07.221
pop. 14,000 | elevation 274 m/899 ft

The picturesque town of Franschhoek is a little bit of France tucked within the breathtaking mountains of the Winelands. Franschhoek, meaning "French corner," was settled in 1688 by French Huguenot refugees who fled religious persecution during the 17th century. Today it's a gourmet and gastronomic mecca in South Africa and boasts some of the best, and most expensive, restaurants in the country. The city is centered on the main Huguenot Street and is navigable on foot, with many good wineries within walking distance from the center of town. Nothing here caters to the budget crowd, but the quaint village and gourmet dining options make it well worth a visit.

⊘ TOURIST INFORMATION

Tourist Information Office *(S 33 54.569 E 019 07.090, The Village Center, Huguenot St)* has a full gift shop and helpful staff. They have free maps as well as brochures for area accommodation and activities.

⊘ MONEY

Huguenot Street has all the major banks including **Standard Bank** *(S 33 54.665 E 019 07.171)*, which has a MoneyGram for money transfers, and ABSA directly across the street. Nedbank and FNB are just down the road.

⊘ INTERNET

Just Franschhoek *(S 33 54.614 E 019 07.114, Village Square, 10am-5:30pm,* ☎*021-876-4353, R7/10mins)* is a souvenir shop next to the Elephant and Barrel Pub that doubles as an Internet café and has three updated computers.
The Kodak Express *(S 33 54.706 E 019 07.218, 28a Huguenot St,* ☎*021-876-4741,* www.photolab. co.za, *8am-6pm Mon-Fri, 8am-4pm Sat, 10am-2pm Sun, R12/15mins)* has five updated computers with printing and webcam/Skype capabilities. Laptop connection is also available.

⊘ SHOPPING

Huguenot Street is lined with boutique clothing stores, handmade craft shops, souvenir booths and high-end art galleries. Take your time exploring the length of the street and keep an eye out for shops that promote conscientious trade.

IMPACT **Tsonga** (*S 33 54.647 E 019 07.161, 40B Huguenot St,* ☎*021-876-3274, www.tsonga.com*) sells chic handmade shoes and bags created through an empowerment program for Zulu women in the Drakensburg foothills.

Franschhoek Farmers' Market (*S 33 54.562 E 019 07.138, Huguenot St,* ☎*073-967-3790, 9am-1pm Sat*) offers a variety of food delights for sale under the trees of the Dutch Reformed Church. Sample smoked cheeses and olives or stock up on organic vegetables, fresh breads and free-range eggs. A delicious way to spend a Saturday morning in Franschhoek.

⊗ SIGHTS & ACTIVITIES

Huguenot Monument (*S 33 54.908 E 019 07.392, cnr Huguenot St & Lambrecht St, 9am-5pm, adult R5, child R1*) is hard to miss at the end of Huguenot Street. Built in 1948, the monument commemorates the contribution of Huguenots to South Africa's history and culture and is surrounded by an expansive and beautifully manicured garden. **Huguenot Memorial Museum** (*S 33 54.824 E 019 07.445, Lambrecht St,* ☎*021-876-2532, 9am-5pm Mon-Sat, 2pm-5pm Sun, adult R10, child R5*) tells the story of the persecution of the French Huguenots, their flight, settlement at the Cape and contribution to South Africa through pictures,

artifacts and a lot of dense text. If you choose to wade through the haphazard displays, you may feel like you've gone through a war or two yourself. In the more relatable **Annex** (*S 33 54.788 E 019 07.420*) across the street, learn more about Franschhoek's local history. View ancient model Khoikhoi homes, get a feel for the town's first residents from their antique portraits, or pop into the attached shop for a souvenir or two. Bring a picnic basket along and lunch in the beautifully landscaped monument next door or get a light bite at the attached Café Antoinette tearoom.

Paradise Stables (*S 33 55.490 E 019 05.493, Robertsvlei Rd,* ☎*021-876-2160, www.paradisestables.co.za, guided tour: 8am or 6pm Mon-Sat, R200/1hr, tour and wine tasting: 9am or 1:30pm Mon-Sat, R500/4hrs*) offers scenic one-hour guided tours on horseback throughout the valley for beginners and experienced riders. You can also opt for a four-hour ride that includes wine tasting at Rickety Bridge Winery and Mont Rochelle for R500.

Manic Cycles (*S 33 54.407 E 019 06.933, Franschhoek Centre, Huguenot St,* ☎*021-876-4956 or* ☎*082-578-3017, www.maniccycles.co.za, 8:30am-5:30pm Mon-Fri, 8:30am-1pm Sat, Sun on request, half-day rental R110, full-day rental R195, standard tour R385/person*) is the place to go for bike rentals or for an organized bike wine tour. The standard tour includes a scenic ride through the valley, wine tasting and a picnic, topped off by a

WEST TO
Moreson Vineyard, Bread & Wine (7km),
Franschhoek Motor Museum (15km)

EAST TO
Cabrière Vineyard
& Haute Cabrière Cellar(800m)

WEST TO
Mont Rochelle
Vineyard (500m),
Mont Rochelle
Hotel (800m)

SOUTH TO
Paradise
Stables (2km)

WESTERN CAPE

500ft
200km

FRANSCHHOEK

TOURIST INFO
Tourist Information Office 1 C2

MONEY
Standard Bank 2 D2

INTERNET
Just Franschhoek ....(see 17)
The Kodak Express 3 D3

SHOPPING
Franschhoek Farmers' Market 4 C2
Tsonga 5 D2

SIGHTS & ACTIVITIES
Annex 6 D3
Huguenot Memorial Museum 7 E3
Huguenot Monument 8 E3
Manic Cycles 9 B1

VINEYARDS
Chamonix 10 A4

SLEEPING
Chamonix Guest Cottages 11 A4
Le Ballon Rouge 12 D3
Le Quartier Français 13 D3
The Map Room 14 D2

EATING & DRINKING
Bouillabaisse 15 D2
Essence Rest. & Coffee Bar 16 D3
French Connection 17 C2
Ici ....(see 13)
Reuben's 18 D3
Tasting Room ....(see 13)
Topsi & Co 19 D2

DRINKING & ENT.
Elephant & Barrel 20 C2
Screening Room ....(see 13)

souvenir bottle of local wine. Specialized tours with a heavier focus on either wine or on biking can be arranged as well.

Franschhoek Motor Museum *(S 33 51.937 E 018 58.719, R45, L'Ormarins Wine Estate, ☎021-874-9000, www.fmm.co.za, 10am-4pm Tue-Fri, 10am-3pm Sat-Sun, R60)* has an impressive collection of cars that represents the history of the automobile in South Africa. Located on the L'Ormarins Estate, it houses over 220 vehicles ranging from antique (pre-1904) vintage (1919-1930) to post-1960 and is a must-see for car lovers. After the hour-long tour you can stop at the estate's tasting center to sample some of their wines for R30.

☼VINEYARDS

Cabrière *(S 33 54.852 E 019 08.143, Franschhoek Pass, ☎021-876-8500, www.cabriere.co.za, 9am-5pm Mon-Fri, 10am-4pm Sat, 11am-4pm Sun, tasting R20-30, cellar tour: 11am & 3pm Mon-Fri, 11am Sat, R50)* was founded in 1684 by French Huguenot Pierre Jourdan, who lent his talents and name to the estate's flagship wines. The tasting center is carved out of the side of the mountain. Cellar tours are offered daily, but it's best to wait until Saturday when the cellar master, armed with a flair for the dramatic, conducts the tour himself. If you can't make the tasting, the renowned Haut Cabrière Restaurant offers the same choice wines and a view overlooking the cellar.

Moreson *(S 33 53.240 E 019 03.494, Happy Valley Rd, ☎021-876-3055, www.moreson.co.za, 11am-5pm, tasting R15)* is a picturesque estate just outside of Franschhoek. You couldn't find a prettier setting for a tasting room, so be sure to take your glass outside. If you're taking a bottle home, try the slightly lower cost Miss Molly label - named for the owner's dog.

Mont Rochelle *(S 33 54.865 E 019 06.387, Dassenberg Rd, ☎021-876-3000, www.mont rochelle.co.za, tastings 10am-7pm, cellar tours 11am, 12:30pm & 3pm Mon-Fri, 11am & 3pm Sat, tasting R20)* is situated in the foothills of the mountains overlooking Franschhoek. The small tasting room serves dry whites and dry reds and the Country Kitchen Bistro can whip you up an afternoon meal under the sun.

Chamonix *(S 33 53.968 E 019 07.685, Uitkyk St, ☎021-876-8400, www.chamonix.co.za, 9:30am-4pm, tasting R15)* has a limited but good selection

of wines, including a Methode Cap Classique and Pinot Noir. Tastings are in an old blacksmith's cottage beside the cellar, with outdoor tables to enjoy the wine. There is also a vineyard restaurant located up the road near the tasting room.

☼SLEEPING

BUDGET

Chamonix Guest Cottages *(S 33 54.016 E 019 07.556, Uitkyk St, ☎021-876-8406, www.chamonix. co.za, s R270, d R540, 4-person R1,000)* are seven Cape Dutch cottages in the middle of the Chamonix vineyard. They each have one or two bedrooms, a living room, kitchen, TV and fireplace and a braai on the outdoor deck. The tasting room and a vineyard restaurant are located within steps of the cottages.

MID-RANGE

The Map Room *(S 33 54.742 E 019 07.091, 21 Cabriere St, ☎021-876-4356 or ☎072-464-1240, www.explorersclub.co.za, d R1,600, 4-person R2,000, wifi, secure parking)* is a sleek and tasteful self-catering house with two spacious bedrooms. The open-plan kitchen and living room has a fireplace and glass doors that open to a deck and braai. The friendly host Jo knows the area well and can help you plan a perfect Franschhoek experience.

Le Ballon Rouge *(S 33 54.684 E 019 07.263, 7 Reservoir St East, ☎021-876-2651, www. ballonrouge.co.za, s/d R700-850, breakfast included, swimming pool)* is centrally located in a historic 1904 Victorian homestead just one block from Huguenot Street. The 10 rooms are warmly appointed and have beautiful en suite bathrooms and access to a courtyard in back. There are also two enormous upper-level Superior Suites with their own private decks.

TOP END

Mont Rochelle Hotel *(S 33 55.093 E 019 06.491, Dassenberg Rd, ☎021-876-2110, www. montrochelle.co.za, s/d R2,300-5,400, breakfast included, swimming pool)* is a 5-star vineyard lodge situated in the foothills of the mountainside overlooking Franschhoek. There are 22 luxury rooms and suites within the Cape Dutch manor house; each has a spacious bathroom and beautiful views. Attached to the hotel is the formal restaurant, Mange Tout.

Le Quartier Français (*S 33 54.754 E 019 07.243, 16 Huguenot St,* 021-876-2151, *www.lequartier. co.za, rooms R3,900-4,600, suites R4,500-9,200, breakfast included, Internet/wifi, swimming pool*) is an elite village oasis in the heart of Franschhoek. Each of the rooms is exquisite, boasting whimsical personal touches and a flair for color; many offer their own private pool or garden. The staff is warm and professional and go above and beyond their duties to ensure that your stay is memorable. Le Quartier is also home to one of the country's finest and most exclusive restaurants, the Tasting Room.

EATING

Reservations are essential to get a table most nights in Franschhoek's top restaurants.

Reuben's (*S 33 54.712 E 019 07.238, 19 Huguenot St,* 021-876-3772, *www.reubens. co.za, 12pm-3pm & 7pm-9pm, mains R90-170*) is a local favorite and consistently one of the more popular restaurants in town. They serve high quality, well-crafted meals focusing on steak and regional meat specialties. The large courtyard fills up in the evenings with families and tourists alike, and everyone is assured to leave satisfied.

Bread & Wine (*S 33 53.240 E 019 03.494, Moreson Wine Farm, Happy Valley Rd,* 021-876-3692, *12am-3pm, mains R50-130*) is nestled in the Moreson Vineyard at the foot of the mountains surrounding Franschhoek. Here you'll find simple but elegantly executed fare that will make you wonder why food can't taste this good all the time. If you forget to make lunch reservations or are on a tight budget, the grocery counter will still satisfy your culinary dreams with especially good bread and antipasto.

Haute Cabrière Cellar (S 33 54.852 E 019 08.143, Franschhoek Pass Rd, ☎021-876-3688, www.cabriere.co.za, Sept-Apr: 12pm-3pm & 7pm-9pm, May-Oct: 12pm-3pm Sun-Thu, 12pm-3pm & 7pm-9pm Fri-Sat, mains R70-170) is dramatically situated in the arched-brick cavern overlooking the Pinot Noir maturation cellar of the Haute Cabrière winery. Chef Matthew Gordon's culinary innovations are meant to be paired with the estate's fine wines and dishes can be served tapas-style or as a full meal. Full of flavor and expertly executed, you'll want to try more than one. We recommend the sesame-crusted tuna tataki accompanied by an Asian salad and ginger dressing - delicious.

Tasting Room (S 33 54.754 E 019 07.243, Le Quartier Français, 16 Huguenot St, ☎021-876-2151, five courses R550, eight courses R700-980) is Franschhoek's premier restaurant and is considered among the top restaurants in the world. That being said, it may be difficult to get a table if you don't make reservations weeks in advance. **Ici** (S 33 54.754 E 019 07.243, Le Quartier Français, 16 Huguenot St, ☎021-876-2151, 7am-10:30am, 12pm-4:30pm & 6pm-10pm, mains R95-110) is the less expensive sister restaurant of (and shares the same kitchen as) the neighboring Tasting Room. You can dine in velvet chairs under colored chandeliers or find a spot on the less painfully chic back terrace.

French Connection (S 33 54.606 E 019 07.118, 48 Huguenot St, ☎021-876-4056, www.frenchconnection.co.za, 12pm-3pm & 6pm-10pm, mains R90-125) has a petite menu of superb meals such as mushroom risotto, roasted duck, veal schnitzel and wildebeest loin. By the same owner as the Haute Cabrière Cellar restaurant, it has fewer frills but an equal emphasis on incredible food. The restaurant offers sidewalk dining and a large selection of local and imported wine.

Topsi & Co (S 33 54.745 E 019 07.201, 7 Reservoir St, ☎021-876-2952, 12:30pm-4pm & 7:30pm-9:30pm Mon & Wed-Sat, mains R60-90) is tucked away from the busy main street and offers unpretentious old world charm with a twist of quirk. The unique, home-style South African specials change daily, but range from venison to warthog loin and a delectable crispy duck. It's a BYOB establishment and your personable host, Topsi, will gladly pop open your wine for no charge. Entrance is off Huguenot Street, down the brick alley next to the FNB.

Bouillabaisse (S 33 54.638 E 019 07.147, 38 Huguenot St, ☎021-876-4430, www.bouillabaisse.co.za, 10am-10pm Mon-Sat, mains R50-90) is a chic and unpretentious restaurant with a wide selection of seafood and Asian-fusion tapas. Watch the chef flame-grill your order in the open kitchen behind the counter.

Essence Restaurant & Coffee Bar (S 33 54.738 E 019 07.237, Shop 7 Huguenot Square, ☎021-876-4135, 7am-7pm Mon-Sat, 7-6 Sun, mains R30-70, wifi) is a casually elegant coffee and lunch spot that offers breakfast, light meals and an array of desserts. Nab a spot on the side porch to get out of the hubbub of Huguenot Street or sit out front for some prime people watching.

✪ DRINKING & ENTERTAINMENT

Elephant & Barrel (S 33 54.611 E 019 07.095, 48 Huguenot St, ☎021-876-4127, www.elephantandbarrel.co.za, 12pm-late) is an English pub and a local Franschhoek watering hole hidden in a large courtyard off of Huguenot Street. Food and cocktails are served at the large dark wood bar inside, but in the evenings the crowd hangs outside in the courtyard.

Screening Room (S 33 54.754 E 019 07.243, Le Quartier Français, Huguenot St, ☎021-876-2151, www.lequartier.co.za/indulgences, 6:30pm Mon & Thu-Sat, 1pm, 6:30pm & 8pm Tue, 5:30pm & 8pm Sun) is a cozy cinematic experience at Le Quartier Français. Their screening room shows a range of classics, cinema nouveau, and new releases as you sip on a complimentary glass of local wine. Book ahead to ensure a spot on their soft, pink leather seats or one of the sofas in the back. Check online for updated listings and screening information. Bookings are essential and can be made at the Touches and Tastes shop in Le Quartier Français between 9am and 5pm.

✪ TRANSPORTATION

There is no public transportation to Franschhoek. The best way to get there is with your own car. The R45 runs straight through town and it's roughly a half-hour drive from both Stellenbosch and Paarl. If you need a taxi, contact **Isak De Wet** (☎078-587-4061) or his son **Colin** (☎073-191-6962, colindewet@gmail.com) who can shuttle you around town or pick you up from Stellenbosch or Paarl (R250). Advance booking required.

PAARL

GPS: S 33 43.873 E 018 57.770
pop. 130,000 | elevation 120 m/394 ft

Paarl Mountain proves a dramatic backdrop to the industrial hub of the winelands and the area's largest city. Notably marked by a behemoth monument, the town is a bastion of Afrikaner culture and heritage and if you look closely you'll see exquisite examples of traditional Cape Dutch architecture still standing side by side with Main Street's car dealerships. While the town itself pales in comparison to the beauty of its neighbors, top-notch surrounding vineyards and exceptional accommodation options make Paarl a pleasant base for wine touring.

𝒊 TOURIST INFORMATION

Paarl Tourism *(S 33 44.419 E 018 57.747, 217 Main St,* ☎*021-872-0685,* www.paarlonline.com, *8am-5pm Mon-Thu, 8am-3:45pm Fri, 10am-1pm Sat-Sun)* has free city maps and a brochure of area vineyards as well as information for accommodation and activities in town and the surrounds.

💰 MONEY

FNB *(S 33 43.858 E 018 57.764, cnr Main Rd & Lady Grey St)* has full banking services and a bureau de change. Farther down the street there is also a **Standard Bank** *(S 33 43.876 E 018 57.877, cnr Fabriek St & Lady Grey St).* **The Paarl Mall** *(S 33 45.911 E 018 58.067, Cecilia St, 9am-7pm Mon-Fri, 9am-5pm Sat, 10am-4pm Sun)* has ATMs for ABSA, Nedbank and Standard Bank.

@ INTERNET

3@1 *(S 33 45.911 E 018 58.067, Shop 84, Paarl Mall, Cecilia St,* ☎*021-863-0726,* paarl@3at1.co.za, *9am-7pm Mon-Fri, 9am-5pm*

Sat, 10am-4pm Sun, R10/15mins) is located near the food court in the Paarl Mall and has five updated computers, laptop connectivity, CD/DVD burning and printing.
Ink-Net *(S 33 43.874 E 018 57.795, 32 Lady Grey Street,* ☎*021-871-1778,* www.inknet.co.za, *8:30am-5pm Mon-Fri, 8:30am-1pm Sat, R30/hr)* offers full IT services and has computers, printers and a fax machine for public use.

🛒 SHOPPING

Paarl Mall *(S 33 45.911 E 018 58.067, Cecilia St,* ☎*021-863-5360,* www.paarlmall.co.za, *9am-7pm Mon-Fri, 9am-5pm Sat, 10am-4pm Sun)* has more than 100 stores and restaurants for all your shopping needs including department stores, fashion, home decor and sports gear. There are also multiple ATMs and a Pick 'n Pay.

⦿ SIGHTS & ACTIVITIES

Taal Monument *(S 33 45.944 E 018 56.550, Gabbema Drive, Paarl Mountain,* ☎*021-872-3441,* www.taalmuseum.co.za, *Apr-Sept: 8am-5pm, Oct-Mar: 8am-8pm, adult R12, child R5)* is a goliath structure perched atop Paarl Mountain. Though it may appear that it is giving a giant middle finger to the world, this monument's symbolism pays tribute to the roots of the Afrikaans language and the three continents that contributed to its evolution and development. Numerous shaded benches surrounding the monument offer a quiet respite. Free guided tours are available upon request.
Paarl Mountain Nature Reserve *(S 33 45.457 E 018 56.842, Jan Phillips Mountain Dr,* ☎*021-872-3658, summer: 7am-7pm, winter: 7am-6pm)* is 1,910 hectares of rugged mountain and plateau of fynbos. The large network of hiking

paths and roads make it extremely accessible. Highlights include the three large granite rocks dotting the peak of the reserve for which the town was named, pristine mountain lakes and the Meulwater Wild Flower Garden, which is perfect for picnics. There are multiple lookout points, but for the best views scale Bretagne Rock - on a clear day you can see False Bay and Cape Town's Table Mountain in the distance. None of the hiking trails are too strenuous, but some can be long, so it's best to consult the trail maps available at the Taal Monument or at the Tourism Information office on Main Street before you head out. For an easy two-hour stroll, try the Circular Route that starts at the Taal Monument. If nothing else, you should at least make sure to drive along the unpaved Jan Phillips Mountain Drive to take in the great views of the city. It's a sight not to be missed.

Afrikaans Language Museum *(S 33 44.056 E 018 57.809, 11 Pastorie Ave, ☏021-872-3441, www.taalmuseum.co.za, 9am-4pm Mon-Fri, adult R12, child R2)* is housed in the former home of Paarl businessman Gideon Malherbe, one of the founding members of the Association of True Afrikaners (ATA). The two-story museum explores the roots of the Afrikaans language and pays tribute to famous Afrikaners and others who struggled to elevate the language to a written form. The nominal multimedia exhibits include a map of the Afrikaner diaspora, various audio lessons, children's games and an oversized scrabble board.

Paarl Museum *(S 33 43.943 E 018 57.851, 303 Main St, ☏021-872-2651, www.museums.org.za/paarlmuseum, 9am-5pm Mon-Fri, 9am-1pm Sat, R5)* has a good collection of antiques, artifacts and photographs that depict the history and development of Paarl.

Wine Valley Horse Trails *(S 33 40.623 E 018 56.023, Rhebokskloof Estate, off Northern Agter Paarl Rd/R45, ☏021-869-8687 or ☏083-226-8735, www.horsetrails-sa.co.za, by appointment only, R280/1hr, R400/2hrs)* offers a variety of packaged tours of the countryside on horseback or quad bikes. Tours can include wine tasting or dinner and can accommodate riders of all ages.

⚘SLEEPING

BUDGET

Berg River Resort *(S 33 47.753 E 018 57.730, ☏021-863-1650, www.bergriverresort.co.za, camping: R170-230, chalets: d R530-900, 4-person R590-1,010)* is located 5 km south of Paarl and has riverside campsites with electricity and 15 self-catering chalets spread over the 1.5 km of river frontage. The river is perfect for swimming or canoeing (canoes are available for rent from the on-site café) and there is a small animal farm and kiddie pool with a waterslide. Head south out of Paarl on Main St/R45. About 1 km after passing under the N1, turn left onto R45/Franschhoek Rd. Continue 1.2 km to the signed left turn into Berg River Resort.

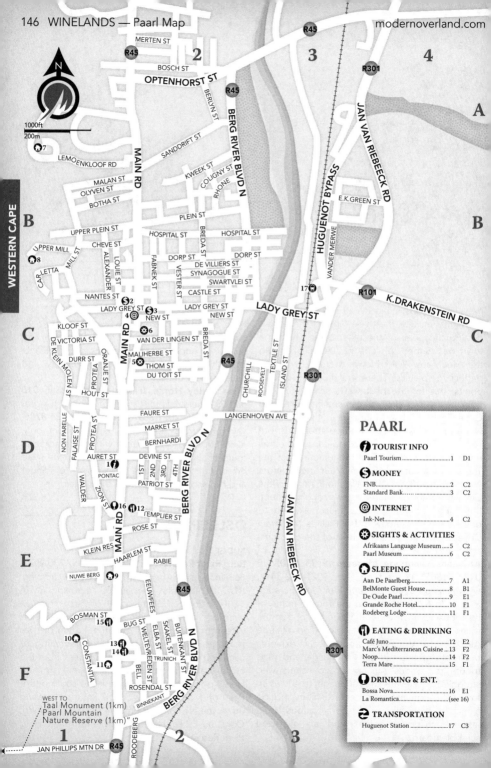

PAARL

TOURIST INFO
Paarl Tourism 1   D1

MONEY
FNB...2   C2
Standard Bank…… 3   C2

INTERNET
Ink-Net...4   C2

SIGHTS & ACTIVITIES
Afrikaans Language Museum 5   C2
Paarl Museum 6   C2

SLEEPING
Aan De Paarlberg............................7   A1
BelMonte Guest House 8   B1
De Oude Paarl....................................9   E1
Grande Roche Hotel.....................10   F1
Rodeberg Lodge 11   F1

EATING & DRINKING
Café Juno 12   E2
Marc's Mediterranean Cuisine ...13   F2
Noop...14   F2
Terra Mare 15   F1

DRINKING & ENT.
Bossa Nova..16   E1
La Romantica..............................(see 16)

TRANSPORTATION
Huguenot Station 17   C3

MID-RANGE

BelMonte Guest House *(S 33 43.670 E 018 57.223, Upper Mill St,* ☎*021-872-9055,* www.belmonteguesthouse.co.za, *s R500-650, d R800-900, breakfast included, Internet/wifi, parking, swimming pool)* is a newly constructed B&B perched on the slopes of Paarl Mountain that has excellent views of the valley below. The six sophisticated and spacious rooms and one private apartment feature paintings by local artists and offer a balcony or private garden access. The pool view can't be beat, there is easy access to Paarl Nature Reserve hiking paths and the organic vegetable garden stocks local restaurants with fresh produce.

Aan De Paarlberg *(S 33 43.299 E 018 57.350, 16 Lemoenkloof Rd off Sitrus St,* ☎*021-872-8215 or* ☎*082-320-0669,* www.aanpaarlberg.co.za, *d R800-1,400, breakfast included, wifi, swimming pool)* is a romantic guesthouse with chic yet rustic décor, tucked away among the rocky slopes of Paarl Mountain outside of the main city center. Each of the luxurious rooms, aptly named after area wine specialties, is uniquely decorated and offers a balcony, private garden or Jacuzzi for your pampering pleasure. The swimming pool and lapa have a braai and there is a fire pit in the nearby courtyard.

De Oude Paarl *(S 33 44.843 E 018 57.7219, 132 Main St,* ☎*021-872-1002,* www.deoudepaarl.com, *s R720, d R1,020, breakfast included, wifi, secure parking, swimming pool)* is a lodge located on the main drag with 26 en suite rooms that each look completely different from one another in décor and floor plan. Rooms surround a courtyard and swimming pool. There is also a steak house restaurant and a tapas and cocktail bar in the building.

Rodeberg Lodge *(S 33 45.181 E 018 57.715, 74 Main St,* ☎*021-863-3202,* www.rodeberglodge.co.za, *s R420, d R660, breakfast included, Internet, secure parking)* is a 1899 Victorian house-turned-B&B, run by two retired attorneys. The lodge has six bright and simple en suite rooms. A hearty South African breakfast is served in the conservatory overlooking the lush backyard garden.

TOP END
Grande Roche Hotel (S 33 45.085 E 018 57.555, Plantasie St, ☎021-863-2727, www.granderoche. co.za, Nov-Mar: R3,025-6,265/room, Apr-Oct: R2,140-4,860/room) offers exceptional service and lavish living in beautifully restored Cape Dutch buildings spread across a massive vineyard estate. Modern suites are tucked into the historic houses and are surrounded by an expanse of immaculate gardens. There are two onsite gourmet restaurants and a central swimming pool sundeck.

❶EATING

Paarl's scenic vineyards offer the best dining options in the area. Many employ gourmet chefs and meals are luxurious affairs when paired with the region's top wines. For dinner at a vineyard, it's best to book ahead. Other tasty options in town include:
Café Juno (S 33 44.599 E 018 57.751, 191 Main Rd, ☎021-872-0697, 7:30am-6pm Mon-Fri, 7:30am-2pm Sat, mains R30-65) is a funky and arty bistro that doubles as an art gallery and winery. Picnic table dining in the front or on the back balcony is perfect for all-day breakfasts or long lunches. During 'Sunset Hour' (4pm-6pm), only snack platters of olives, hummus, cheeses and baguettes are available, but they are a tasty accompaniment to Juno wines.
Terra Mare (S 33 45.023 E 018 57.707, 90a Main Rd, ☎021-863-4805, 10am-11:45pm Tue-Sat, mains R80-120) is an upscale second story restaurant with attentive service, exceptionally fresh fare and a hip vibe. The menu boasts a mix of Mediterranean and Italian fare, a variety of tapas and a large selection of fine local wines.
Marc's Mediterranean Cuisine & Garden (S 33 45.129 E 018 57.728, 129 Main St, ☎021-863-3980, www.marcsrestaurant.co.za, 11am-3:30pm & 6pm-10pm Mon-Sat, mains R60-125) broadly terms Mediterranean everything from Alsacean tarte flambée to Lebanese mezze, but the fare is delicious and is served in healthy portions. The restaurant has a warm and simple front room but head straight back to its namesake garden for lovely alfresco dining.
Noop (S 33 45.139 E 018 57.728, 127 Main St, ☎021-863-3925, 11am-11pm Mon-Fri, 6pm-11pm Sat, mains R80-130) is a local favorite with a large menu of salads, pizza, pastas, sushi, steak and a

full page of desserts. Courtyard seating caters well to families and large groups. Meals start off with gourmet bread, fresh olive oil and balsamic vinegar infused with anise.

❶DRINKING & ENTERTAINMENT

Bossa Nova (S 33 44.608 E 018 57.729, 166 Main Rd, ☎021-872-9861, 9am-2am Sun-Thu, 9am-4am Fri-Sat) is a cross between a wine cellar and sports bar that has specials on pizza and Jack Daniel's. It draws a sizeable crowd on the weekdays but is the heart of Paarl nightlife on the weekends. Find it above the La Romantica Bar.
La Romantica (S 33 44.608 E 018 57.729, 166 Main Rd, ☎021-872-9283, 9am-2am) is a sports bar that serves brandy and oysters (R90/12). It was previously a 23-and-over cigar bar but is now open to a greater cross section of the general public.

❷TRANSPORTATION

❸ Bus
Shell Monument Motors (S 33 46.003 E 018 57.637, cnr Main Rd & South St) is the stop for long distances buses: **Intercape** (☎086-128-7287, www.intercape.co.za), **Greyhound** (☎083-915-9000, www.greyhound.co.za) and **TransLux/City-to-City** (☎086-158-9282 or ☎011-774-3333, www.translux.co.za). Service to and from Cape Town passes through town multiple times a day (50min, R150).

❸ Train
Paarl has two train stations. **The Paarl Railway Station** (S 33 45.893 E 018 57.871, Station St) is in the south of town behind the Paarl Mall. **Huguenot Station** (S 33 43.793 E 018 58.611, cnr Huguenot Bypass/R301 & Drakenstein Rd) is more centrally located and the main commuter hub for Paarl residents. Both are serviced by **Cape Town's Metrorail** (☎080-065-6463, www.capemetrorail. co.za) on the green Cape Town-Bellville-Wellington-Stellenbosch-Strand line nearly every hour. If travelling by train between Stellenbosch and Paarl, you'll have to transfer at Muldersvlei Station. The trip from Cape Town takes about one hour and 20 minutes (first class R16).

❸ Taxi
Paarl Taxis & Tours (☎021-872-5671).

WESTERN CAPE

WHALE COAST

The Whale Coast is the coastline that stretches roughly from Pringle Bay in the west to L'Agulhas in the east. Its moniker derives from the numerous Southern Right and Humpback Whales that come from the cold waters of the sub-Antarctic Ocean and make their way north to the warmer and protected bay near Hermanus where the females calve and nurse their newborn. This stretch of coast provides some of the finest shore-based whale watching in the world.

HERMANUS

GPS: S 34 25.174 E 019 14.553
pop. 50,000 | elevation 23 m/75 ft

The cliff-side town of Hermanus is the whale watching capital of South Africa. The former fishing village has become increasingly more developed in recent years to cater to the tourist crowd that flocks to the city during the calving season (July-October) when whales come into Walker Bay. Between August and September, you are almost guaranteed to spot a whale, sometimes with its newborn calf. There are hundreds of B&B and guesthouses in town, many of which overlook the ocean, making it almost possible to whale watch from bed.

is lined with large flip-picture books that showcase B&B accommodation options, restaurants and activities in the area. The staff is helpful and can assist you with bookings. Free maps of Hermanus are available. For after-hours accommodation assistance call ☏*079-492-1949*.

⊗MONEY

There are several banks and ATMs along Main Road for quick withdrawals and currency exchange. **FNB** (*S 34 25.188 E 019 14.543, Main Rd*) is the most central and has a bureau de change, but head towards Westcliff Street and you will find a Standard Bank, Nedbank and ABSA.

❼TOURIST INFORMATION

Hermanus Tourism Office (*S 34 25.008 E 019 14.599, Old Station Bldg, cnr Mitchell St & Lord Roberts St, ☏028-312-2629, www.hermanus.co.za, 8am-6pm Mon-Fri, 9am-5pm Sat, 11am-3pm Sun*)

@INTERNET

Main Street Computing (*S 34 25.177 E 019 14.356, 69 Main Rd, ☏028-313-1574, 8:30am-6:30pm Mon-Fri, 8:30am-4pm Sat, R5/20mins*) is located next door to the ABSA. There are nine

updated computers and five spots for laptops. Printing, webcams, and CD/DVD burning are also available.
Computer Connections & Internet Café *(S 34 25.198 E 019 14.350, 38 Main Rd, ☏028-312-4683, 8am-6:30pm Mon-Fri, 8:30am-4pm Sat, 9am-2pm Sun, R5/20mins)* is located across the street from Main Street Computing and has 13 updated computers, with plans to expand. There are also laptop connections, printing, CD/DVD burning and Skype/webcams.

☉SHOPPING

Marine Drive and High Street are lined with high-end clothing and décor boutiques.
Market Square *(S 34 25.204 E 019 14.565, cnr Market St & Marine Dr)* has a daily market of handmade crafts and souvenirs oriented towards tourists. Market Street is lined with small outdoor cafés where you can grab a drink while considering your purchases.
High Street Close No. 3 *(S 34 25.159 E 019 14.532, High St)* is a tree-lined alley just off High Street in the center of town. A small café, art gallery, antique shop and craft stores line the gravel pathway, which feels like a secret garden amid the hubbub.

✪SIGHTS & ACTIVITIES

Whale cruises are a must if you're visiting Hermanus between May and January.
Southern Right Charters *(S 34 26.049 E 019 13.480, New Harbour, ☏082-353-0550, www. southernrightcharters.co.za, Jun-Dec: 7am, 9am, 12pm, 3pm, 7pm, 2hr R600)* and **Bee Company** *(S 34 26.049 E 019 13.480, New Harbour, ☏028-313-*

2722, www.hermanus-whale-cruises.co.za, May-Jan 7am, 9am, 12pm, 2pm, 4pm, 2hr adult R600) tour Walker Bay during the whale watching high season and do eco-tours of the local marine life during the rest of the year.
Hermanus Whale Festival *(☏028-313-0928, www. whalefestival.co.za, end of Sept)* draws thousands of tourists to Hermanus every spring to celebrate the return of the Southern Right whales to Walker Bay. To supplement the main attraction, the four-day festival is choc-full of craft stalls, live concerts and entertainment and educational events, much of which is geared towards children. If you can brave crowded streets and high prices, you will have a blast, but if you want to check out the whales in the absence of large crowds, the best time to head to Hermanus is the first week of October. The whales will still be there, but the hordes of tourists will have all gone home.
Walker Bay Adventures *(S 34 25.210 E 019 14.632, Old Harbour, ☏082-739-0159, www. walkerbayadventures.co.za, 2hr R300/person offers sea kayaking trips that launch from the Old Harbour)*. On a good day you can paddle feet from whales, seals, dolphins, penguins and sea birds. Walker Bay Adventures also does a variety of other outdoor and ocean adventure activities.
Shark Cage Diving that is promoted along the southern coast occurs about 25 km southeast of Hermanus in Gansbaai. There are a handful of operators that will take you out for a day drip where you climb into a metal cage tied to the side of the boat. The water is chummed with small fish to attract the sharks and fish heads or dummy bait is thrown out and pulled in by rope to bring the Great Whites right in front of you.
Shark Diving Unlimited *(S 34 36.874 E 019 21.311, 1 Swart St, Kleinbaai, ☏028-384-2787 or ☏082-441-4555, www.sharkdivingunlimited.com, R1,350)* is one of the more reputable shark cage diving operators. They offer a three to four-hour boat trip that includes lunch, and a shuttle will pick you up from Hermanus for an additional R150.
Great White Shark Tours *(☏028-384-1418, www.sharkcagediving.net, R1,350)* is also a recommended shark diving operator. They offer pickup from Hermanus for an extra R110/person.
Walking and hiking is breathtaking in this area. The beautiful 10 km Cliff Path Walking trail will take you through town and past three white sand beaches. Grotto Beach is popular for surfing and sunbathing; all along the way you'll have fantastic

Setting the Record Straight: The Cage Diving Controversy

In recent years there has been much controversy over shark cage diving and whether or not it contributes to the rise of shark attacks in South Africa. Many have argued that the practice of chumming and using baited ropes to lure sharks towards boats causes sharks to associate humans with food and is detrimental to Great Whites and humans alike. Socially conscious travelers should be aware of this controversy and know the facts before they take the big plunge.

The Save our Seas Foundation, a reputable international shark awareness, conservation and education organization argues that cage diving is actually beneficial because it shatters the "Jaws" image that most people have of Great Whites. By offering unique encounters with the animals and encouraging increased understanding of their natural behavior, the foundation hopes that these interactions will lend further appreciation for the animals they call the "custodians of the sea." White shark biologist Alison Kock, co-author of "South Africa's White Shark Cage-Diving Industry - Is There Cause For Concern?" affirms that cage diving, when done responsibly and lawfully, does not cause sharks to equate humans with food. Conditioning, she argues, would only arise if sharks received a significant and reliable food reward, which is against the law. Chumming the water involves very little food and is mostly a pungent brew of fish oils with a scent that attracts the sharks. Baiting is also permitted, and necessary, to lure sharks within range of visibility. Many sharks have no interest in the bait and leave for deeper waters, while others seem to be suckers for fish heads and will circle the boat cautiously several times. Even if they get the bait, this is not enough food to pose a large threat of conditioning (such little food may actually be a disappointment for the sharks). However, some signs of positive conditioning have been observed in a handful of sharks in Mossel Bay, prompting a tightening of regulations. Still, it is highly improbable that this conditioning would put swimmers and surfers in danger. There is little similarity between cage diving boats, which are larger than sharks and therefore intimidating, and a human swimming by. In short, though Great Whites are smart, they aren't that smart.

Yet the controversy remains relevant to companies that do not operate within the confines of their permits and illegally feed sharks as a sort of "feeding show" to impress clients. Make sure that you only go with accredited companies. When in doubt, ask them if they feed the sharks, or ask around to feel out a company's reputation. But if shark diving interests you, do not let noise of the controversy deter you. They are magnificent animals and an up-close encounter should not be missed.

For more information check out: **www.saveourseas.com/cage-diving**.

views of the bay and marine wildlife. **Fernkloof Nature Reserve** (*S 34 24.083 E 019 16.044, Fir Ave,* 028-384-8000, *www.fernkloof.com, 7am-7pm, free*) has more than 60 km of walking trails with views of the bay and some of the biggest carnivorous plants in the world. **Market Square** (*S 34 25.204 E 019 14.565, cnr Market St & Marine Dr*) and the neighboring Old Harbour have three museums (adult R15, child R5 for entrance to all three, 8am-4:30pm Mon-Sat, 12pm-4pm Sun) perhaps best saved for a rainy day. **Whale House** (*www.oceansofafrica.co.za*) is the newest of the three, with multimedia and large graphic displays on the whales of Hermanus. The best use of your time is the 20-minute video for the basics on the regional whale life and tips on prime spots to view them in the area (10am, 12pm & 3pm Mon-Sat, 12pm & 3pm Sun). **De Wet's Huis Photo Museum** (028-313-0418) has a collection

of black and white photos and furniture from the town's booming fishing days, housed in a historic schoolhouse. **The Old Harbour Museum** (*S 34 25.210 E 019 14.632*) is across Marine Drive toward the ocean and is housed at the foot of the cliffs, down the stairs from a war memorial. The displays on the area's fishing history feel less loved than its neighboring Whale House – at the time of review the local fish breeds were missing from their aquariums with no word on when they would return.

⊙ SLEEPING

Hermanus has over 300 guesthouses and B&Bs to cater to every whale watcher's needs and desires. For additional options, stop at the tourism office and page through their many accommodation picture books.

WESTERN CAPE

Indian Ocean

HERMANUS

🛈 TOURIST INFO
Hermanus Tourism Office 1 A4

💲 MONEY
FNB..2 B4

@ INTERNET
Computer Connections...............3 B3
Main Street Computing..............4 A3

🛍 SHOPPING
High Street Close No. 3..............5 A4
Market Square ....(see 7)

✦ SIGHTS & ACTIVITIES
Bee Company............................6 E1
De Wet's Huis Photo Museum....(see 7)
Market Square 7 B4
Old Harbour Museum 8 B4
Southern Right Charters ....(see 6)
Walker Bay Adventures ....(see 8)
Whale House ....(see 7)

🛏 SLEEPING
Auberge Burgundy.....................9 B4
Avalon on Sea 10 B2
Hermanus Backpackers 11 B2
La Fontaine.............................12 B3
Ocean Eleven 13 C2
Quarters Hotel 14 B4
Windsor Hotel 15 B4
Zoete Inval Travellers Lodge.......16 A2

🍴 EATING
Bientang's Cave 17 A4
Fisherman's Cottage ....(see 7)
Mediterra................................18 A4
Paradiso 19 A4
Savannah Café 20 A4
Tapas 21 B4
The Burgundy Restaurant ....(see 21)

🍷 DRINKING & ENT.
Bojangles.................................22 B4
Shimmi...................................23 A4
Zebra Crossing 24 B4

⮂ TRANSPORTATION
Minibus Taxi Rank 25 A3

BUDGET
Hermanus Backpackers (*S 34 25.230 E 019 13.974, 26 Flower St,* ☎*028-312-4293,* www. hermanusbackpackers.co.za, *dm R100, s R175, d R320-350, bar, shuttle to Baz Bus, Internet, parking, swimming pool*) is a colorful backpackers with a loungy TV and living room area shared with the resident cat and dog. Behind the house, the large yard has a swimming pool, braai, tables, a fire pit to sit around at night and a bar and pool table. The managing staff and their friends are laid-back and friendly and frequently head out to sandboard or catch the surf.

Zoete Inval Travellers Lodge (*S 34 25.116 E 019 13.821, 23 Main Rd,* ☎*028-312-1242,* www. zoeteinval.co.za, *dm R100, s R325, d R350, shuttle to Baz Bus, Internet, Jacuzzi, secure parking*) is a quiet backpackers off the Main Road that's a lovely place for a mellow night, but not a place to party. When you're ready to chill, hop in the Jacuzzi, a hammock or kick back in one of the multiple lounge rooms. They have one en suite room that offers more privacy for families or groups of friends.

MID-RANGE
La Fontaine (*S 34 25.239 E 019 14.245, 33 Marine Dr,* ☎*028-312-4595,* www.lafontaine.co.za, *d R1,100-1,450, breakfast included, Internet/wifi, secure parking, swimming pool*) is an exquisite B&B with all the touches of home. Perfectly perched to overlook the cliffs, its sea-facing rooms have a large balcony to view the whales in the bay below, while others open to a lovely garden and swimming pool. Breakfast is best enjoyed on the patio to take in the views as you sip your coffee.

Avalon on Sea (*S 34 25.320 E 019 14.070, 1 Marine Dr,* ☎*028-313-0959,* www.avalononsea. co.za, *s R550, d R750, breakfast included, Internet/ wifi, secure parking, splash pool*) is a cozy and well-situated guesthouse run by a gracious couple who are happy to arrange activities for you. It has three double rooms with gorgeous ocean views of Walker Bay as well as family friendly accommodation. The pool is nothing you can do laps in, but is private and perfect for lounging.

Windsor Hotel (*S 34 25.265 E 019 14.429, 49 Marine Dr,* ☎*028-312-3727,* www.windsorhotel. co.za, *breakfast, Internet/wifi, secure parking, sea-facing rooms: R600-1,200/person, non-sea-facing: R480-960/person*) is a historic Hermanus establishment that's looking a little worn but

has unbelievable ocean views. Ask for a third-floor room for the best vantage point for whale watching. Some second-floor rooms have a balcony for no additional cost.

TOP END
Auberge Burgundy (*S 34 25.253 E 019 14.547, 16 Harbour Rd,* ☎*028-313-1201,* www.auberge. co.za, *R780-R1,040, breakfast included, wifi, secure parking, swimming pool*) is an enchanting guesthouse in the Provençal style, just steps from both the city center and the sea. If the ivy-laden back terraces and crisp white linens don't delight you, the spectacular views and rooftop pool will. Rooms 14, 15, 16 and the penthouse are poolside.

Ocean Eleven (*S 34 25.422 E 019 14.057, 11 Westcliff Rd,* ☎*028-312-1332,* www.oceaneleven. co.za, *s R1,100, d R2,000, suites R2,400, apt R3,300, breakfast included, Internet/wifi, secure parking, swimming pool*) is the most elegant guesthouse in Hermanus. Each of the 11 spacious rooms look out right over the cliff to the ocean and the front of the house has a direct entry to the cliff path. They also offer two luxury suites and an apartment for four, outfitted with French doors, a spacious living area and private patio.

Quarters Hotel (*S 34 25.228 E 019 14.549, on Market Square,* ☎*028-313-7700,* www.quarters. co.za/quarters-hermanus, *s R1,600-1,800, d R2,300-R2,700, apt R3,700, breakfast included, Internet/wifi, secure parking, swimming pool*) is a posh hotel located in the heart of downtown Hermanus. Suites offer private balconies and full kitchens and every room affords you the opportunity to take a bubble bath right next to your bed. If you can, book suite numbers 14 and 8 for the best sea views.

WESTERN CAPE

❶EATING

Fisherman's Cottage (*S 34 25.216 E 019 14.540*, *Lemm's Corner, Market Square*, ☏*028-312-3642*, *6:30pm-9:30pm, mains R115-155*) is a Hermanus mainstay that has recently come under new ownership. Though under remodeling at the time of research, new owners Maurice and Erma promised to keep the cozy classic kitsch of the eatery while expanding the seafood menu.

The Burgundy Restaurant (*S 34 25.244 E 019 14.566*, *Marine Dr*, ☏*028-312-2800*, *8am-9pm, mains R80-140*) is a French country kitchen that serves up continental favorites in an understated dining room of cozy rugs, enclosed porches and beamed ceilings. Tapped as one of the best restaurants in the area, Burgundy's strength is preparing straightforward main dishes that allow the flavors of the high-quality base ingredients to shine through. If you have room for dessert, don't miss the Malva pudding, a mouthwatering warm South African trifle.

Mediterra (*S 34 25.139 E 019 14.622*, *87 Marine Dr*, ☏*028-313-1685*, *6pm-late Mon-Sat, 12pm-late Sun, mains R120-150*) is one of the more formal dining options in Hermanus. The good fresh food is served in a second-story dining room overlooking the water. Choose from either a selection of tapas or a two or three-course meal of fresh seafood, steak and a large selection of desserts.

Tapas (*S 34 25.231 E 019 14.563*, *Market Square*, ☏*028-312-4840*, *11am-9pm, mains R25-90*) is an upbeat restaurant and wine bar located in the heart of downtown. Live music sets the mood most nights as patrons nibble Mediterranean-inspired tapas and unwind after a long day. Don't be surprised if, by the end of the night, satisfied customers are dancing in the square.

Savannah Café (*S 34 25.050 E 019 14.629*, *25 High St*, ☏*028-312-4259*, *www.savannahcafé. co.za*, *8am-5pm Mon-Fri, 8am-3pm Sat-Sun, mains R40-60*) serves breakfast and lunch with a dose of dressed-down elegance. Lunch fare and comfort food are heavy on cheese, which is usually a good thing.

Bientang's Cave (*S 34 25.150 E 019 14.668*, ☏*028-312-3454*, *Below Marine Dr, 9am-4pm, www.bientangscave.com, mains R50-140*) is a seafood restaurant built inside a cave in the cliff near Old Harbour. Just feet away from penguins, gulls and (on a good day) breeding whales, this eatery is well known for its breathtaking scenery, but you better like your fish fried.

Paradiso (*S 34 25.149 E 019 14.613*, *83 Marine Dr*, ☏*028-313-1153*, *4:30pm-late Mon-Fri, 11:30am-late Sat-Sun, mains R55-105*) is a casual Italian restaurant with outdoor seating. It's known for its pasta and thin crust pizza, but also has a selection of seafood and steaks.

❶DRINKING & ENTERTAINMENT

Zebra Crossing (*S 34 25.205 E 019 14.509*, *cnr Main Rd & Long St*, ☏*028-312-3906*, *9am-late*) is one of the better libation destinations in town. It is a small cozy bar with occasional live acoustic music, where you rub shoulders with the locals. Breakfast, light meals and pub grub can be ordered from the small kitchen.

Shimmi (*S 34 25.177 E 019 14.604*, *Village Square, Marine Dr*, ☏*083-235-0881*, *www.shimmi. co.za*, *4pm-1am Mon-Sat, cover R30*) is a retro-chic lounge and club that attracts the party crowd. If there is a place to be seen out at night in Hermanus, this is it.

Bojangles (*S 34 25.213 E 019 14.502*, *121 Main Rd*, ☏*028-313-1406*, *9am-late Tue-Sun, 4pm-1am Mon, cover*) does its best to pull off a Hermanus club scene and attracts a mixed crowd with a DJ, dance floor and events such as karaoke, "talent" competitions and ladies night. Next door to Bojangles is their unlicensed mini-casino where you can get drinks and play the slots.

❷TRANSPORTATION

❸Bus

There is currently no bus service directly to Hermanus. You can arrange a shuttle through both hostels (*30mins, R40 one-way*) to and from the nearest **Baz Bus stop** (☏*021-439-2323*, *www. bazbus.com*) in Bot River.

Hermanus Tours (☏*072-062-8500*, *www.hermanus tours.com*, *R850/car*) can arrange a direct shuttle to and from Cape Town.

❸Minibus Taxi

Minibus Taxi Rank (*S 34 25.134 E 019 14.342*, *cnr Magnolia Ave & Paterson St*) has service to Zwelihle (*5mins, R5*) where you can transfer to a minibus to Cape Town (*1.5hr, R60*).

Route 62 & The Little Karoo

Route 62 is an iconic inland drive that is a common alternative to the coastal N2. The route takes you though winding mountain passes and lush valleys, past vineyards and orchards, and through the hot and dry valley of the Little Karoo (or Klein Karoo in Afrikaans), a region squeezed between the Swartberg and the Langeberg Mountains. The valley is home to a string of small historic towns that line the route, each with their own character and charm.

MONTAGU

GPS: S 33 47.176 E 020 07.194
pop. 10,000 | elevation 231 m/758 ft

The little town of Montagu marks the gateway to the Klein Karoo on Route 62. The shops and restaurants that line Long and Bath Streets haven't changed much in 50 years and while strolling downtown it's easy to imagine that this town has been forgotten by time. The area surrounding Montagu is rife with natural wonders - local rock formations in the stunning Cogman's Kloof Pass provide some of the best rock climbing and hiking in the Western Cape. Most of the town's restaurants and accommodation are located on Long Street and Bath Street (alternatively called Brown Street and Bad Street).

❶ TOURIST INFORMATION

Montagu - Ashton Tourism *(S 33 47.248 E 020 07.102, 24 Bath St,* ☎*023-614-2471,* www.tourismmontagu.co.za, *8am-6pm Mon-Fri, 9am-5pm Sat, 9:30am-5pm Sun)* has free maps of the city and brochures for area activities and accommodation. They also have an updated menu for most of the town's restaurants.

❸ MONEY

Standard Bank *(S 33 47.215 E 020 07.260, 46 Bath St)* has full banking services with an outside ATM and a bureau de change. ATMs can also be found at each of the supermarkets along Bath Street.

◉ INTERNET

Printmor *(S 33 47.156 E 020 07.543, 61 Bath St,* ☎*023-614-1838, 7:30am-5:30pm Mon-Fri, 8am-1pm Sat, R8/15mins)* has five computers along with printing services.
Internet @ the Office *(S 33 47.210 E 020 07.362, 54 Bath St,* ☎*023-614-3619, 8am-5pm, R8/15mins)* has three computers and wireless connectivity for laptops. Their services include printing, CD burning, Skype capabilities and wedding photography.

WESTERN CAPE

🛍SHOPPING

Arts and crafts stores are all over town – the tourist information office can provide you a map that denotes where you can find them. **Art Africa** (S 33 47.248 E 020 07.102, 24 Bath St, 023-614-3154, 8am-6pm Mon-Fri, 9am-5pm Sat, 9:30am-5pm Sun) and **Art Studio & Gallery** (S 33 47.246 E 020 07.123, 6 Bath St, 023-614-3978, by appointment only) are just next to the tourism office and **Jessica's** (S 33 47.166 E 020 07.450, 47 Bath St, 023-614-1805, www.jessicasrestaurant. co.za, 6:30pm-10pm) is a fine restaurant that doubles as an exhibition space for Montagu Art Association artists.

Montagu Books & CDs (S 33 47.212 E 020 07.295, 48 Bath St, 023-614-2772, 9am-5pm Mon-Fri, 9am-1pm Sat) is a quick stop if you're running low on used books or (mostly classical) music.

Kohler Street has two antique and décor shops if you're looking for some local treasures.

⚙SIGHTS & ACTIVITIES

Montagu is a hiking and rock climbing hotspot. There are three main hiking trails that depart from **Ou Meul** (S 33 46.748 E 020 06.751, Tanner St). The 2.2 km Lover's Walk (R11) will drop you off at the Avalon Springs Hotel for a swim. Bloupunt (15.6 km) and Cogman's Kloof (12.1 km) trails will take you the whole day (R18). Hiking maps are available at the tourism information office. To get to Ou Meul, take Barry St north and turn left on Mill St. Follow Mill St until you reach your first right, Tanner St. Turn right on Tanner St and go straight until you see the Ou Meul, which has a big wheel out front.

Rock climbers should be satisfied with over 300 bolted routes within walking distance of town. The guys at **De Bos** (S 33 47.354 E 020 06.760, Bath St, 023-614-2532, www.debos.co.za) rent out climbing gear (R200 for ropes, harness, quickdraw and shoes), but the shoe selection is limited and bringing you own is advised. They also can provide you with a route map or you can download it from their website. If you're interested in a hiking or climbing guide, try **Justin Lawson** (023-614-3193 or 082-696-4067).

Hot mineral springs (S 33 45.959 E 020 07.041, Avalon Springs Resort Hotel, Uitvlucht St, 023-614-1150, 10am-6pm Mon-Fri, 10am-1pm & 3pm-9pm Sat-Sun, adult R70, child R50) are touted as one of Montagu's top attractions, but don't expect a peaceful or natural bath. This highly commercialized attraction pumps the 43°C/109°F mineral water from its underground spring into a number of modern swimming pools. Day visitors are restricted to the busy family pool section. Ask to enter the section of the springs reserved for hotel guests if you're craving a quieter dip.

Donkey Cart Rides (S 33 47.433 E 020 06.759, Route 62 Farmstall & Restaurant, 1 Long St, 023-614-2209, adult R25, child R10) are another one of Montagu's unique activities on offer. Scenic rides can be arranged along R62 or through the town, with stops at a local restaurant or pub.

Tractor trips by Protea Farm (S 33 42.364 E 019 52.665, 023-614-3012, www.proteafarm. co.za, 10am & 2pm Wed & Sat, booking essential, adult R80, student R40, child R35) take you on a three-hour roundtrip climb to the summit of the Langeberg mountain range. Enjoy gorgeous views and a snack at a hut on the top. Protea Farm also serves a traditional South African lunch called Potjiekos (adult R90, child R35, student R60).

Montagu Cycle Hire (S 33 47.369 E 020 06.457, 1 Kloof St, 083-702-5465) can arrange bike rentals (R75/day) and owner Allan Brown can guide you through the six scenic trails available in the surrounding area.

Montagu Museum (S 33 47.345 E 020 07.251, 41 Long St, 023-614-1950, mmuseum@telkomsa. net, 9am-5pm Mon-Fri, 10:30am-12:30pm Sat-Sun, adult R5, child R2) is housed in a 1907 church. Apart from the gorgeous building, this is a motley collection of town history, including old-fashioned wedding dresses, antique china and pictures from Montagu's devastating floods, predominantly the flood of 2008. Check out the wall of purchasable Khoi and San herbal remedies the museum has been researching for more than 20 years.

Joubert House (S 33 47.373 E 020 07.107, 25 Long St, 023-614-1774, 9:30am-5pm Mon-Fri, 10am-12pm Sat-Sun, adult R5, child R2) is a 1853 farmhouse furnished with original pieces and displayed in the style of late 19th century country life. The house is the oldest in Montagu and was nearly destroyed in the flood of 1981, but was fully restored and opened as a museum with community support. The curator will give you a guided tour through the house for no extra charge.

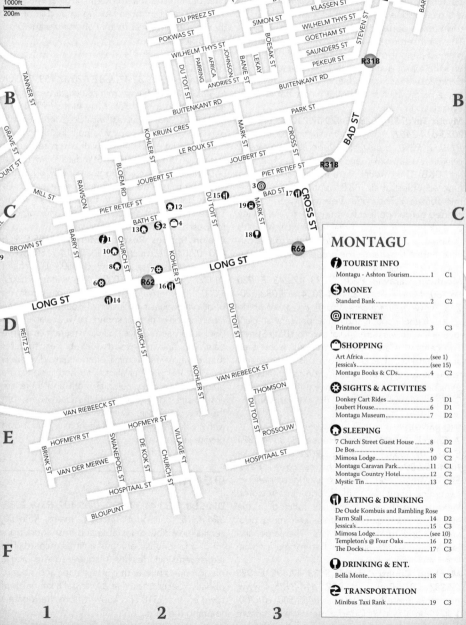

WESTERN CAPE

MONTAGU

TOURIST INFO

Montagu - Ashton Tourism.............1 C1

MONEY

Standard Bank....................2 C2

@ INTERNET

Printmor....................3 C3

SHOPPING

Art Africa...........................(see 1)
Jessica's...........................(see 15)
Montagu Books & CDs...................4 C2

SIGHTS & ACTIVITIES

Donkey Cart Rides......................5 D1
Joubert House..........................6 D1
Montagu Museum.......................7 D2

SLEEPING

7 Church Street Guest House....8 D2
De Bos..................................9 C1
Mimosa Lodge.......................10 C2
Montagu Caravan Park............11 C2
Montagu Country Hotel...........12 C2
Mystic Tin............................13 C2

EATING & DRINKING

De Oude Kombuis and Rambling Rose
Farm Stall...........................14 D2
Jessica's.............................15 C3
Mimosa Lodge....................(see 10)
Templeton's @ Four Oaks.......16 D2
The Docks............................17 C3

DRINKING & ENT.

Bella Monte.........................18 C3

TRANSPORTATION

Minibus Taxi Rank..................19 C3

WESTERN CAPE

☺SLEEPING

BUDGET

De Bos (S 33 47.354 E 020 06.760, 8 Brown St, ☏023-614-2532, www.debos.co.za, camping R40/person, dm R80, s R180, d R350, swimming pool) is a picturesque farm located on the west end of town that is perfect for a rustic weekend getaway. The rural setting is complete with horses and a peacock, and it offers quaint private bungalows, en suite rooms and campsites. Most unique is the backpackers accommodation in the converted horse barn, which may be the nicest stable you'll ever sleep in.

Mystic Tin (S 33 47.236 E 020 07.210, 38 Bath St, ☏023-614-2461, www.themystictin.co.za, dm R110, d R390, breakfast included, bar, Internet, parking) is a funky and crunchy backpackers and B&B. The owners are a friendly couple who have doubled their B&B venture as a home microbrewery. They offer free tastings in a large shaded garden perfect for lounging; try the honey or dark brew. A simple breakfast is included with the double en suite rooms. One of the rooms can accommodate a family or group of four for the price of a regular double.

Montagu Caravan Park (S 33 47.243 E 020 06.780, Middle St, ☏023-614-3034 or ☏082-920-763, www.montagucaravanpark.co.za, camping R130, chalets R350) is the municipal caravan park located on the western end of town on Bath Street. The campsites are clean with braais, water taps and electricity at each site but this place seems to be more of a quiet destination for caravaning pensioners. A better experience might be had at De Bos, located right beside the caravan park.

MID-RANGE

7 Church Street Guest House (S 33 47.321 E 020 07.165, 7 Church St, ☏023-614-1186 or ☏084-507-8941, www.7churchstreet.co.za, s R395-525, d R890-1,050, breakfast included, parking, swimming pool) has its main lodge in a restored Victorian home and four units located in the expansive back garden, with a swimming pool and a pond that attracts birds. The large and lovely rooms have spacious bathrooms, percale linen and high ceilings.

Montagu Country Hotel (S 33 47.192 E 020 07.287, 27 Bath St, ☏023-614-3125, www.montagucountryhotel.co.za, s R450-580, d R700-1,400, breakfast included, Internet/wifi, secure parking, swimming pool) is the only authentic art deco hotel in town. Though it looks a little worse for wear, the kind staff, comfortable rooms and lush garden make it a fine place to stay. The luxury rooms are attractive, and the Victorian Villa built behind the main hotel in 1905 is spacious, light and airy. For those looking to be pampered, there is a wellness center that offers massages and aromatherapy.

TOP END

Mimosa Lodge (S 33 47.268 E 020 07.153, Church St, ☏023-614-2351, www.mimosa.co.za, Sept-Apr: s R675-1,190, d R990-1,750, May-Aug: s R970-1,485, d R1,580-2,340, breakfast included, Internet/wifi, parking, swimming pool) was built in 1859 and is now a national monument with a top restaurant located on the ground level. Standard rooms on the upper level of the main lodge are lovely, but you'd do better to request one of the more recently built rooms behind the lodge in the rambling garden. These are tasteful, modern and airy and some of the best accommodations in town.

Avalon Springs Resort Hotel (S 33 45.959 E 020 07.041, Uitvlucht St, ☏023-614-1150, www.avalonsprings.co.za, wkday: d R500-700, chalet R1,000, wkend: d R1,000-1,400, suites R1,600-1,800, Internet/wifi, secure parking, swimming pool) offers guests exclusive 24-hour access to the nicer section of the hot springs as well as an indoor pool, luxury spa services, a full restaurant and three bars. The one-stop resort does its best to cater to the whole family and offers many diversions for kids and parents alike. The hotel rooms are plagued by a tacky colonial motif and there are arm chairs oddly placed in the bathrooms, but the new Mountain Chalets are more updated with sleek furnishings, a full kitchen, and your own private jacuzzi.

⑪EATING

Die Stal (S 33 44.332 E 020 05.409, R318, ☏082-324-4318, 8am-5pm Tue-Sun, mains R55-100) serves incredibly delectable and fresh food, right off of a farmhouse porch in a citrus orchard. The large menu includes freshly squeezed fruit juice, a ploughman's platter that is to die for, and a board of daily specials. You'll find Die Stal 8 km north of town on the R318 and know it from the roosters roaming the yard.

Jessica's (*S 33 47.166 E 020 07.450, 47 Bath St,* ☏023-614-1805, www.jessicasrestaurant.co.za, *6:30pm-10pm, Oct-Apr: 11:30am-2:30pm Wed-Sun & 6:30pm-10pm, mains R80-130*) is a family-run operation with a surprising Asian bent. In the intimate dining room or the romantic back terrace, you can't miss the proprietors' incredible attention to detail – from perfectly piled mashed potatoes to lap blankets for chilly nights. Game is served tender and perfectly sauced; The Panaeng curry is delicate with vegetables that taste straight from the garden. During the day, Jessica's doubles as a gallery for local artists.

Templeton's @ Four Oaks (*S 33 47.350 E 020 07.299, 46 Long St,* ☏023-614-2778, *11am-3pm & 6pm-late Mon-Sat, mains R95-115*) was rated by Eat Out as one of the top 20 restaurants in South Africa. The small menu features artful new twists on traditional local dishes and Cape Malay meals. The intimate dining rooms are flanked by paintings and the leafy courtyard is charming. There is also a small cocktail bar where you can enjoy an aperitif or digestif.

The Docks (*S 33 47.154 E 020 07.637, 80 Bath St,* ☏023-614-3360, *5pm-9:30pm Tue-Fri, 10am-9:30pm Sat, 10am-3pm Sun, mains R30-90*) looks more like a swinging Floridian retiree's house than a serious eating establishment. Pop in if you want to groove to some Elvis ballads while lounging on patio furniture around the pool. Perhaps more thought was put into the music playlist than the food, so don't expect more than your grandma could whip up.

Mimosa Lodge (*S 33 47.268 E 020 07.153, Church St,* ☏023-614-2351, www.mimosa.co.za, *8am-10am & 7pm-10pm, 4 courses R260, w/ wine R375*) is one of Montagu's finest restaurants. The menu changes each day but the food is consistently good. Guests are welcome to arrive at 7pm for an aperitif and the set 4-course meal starts between 7:30-8pm. The food is slow-cooked and combines fresh local produce with a high quality meat or fish. A new wine is paired with each course.

De Oude Kombuis and Rambling Rose Farm Stall (*S 33 47.380 E 020 07.134, 36 Long St,* ☏023-614-3438, www.oudekombuis.co.za, *8am-4pm, mains R30-60*) is a farm restaurant in the center of town. The country dining room serves up fresh-baked bread, savory pies, tramezzinis and salads with ingredients picked from right outside.

❶DRINKING & ENTERTAINMENT

Bella Monte (*S 33 47.250 E 020 07.551,* ☏023-614-2941, *5pm-late Mon-Fri, 10am-late Sat*) is a local haunt, usually full of neighbors flirting by the lightly stocked bar or watching the TVs stacked precariously atop stools on the countertop. The side room has a pool table and is sometimes host to live music.

❷TRANSPORTATION

There are currently no direct buses to Montagu, but long distance **TransLux and City-to-City Buses** (☏086-158-9282 or ☏011-774-3333, www.translux.co.za) service Ashton, just 10 km away, on their Cape Town-Port Elizabeth route. **Minibuses leave from OK Foods** (*S 33 47.180 E 020 07.511, cnr Bath St & Mark St*) to get to/from Ashton (*10min, R8*). Most accommodation options in town also can arrange shuttle services to/from Ashton, but you must book in advance.

Brown's Transport (☏072-750-3125) in Ashton also operates a private shuttle between Cape Town and Montagu (*2hr, R150*).

OUDTSHOORN
GPS: S 33 35.322 E 022 12.241
pop. 90,000 | elevation 352 m/827 ft

Situated in the heart of Klein Karoo (or Little Karoo), Oudtshoorn is a quirky commercial center surrounded by the stunning peaks of the Swartberg Mountains. The sleepy farm town rose to fame in the late 1800s when, in response to high demands for lavish fashions in Europe and the Americas, it became the world's largest supplier of ostrich feathers. Ostriches - and ostrich riding - are still some of Oudtshoorn's primary draws, but the area is home to other diversions that are just as unique. Make a visit to the vast dripstone caverns of the Cango Caves or revel with thousands during the country's largest Afrikaner cultural festival in April.

❼TOURIST INFORMATION

Oudtshoorn Tourism Bureau (*S 33 35.542 E 022 12.081, cnr Voortrekker St & Baron van Reede*

WESTERN CAPE

OUDTSHOORN

TOURIST INFO
Oudtshoorn Tourism Bureau.......1 D3

MONEY
FNB...2 D4
Standard Bank 3 D4

INTERNET
Café Brulé.............................(see 20)
Internet & Art Gallery...................4 D4
MD Computer Systems 5 B4
Oudtshoorn Media & IT..............(see 8)

SHOPPING
Klein Karoo Ostrich Co-op..........6 F1
Lugro Ostrich 7 F4
Queen's Riverside Mall 8 D3

SIGHTS & ACTIVITIES
4x4 Botanical Tours......................9 D2
CP Nel Museum..........................10 D3

SLEEPING
Adley House...............................11 C2
Attakwas Cottage.......................12 D2
Backpacker's Paradise 13 A4
Gum Tree Lodge 14 D3
Hlangana Lodge 15 A4
Karoo Soul Travel Lodge.............16 F4
Kleinplaas Holiday Resort............17 A4
La Pension 18 C2
Oakdene Guesthouse..................19 B4
Queen's Hotel 20 D3

EATING & DRINKING
Bello Cibo..................................21 B4
Café Brulé..............................(see 20)
Jemima's Restaurant....................22 C4
Kalinka......................................23 B4
La Dolce Vita 24 C4
Nostalgie...................................25 C4

DRINKING & ENT.
Lemon'n Lime............................26 E3
Upper Deck................................27 D4

TRANSPORTATION
Bus Station ....(see 8)
Minibus Taxi Rank 28 D4

NORTH TO
Cango Wildlife Ranch (2.5km)
Cango Caves (30km)

NORTH TO
Highgate Ostrich
Show Farm (13km)

1000ft
200m

St, ☎044-279-2532, www.oudtshoorn.com, 8am-5:30pm Mon-Fri, 9am-5pm Sat, 10am-5pm Sun) can provide you with maps of the area and assist with accommodation and activities.

💲 MONEY

FNB (S 33 35.323 E 022 12.327, cnr Church St & High St) has a bureau de change and ATMs. **Standard Bank** (S 33 35.322 E 022 12.240, Church St) is located just one block down from the FNB.

🌐 INTERNET

Internet & Art Gallery (S 33 35.354 E 022 12.194, 37 Baron van Reede St, ☎044-279-3007, 8am-6pm Mon-Fri, 9am-5pm Sat, R1/min), formerly the Cyber Ostrich, has six computers and a collection of art for sale. You can also connect a laptop.
Oudtshoorn Media & IT (S 33 35.479 E 022 12.054, Queen's Riverside Mall, 8am-5pm Mon-Fri, 8am-1pm Sat, R15/30mins) offers four private booths for Internet use and Skype phone calls. Laptop connectivity is available as well as printing and CD/DVD burning.
MD Computer Systems (S 33 34.816 E 022 12.294, 127 Baron van Reede St, ☎044-279-1769, 8:30am-5pm Mon-Fri, 9am-12pm Sat, R15/30mins) is a computer repair company that also has four public computers and wireless for laptops. Printing, faxing and copying services are also available.
Café Brulé (S 33 35.483 E 022 12.158, Queen's Hotel, 11 Baron van Reede St, ☎044-279-2412, www.queenshotel.co.za/cafebrule.php, 7am-5pm) at the Queen's Hotel offers free wifi while you sip your coffee, and serves delicious light meals and fresh baked bread everyday. Pick up a piece of their chocolate cake with the money you save on Internet.

🛒 SHOPPING

Klein Karoo Ostrich Co-op (S 33 35.805 E 022 11.329, 7:30am-5pm Mon-Fri, 9am-12pm Sat) is a high-end boutique on the edge of town that showcases ostrich leather and feather goods from a variety of local craftsmen. Decoupage eggs, fine apparel and accessories, jewelry and bins of colored feathers are all fair game at this tourist-oriented ostrich showcase.
Lugro Ostrich (S 33 35.904 E 022 12.340, 133 Langenhoven Rd, ☎044-272-7012, www.lugro-ostrich.co.za, 9am-5pm Mon-Fri, 9am-1pm Sat) hand stitches and sells high quality ostrich leather accessories.
Queen's Riverside Mall (S 33 35.533 E 022 11.983, 14 Voortrekker Rd) has a Pick 'n Pay, movie theaters, and a variety of smaller shops.
Art galleries and craft shops dot the length of Baron van Reede Street, particularly next to the Queen's Hotel.

⚲ SIGHTS & ACTIVITIES

Highgate Ostrich Show Farm (S 33 39.504 E 022 08.141, off R328, ☎044-272-7115, www.highgate.co.za, 7:30am-5pm, adult R66, child R32) has been in the ostrich-raising business for nearly 100 years. They offer 1.5-hour tours where you can see the nests, eggs (they are so tough that you can stand on them), incubators and baby chicks. After feeding the ostriches, you get to watch "ostrich jockeys" race a few birds down the racetrack. They make it look easy, but you can try riding one yourself and see how challenging it can be to keep your balance on these large awkward birds. Tours start roughly every 20 minutes. Head south out of town on the R328. After about 9 km, take a left turn onto an unnamed road with signs pointing you to Highgate and continue 2.5 km to the farm.
CP Nel Museum (S 33 35.526 E 022 12.141, 3 Baron van Reede St, ☎044-272-3676, 8am-5pm Mon-Fri, 9am-1pm Sat, adult R15, child R3) is Oudtshoorn's best-kept secret when it comes to in-town tourist attractions. This is a well-curated eclectic collection of antiquities that showcases both town history and the highlights of ostrich farming through the ages. Wander through turn-of-the-century replica stores, homes and a Jewish synagogue. Particularly dazzling is the display case of feather-accented high fashions sported by ostrich baronesses of yesteryear.
Cango Caves (S 33 23.607 E 022 12.833, R328, ☎044-272-7410, www.cangocaves.co.za) are a 2-km-long series of underground caverns, which have formed over the past 20 million years from rainwater dissolving limestone rock into intricate caverns and passageways. They offer a standard tour (1hr, adult R60, child R30) through the caves

WESTERN CAPE

starting every hour from 9am-4pm. The Adventure tour *(1.5hrs, adult R75, child R50)* departs hourly from 9:30am-3:30pm, but you must be "fit, lean and flexible" to go on the adventure tour, which involves crawling through small rock passages - unfit and overweight individuals are explicitly not allowed on the adventure tour as people have become stuck in the narrow passages. If you are unsure if you will physically fit through the narrow passages, there are life-size displays of the holes that you will have to crawl through. No cameras or bags are allowed on the adventure tour. Inside the main entrance building there are displays and a short video on the formation of the caves. There is also a restaurant at the facility that overlooks the surrounding mountains.

IMPACT **Cango Wildlife Ranch** *(S 33 33.991 E 022 12.771, Baron van Reede/R328,* ☎*044-272-5593, www.cango.co.za, 8am-4:30pm, adult R100, child R60)* is a one-of-a-kind wildlife experience in the Western Cape. While elsewhere you can dive with sharks, only here can you go croc cage diving, where you get up close and personal with 4-meter crocodiles in a large, heated pool.

The ranch is a vital facility for endangered species and the ranch believes that the best conservation education is interaction with the animals. Adults can hang out with tigers, lions, jaguars and cheetahs, kids will have a ball at

the Kiddies Farmyard where they can cuddle with bunnies, and the whole family can stroll through the snake park. You can wander around the ranch on your own, but to get the most out of your experience join a one-hour tour. 'Natural Encounters' or up-close time with the big cats costs extra and should be booked in advance to avoid last-minute disappointment. Proceeds from Natural Encounters go toward funding conservation and captive breeding programs.

Buffelsdrift Game Lodge *(S 33 31.741 E 022 15.132, off R328,* ☎*044-272-0106, www.buffelsdrift.com)* is just 7 km out of town en route the Cango Caves and offers a chance to view the Big 5. You can feed elephants (adult R180, child R90) or organize a nature walk (adult R440, child 220), but the biggest draw is their safaris. Horseback safaris (R430) let you ride while looking at the animals. The bush safaris (adult R440, child R220) led by an experienced guide are their signature trips. If you organize your safari in the late afternoon, you can have a sundowner in the wilderness. If nothing else, visit the lodge for a scenic sundowner on the deck, where you can watch the hippos in the lake below. You can also stay in one of their luxury tents (s R1,270-2,260, d R1,740-3,300, breakfast included, Internet, secure parking, swimming pool).

De Zeekoe Meerkat Tours ☎*044-272-6721, www.dezeekoe.co.za/meerkattours.htm, sunrise, R550, no children under 10)* offers you a unique glimpse into the lives of wild meerkats in their natural habitat. You will hardly be noticed or paid any attention as you observe

Oudtshoorn's April Arts Festival

Klein Karoo Nasionale Kunstefees (044-203-8600, **www.kknk.co.za**, April).

In 1994, prominent members of the Oudtshoorn community envisioned a festival that would celebrate Afrikaner heritage and modern culture. From this vision the Klein Karoo Nasionale Kunstefees (KKNK), or the Klein Karoo Arts Festival, was born. Every April, swarms of people from near and far find their way along scenic Meiringspoort Pass and descend upon Oudtshoorn for the largest Afrikaans cultural event of the year. Cutting-edge performances showcase the best in Afrikaans theatre, music and artistic expression. Acts range from classical to modern, avant-garde to mainstream, cabaret to opera and everything in between. Festival stalls overflow with colorful crafts, fine art, photography, clothing and other funky finds.

You don't need to know Afrikaans to have a good time. The festival is inclusive of a broad spectrum of people and attracts an eclectic multicultural crowd. The purpose is to enjoy the arts, culture and creative inspirations borne from the Afrikaans language and enjoy some of the most delicious ostrich dishes that Oudtshoorn's gourmet chefs have to offer.

The weeklong festival consumes the town every year in early April. Check out their website for listings of this year's acts and events.

the little creatures forage and play. The new meerkat guide, Devey, is an expert in his field and can explain the intricacies of meerkat social structures and behavior. His calm and friendly manner has earned the trust of local meerkats and residents alike. The day before the tour, Devey will set out in search of a meerkat gang and inform you where to meet the next morning. Tours leave at sunrise but are dependent on weather. Pictures are allowed with Devey's permission.

Joyride (*S 33 34.798 E 022 12.325*, 148 Baron van Reede St, ☎044-272-3436, www.backpackersparadise.net, R150-280) is run out of Backpackers Paradise and offers a variety of bike trips down the scenic Swartberg Pass and to local attractions such as the Cango Caves, ostrich farms, and the Wildlife Ranch. It's a great way to see all the area sights and enjoy the peaceful surroundings of the Little Karoo. For the less

outdoorsy, bus tours are also on offer. Entrance fees to attractions are not included in the price but are obtained at a discount. All trips leave promptly at 8:15am.

4x4 Botanical Tours (*S 33 35.335 E 022 11.687*, 192 Jan van Riebeeck Rd, ☎044-272-5114, www.attakwas.co.za, with overnight camping: R200/vehicle/day, no camping: R250) are available through Attakwas Cottage. The owner, Katot, can act as a guide for large groups on one-day and four-day treks through the botanical conservation area, but you must provide your own vehicle.

⊙SLEEPING

BUDGET

Backpacker's Paradise (*S 33 34.798 E 022 12.325*, 148 Baron van Reede St, ☎044-272-3436, www.backpackersparadise.net, camping R50/person, dm R100, d R270, bar, shuttle to Baz Bus, Internet, secure parking, swimming pool) is a large complex where transient travelers become part of an impromptu community. The social and easygoing atmosphere is fueled by the bar and daily ostrich braais. Staff is helpful with suggestions for things to do in town and also run Joyride bike and other tours from the hostel. All-you-can-eat ostrich egg breakfasts are available when in season.

Karoo Soul Travel Lodge & Cottages (*S 33 35.844 E 022 12.345*, 170 Langenhoven Rd, ☎044-272-0330, www.karoosoul.com, dm R100, d R300-380, Internet/wifi, secure parking, swimming pool) is a surprisingly polished backpackers and lodge just south of the center of town. You can relax in a hammock or go for a dip as you take in the Oudtshoorn's wide views. The quaint cottages are an excellent deal for your money and can accommodate additional people for an additional R100/person. The staff is personable and your stay comes with vouchers for discounts on local attractions.

Oasis Shanti (*S 33 35.411 E 022 12.781*, 3 Church St, ☎044-279-1163, www.oasisshanti.com, camping R50/person, dm R80, s R150, d R220-R250, Internet, secure parking, swimming pool) is a barebones but adequate backpackers. There is a large swimming pool and a small balcony with a braai and it's a good budget option if you are looking for a quiet place up the hill, but the place has not won any awards for ambience.

Attakwas Cottage (*S 33 35.335 E 022 11.708*,

192 Jan van Riebeeck Rd, ☎*044-272-5114,* www. attakwas.co.za, *camping R50/person, guesthouse R130-190/person, breakfast included, secure parking)* is a compound of simply furnished self-catering cottages that you can rent out in full or just by the bed. The guesthouse's owners pride themselves in providing rustic charm and high-quality beds and linens at reasonable rates. The estate also has campgrounds with toilets, hot showers and running water. The owner can act as a guide through the nearby botanical conservation area if you have your own vehicle.

MID-RANGE

Oakdene Guesthouse *(S 33 34.991 E 022 12.259, 99 Baron van Reede St,* ☎*044-272-3018 or* ☎*082-417-3871,* www.oakdene.co.za, *s R595-750, d R800-1,100, breakfast included, Internet, secure parking, swimming pool)* is a luxury six-room guesthouse with a polished yet rustic feel. The charming and spacious accommodations are complemented by antique brass furnishings, a beautiful wild garden and a private swimming pool. The kitchen and dining room will make you feel like you've stepped back in time into a beautiful old country home.

La Pension *(Ⓖ 33 35.244 E 022 11.619, 169 Church St,* ☎*044-279-2445,* www.lapension.co.za, *s R440-580, d R880-1,160, breakfast included, Internet/wifi, secure parking, swimming pool & sauna)* is an elegant and stately guesthouse that feels like home, except better. The family-run establishment boasts perfectly manicured lawns, snowy-white linens and comfortable common areas that you can unwind in with pleasure.

Gum Tree Lodge *(S 33 35.306 E 022 12.087, 139 Church St,* ☎*044-279-2528,* www.gumtreelodge. co.za, *s R295, d R590, breakfast included, Internet, secure parking, swimming pool)* is a country cottage just steps from downtown. The clean and well-appointed rooms open to a covered veranda fragrant with lavender. The pool and braai area overlook a small river and suspension bridge – a lovely view for a sundowner from the guesthouse's full bar.

Adley House *(S 33 35.280 E 022 11.685, 209 Jan van Riebeeck Rd,* ☎*044-272-4533,* www. adleyhouse.co.za, *s R750, d R1,200, breakfast included, Internet, secure parking, swimming pool)* is a Victorian manor house that feels caught in yesteryear. Elaborate furnishings and original architectural features like in-room fireplaces will thrill those who want a taste of what the glory days of the world's ostrich capital were like. For non-history buffs, the house may be a bit fussy.

Kleinplaas Holiday Resort *(S 33 34.562 E 022 12.314, cnr Baron van Reede St & North St,* ☎*044-272-5811,* www.kleinplaas.co.za, *camping R240, 4-person chalet R680-780, 6-person chalet R1,040, breakfast included, wifi, secure parking, swimming pool)* has 51 self-catering chalets and over 40 campsites for caravan or tent camping in a quiet, gated community. It's a good no-frills budget option for longer-term stays or groups, but don't come expecting to be wowed by the atmosphere. There are braai facilities and a nice swimming pool on the premises. All campsites are shaded by trees and have electrical outlets.

TOP END

Queen's Hotel *(S 33 35.483 E 022 12.158, 11 Baron van Reede St,* ☎*044-272-2101,* www. queenshotel.co.za, *R850-1,350, Internet/wifi, secure parking, swimming pool)* is a luxury hotel situated in a historic 1880s Oudtshoorn building in the heart of downtown. Its crisp and classic decor and spacious en suite rooms lend the hotel an old world charm, and its ivy-lined courtyard and swimming pool have an air of seclusion. You can dine at the attached Colony Restaurant and the popular Café Brulé is just downstairs.

Hlangana Lodge *(S 33 34.569 E 022 12.393, cnr Baron van Reede St & North St,* ☎*044-272-2299,* www.hlangana.co.za, *s R700-810 d R950-1,190, breakfast included, Internet/wifi, secure parking, swimming pool)* is a private resort lodge on more than a hectare of beautifully landscaped grounds. The staff prides itself in professionalism and attention to detail. Light-filled standard rooms open directly to the pool and superior rooms onto the lush garden. Standard rooms can accommodate children for an additional fee.

🍴 EATING

Bello Cibo *(S 33 34.816 E 022 12.319, 146 Baron van Reede St,* ☎*044-272-3245,* www. bellocibo.co.za, *11am-10pm Mon-Sat, mains R25-100)* is a charming restaurant patronized mostly by locals and known for its flavorful and fresh Mediterranean fare. Gourmet wood-fired pizza is perfectly crisped and their homemade specialties and pastas are divine.

Kalinka (*S 33 35.025 E 022 12.248*, *93 Baron van Reede St*, ☎*044-279-2596*, *www.kalinka.co.za*, *6pm-10pm, mains R80-150*) is a chic restaurant on the main drag. Dramatic floor-to-ceiling windows and a superbly blended menu of local meats and organic homegrown vegetables leave no question that this is one of Oudtshoorn's better establishments. But the gracious and easygoing staff prevent this rare treat of a restaurant from feeling pretentious.

Café Brulé (*S 33 35.483 E 022 12.158*, *Queen's Hotel, 11 Baron van Reede St*, ☎*044-279-2412*, *www.queenshotel.co.za/cafebrule.php*, *7am-5pm, mains R25-50*) is a cute café and bistro under the Queen's Hotel that serves breakfast and light lunches. It's the best place in town for coffee and its desserts are delightful.

Jemima's Restaurant (*S 33 35.087 E 022 12.262*, *94 Baron van Reede St*, ☎*044-272-0808*, *www.jemimas.com*, *11am-3pm & 6pm-9:30pm Mon-Fri, 6pm-9:30pm Sat-Sun, mains R80-150*) is a high-end restaurant that maintains an intimate and cozy feel. Light lunches, salads and tapas platters combine the best from the pasture, sea and earth. Dinner focuses more on fine meats, but there are also vegetarian, gluten-free and nut-free options. The seating near the back garden is best.

Nostalgie (*S 33 35.205 E 022 12.236*, *74 Baron van Reede St*, ☎*044-272-4085*, *info@ nostalgiebnb.com*, *6:30am-10pm Mon-Sat, mains R20-50*) offers delicious food at a great value. Every part of this restaurant has been given time and thought, from the vinyl LP place settings to the perfectly grilled vegetables. Try the beef lasagna or the old fashioned bobotie.

La Dolce Vita (*S 33 35.298 E 022 12.220*, *60 Baron van Reede St*, ☎*044-279-3269*, *www. thesweetlife.co.za*, *9am-2am Mon-Sat, mains R40-R80*) is a popular outdoor restaurant and bar with great prices on burgers, grills, pastas and light meals. It's the kind of place where you can come for some cheap eats and stay all night.

❶ DRINKING & ENTERTAINMENT

Upper Deck (*S 33 35.307 E 022 12.218*, *cnr*

Church St & Baron van Reede St, ☎*044-272-0072*, *11am-2am Mon-Thu, 7pm-4am Fri-Sat*) is a large upmarket lounge and after-hours club with plush leather sofas and an open dance floor that bumps until the wee hours of the morning. Sometimes even the poles are put to use.

Lemon'n Lime (*S 33 35.622 E 022 12.064*, *Vrede St*, ☎*044-272-7482*, *lemonnlime@telkomsa.net*, *8am-2am*), dubbed "lemon 'n slime" by some, is open all day for standard bar food, but gets packed with thirsty locals in the evening. It has a large open courtyard with picnic tables, multiple bars, fire pits, and pool and foosball tables. Live DJs pump up the rowdy night crowd nightly and the small outdoor stage occasionally hosts live music.

➋ TRANSPORTATION

❶ Bus

Long distance buses depart from the **Queen's Riverside Mall parking lot** (*S 33 35.491 E 022 12.029*, *Voortrekker St/R328*). **Intercape** (☎*086-128-7287*, *www.intercape.co.za*) has service to/ from Cape Town (R250) via Mossel Bay (R150) and Johannesburg (R520-R700) via Graaff-Reinet (R200-R400). **Greyhound** (☎*083-915-9000*, *www.greyhound.co.za*) has service to/from Johannesburg (R400). **City-to-City** (☎*086-158-9282* or ☎*011-774-3333*, *www.translux.co.za*) has service to/from Johannesburg (R370). To reach other costal destinations take the City-to-City bus to Mossel Bay (R90) and transfer to other buses.

Bus tickets can be purchased at the **Checkers** (*S 33 35.517 E 022 12.234*, *cnr High St & Voortrekker St*, ☎*044-203-5500*) or **The Travel Chain** (*S 33 35.468 E 022 12.179*, *24 Queens Mall, Baron van Reede St*, ☎*044-279-2946*, *8am-5pm Mon-Fri*).

Backpacker's Paradise arranges shuttles to/ from George (R100) for the **Baz Bus** (☎*021-439-2323*, *www.bazbus.com*).

❷ Minibus

Minibus Taxi Rank is located behind the Spar (*S 33 35.366 E 022 12.402*, *Unie St*), where you can catch local and long distance minibuses with daily departures to George (R40) and Cape Town (R200).

WESTERN CAPE

PRINCE ALBERT

GPS: S 33 13.421 E 022 01.790
pop. 1,500 | elevation 620 m/2,034 ft

Prince Albert is a small country enclave nestled beside the rocky Swartberg Mountains. The spectacularly steep Swartberg Pass, with its switchbacks supported by hand-packed stone walls, is a legendary challenge for Klein Karoo joy riders. Perhaps because this sleepy town has little to offer as far as mainstream attractions it is beloved by intrepid travelers searching for a break from the tourist mill. Church Street is lined with shops, galleries, antique stores and a handful of restaurants that make for a leisurely afternoon of poking around. But to truly appreciate the slow and contemplative beauty of Prince Albert, you'll have to unwind here for a few days.

❶ TOURIST INFORMATION

Tourist Information Office *(S 33 13.467 E 022 01.818, Church St,* 📞*023-541-1366,* www.patourism.co.za, *9am-5pm Mon-Fri, 9am-1pm Sat)* has a pamphlet on the history of the town, a free town map and a great staff that can provide you with a list of places to stay and eat in town.

⑨ MONEY

ABSA *(S 33 13.673 E 022 01.839, cnr Church St & Parsonage St)* has an ATM and is the only bank in town.

@ INTERNET

Lazy Lizard *(S 33 13.803 E 022 01.875, 9 Church St,* 📞*023-541-1379,* www.geocities.com/jpbol, *R1/min)* is a café, craft and specialty food shop with an Internet café in the upper loft.

⟳ SHOPPING

Prince of Africa *(S 33 13.390 E 022 01.767, Church St,* 📞*023-541-1016, 9am-5pm)* specializes in quality mohair products including colorful soft blankets, socks, scarves and hand knit sweaters. The shop is located beside the Swartberg Hotel.

✪ SIGHTS & ACTIVITIES

Fransie Pienaar Museum *(S 33 13.475 E 022 01.822, Church St,* 📞*023-541-1172, 9:30am-12:30pm & 2pm-5pm Mon-Fri, 9am-12:30pm Sat, 10:30am-12pm Sun, adult R10, child R2)* is a cultural history museum that depicts the history of the town with a variety of displays of typewriters, sewing machines, clothing, churches and military items.

African Relish *(S 33 13.578 E 022 01.850, 34*

Go To Hell

Die Hell (S 33 21.519 E 021 41.386), also known as Gamkaskloof, is a small mountain valley located in the Swartberg Mountains near Prince Albert. It was once home to a small community that lived in virtual isolation for 130 years. Access to the village was only possible on foot or by riding a horse. The community survived by producing dried fruit and honey, which was hauled out of the village on donkeys.

The first dirt road to the village was constructed in 1962 and with their newfound access and communication with the outside world the youth of the community began to leave. The last remaining permanent resident of the farming community left in 1991. Today it is a quiet village of mostly abandoned homes and fruit orchard relics from back in the day.

In 1998, Annetjie Joubert, who was born and raised in the community, returned and converted two simple farmhouses into guesthouses (S 33 21.519 E 021 41.386, *023-541-1107*, **www.diehel.com**, camping R130, farmhouse R180/person) one of the farm houses it fitted with solar lighting and gas cooking facilities (the village does not have electricity, while the other farmhouse only has candles and paraffin lamps). Annetjie also runs a small shop selling dried fruits, preserves and cold beer. Meals can be arranged with a little notice at the licensed bush restaurant.

The access road to Die Hell is located 18 km from Prince Albert and 53 km from Oudtshoornon off of the Swartberg Pass Road at S 33 20.372 E 022 02.274. The dirt road leading to the village is only 45 km but usually takes two and a half hours to drive each way and can be rather difficult after it rains. For an update on the road conditions call the Nature Conservation (*044-802-5310*).

Church St,☎023-541-1381, www.africanrelish.com) is a recently opened restaurant and recreational cooking school. It is a fresh addition to downtown Prince Albert with a beautiful open plan kitchen overlooking a garden and surrounded by olive trees. Take a single or multi-day course and learn about South African culinary culture and the finer details of local cuisine. They also offer all-inclusive packages that include lodging (see below) as well as area excursions such as hiking and walks through botanical gardens.

SLEEPING

Kuis House *(S 33 13.538 E 022 01.807, 51 Church St, ☎023-541-1675 or ☎082-549-3695, R175/person)* is an authentic old Prince Albert cottage that is now rented out as basic self-catering accommodation. The house has three bedrooms, a kitchen and a small living room. The huge backyard lawn and garden has a lounge area and a braai.

Saxe-Coburg Lodge *(S 33 13.353 E 022 01.789, 60 Church St, ☎023-541-1267, www.saxecoburg. co.za, s/d R600-800, breakfast included, swimming pool)* is a historic Victorian B&B with spacious freestanding rooms surrounded by a plush lawn and garden with a swimming pool. The rooms all have TV, AC and a private patio. The hosts are avid hikers and are more than willing to take you out for a day hike in the surrounding area.

Swartberg Hotel *(S 33 13.379 E 022 01.764, 77 Church St, ☎023-541-1332, www.swartberg.co.za, s R380-R450 d R625-740, breakfast included, swimming pool)* was built for travelers in 1864 and remains the town's only hotel. It has a handful of rooms in the main building and five thatched two-bedroom cottages set behind the hotel in the garden. The hotel is home to The Coffee Shop & Victoria Room restaurant (see below) as well as a Ladies Bar.

African Relish *(S 33 13.578 E 022 01.850, 34 Church St, ☎023-541-1381, www.africanrelish. com, s R660, d R1,000)* offers some of the smartest accommodation in town inside individual cottages within walking distance of Church Street. These historically significant houses have received a recent facelift to set off their rustic charm with modern style and convenience, including a full modern kitchen and a private back yard and garden to relax in.

EATING

Karoo Kombuis *(S 33 13.409 E 022 01.878, 18 Deurdrift St, ☎023-541-1110, 7pm-late Mon-Sat, mains R75-85)* serves homemade traditional South African food such as Karoo lamb, bobotie, and chicken pie with fresh veggies and dessert in their cozy and quaint dining room. They are not licensed so remember to bring your own wine.

IMPACT **African Relish** *(S 33 13.578 E 022 01.850, 34 Church St, ☎023-541-1381, www. africanrelish.com, 7pm-late Wed-Sat, mains R75-105)* is a recreational cooking school and restaurant specializing in regional Karoo dishes such as Karoo lamb, venison and ostrich, all with a focus on quality ingredients. If it is not from the organic garden behind the restaurant the produce and meat come from local farmers.

The Coffee Shop & Victoria Room *(S 33 13.379 E 022 01.764, 77 Church St, ☎023-541-1332)* are two of the Swartberg Hotel eateries overlooking Church St. The Coffee Shop (7:30am-6pm, mains R25-55) serves all-day breakfast, sandwiches and light meals. The Victoria Room (7pm-10pm, mains R75-95) is the more formal evening restaurant with indoor and outdoor seating and a small menu featuring traditional South African dishes such as oxtail potjie, bobotie and lamb.

Café Albert *(S 33 13.458 E 022 01.815, Church St, ☎023-5411-175, 9am-4pm Tue-Sat, 9am-2pm Sun, mains R25-40)* serves espresso and coffee as well as all-day farm fresh breakfasts and freshly baked pastries. The light meals are made from seasonal ingredients with an emphasis on Karoo flavors.

TRANSPORTATION

Public transport into and out of Prince Albert is limited.

The Shosholoza Meyl *(www.shosholozameyl. co.za)* has an economy Cape Town - Johannesburg Train that stops at the Prince Albert Station 45 km northwest of town. From there you can arrange transport to Prince Albert via **Onse Rus Guesthouse** *(☎023-541-1380, www.onserus.co.za)* regardless of whether you plan to stay there or not.

Van Rooyen Transport *(☎023-541-1907 or ☎072-337-3149)* is a taxi service that can assist in regional transport.

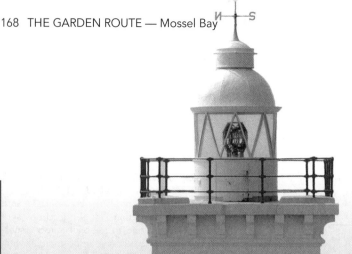

THE GARDEN ROUTE

The Garden Route is the most popular coastal driving route in the country. It stretches from Mossel Bay in the west to the surfing mecca of Jeffreys Bay just across the province line into the Eastern Cape. Dramatic cliffs, soft sand beaches and the verdant wilderness of the Langeberg Mountains frame the route as you drive. The region's beauty and natural wonders beg to be explored through adventure activities, water sports and hiking trails.

MOSSEL BAY

GPS: S 34 10.976 E 022 09.049
pop. 80,000 | elevation 31 m/102 ft

Mossel Bay has been a traveler hot spot for centuries – the first contact between Southern Africans and Europeans occurred on Santos Beach in 1488. But since the opening of a large oil refinery in the '80s, tourism in Mossel Bay has been down at the heels. If you ignore the industrial sprawl on the edges of the city, it's easy to appreciate the beautiful architecture, unhurried warmth and rough-and-tumble lifestyle that attracts fishermen, bikers and South African families alike. But the wide and sandy swaths of swimming and surfing beaches that pepper the coastline are reason enough to pay the town a visit.

❼ TOURIST INFORMATION

Tourist Information Office (*S 34 10.804 E 022 08.575, Market St,* ☎044-691-2202, *www.mosselbay.net, 8am-6pm Mon-Fri, 9am-5pm Sat-Sun*) has free city maps and plenty of brochures for area sights, activities and accommodation. But other than telling you where something is located, the three-person staff seems largely unhelpful.

❺ MONEY

FNB (*S 34 10.869 E 022 08.543, cnr Church St & Bland St*) has a branch with ATMs and a currency exchange.

ABSA Bank (*S 34 10.971 E 022 08.765, cnr Marsh St & Meyer St*) has a bureau de change and ATMs.

@INTERNET

Majestic Internet *(S 34 10.956 E 022 08.817, Spur Center, Marsh St, ☎044-691-3768, 8am-8pm Mon-Fri, 9am-6pm Sat, 10am-6pm Sun, R10/30mins)* has a dozen updated computers for Internet and gaming, and offers printing and copy services. Laptops are allowed to be connected.

PostNet *(S 34 10.867 E 022 08.578, Bayside Center, cnr Church St & Bland St, ☎044-690-7779, R15/15min)* has four computers and allows laptops to be connected.

⟳SHOPPING

Déjávu Vintage House *(S 34 10.974 E 022 09.184, 7 Marsh St, ☎082-415-9588, 8:30am-5pm Mon-Fri, 9am-1pm Sat)* is a great find for vintage and antique lovers, as the house has two floors of clothing and curios for sale. The attic is also used as an impromptu tearoom and ladies can rent hats and gowns of yesteryear so they may nibble on scones in proper form. The shop also screens old movies twice a month.

Mossel Bay Craft Art *(S 34 10.802 E 022 08.600, 3 Market St, ☎044-691-1761, 9am-5pm Mon-Fri, 9am-3pm Sat-Sun)* is a maze of studios for local artisans who sell their wares as they work. Don't mistake this for a glorified street market - these are serious artists who also teach classes on their crafts.

Bayside Center *(S 34 10.867 E 022 08.578, cnr Church St & Bland St)* is a collection of smaller shops with a Pick 'n Pay, Internet, and Nedbank and Standard Bank ATM.

Langeberg Mall *(S 34 11.049 E 022 06.918, Louis Fourie Rd/R102)* is 6 km from town and your best bet if you're looking for one-stop shopping.

✪SIGHTS & ACTIVITIES

Bartolomeu Dias Museum Complex *(S 34 10.809 E 022 08.497, Market St, ☎044-691-1067, www.diasmuseum.co.za, 9am-4:45pm Mon-Fri, 9am-3:45pm Sat-Sun, adult R10, child R3)* encompasses historical landmarks and museums in one complex overlooking the beach. It was here that Portuguese explorer Bartolomeu Dias first landed his ship in 1488 and subsequent travelers anchored to gather water and trade with the local Khoi population.

In the pleasant walk around the Ethno-botanical Garden and Braille Trail, you can learn about the historic and homeopathic uses of South African plants, or venture towards the beach to view replicas of early Mossel Bay cottages and visit the Mecca-facing graves of early Muslim residents. The Post Office Tree is the site where Portuguese captain Pedro de Ataide famously left a letter in a shoe under a large tree to document the ordeal he and his shipmates suffered during a bad storm on their voyage. A year later, the letter was found by another Portuguese sailor and thus the first post office in South Africa was born. Today the site itself it not much to write home about, but if you must, you can post your letter in the stone boot after you obtain the proper postage down the street.

Maritime Museum *(S 34 10.799 E 022 08.493, Bartolomeu Dias Museum Complex, Market St, ☎044-691-1067, www.diasmuseum.co.za, 9am-4:45pm Mon-Fri, 9am-3:45pm Sat-Sun, included in museum complex entrance)* is home to a full-size replica of the original Bartolomeu Dias caravel. The venture was jointly commissioned by the South African and Portuguese governments in 1988 to mark the 500-year anniversary of the first Portuguese landing. The replica was sailed down from Portugal, following Dias's original route, before being pulled ashore and into the heart of the museum. You can board the ship for an extra R15. While the ship's presence may steal the show, the exhibits of Portuguese early nautical technology and exploration are overflowing with information and the collection of early cartography is great for map nerds. Upstairs is also a motley collection of Mossel Bay antiques and artifacts.

Shell Museum & Aquarium *(S 34 10.846 E 022 08.412, Market St, ☎044-691-1067, www.diasmuseum.co.za, 9am-4:45pm Mon-Fri, 9am-3:45pm Sat-Sun, included in museum complex entrance)* is a lot of fun for kids. There are multiple aquariums and a touch tank that allows you to feel sea anemones or pick up hermit crabs. And all the information about shells that you never knew you didn't know.

Cape St Blaize Lighthouse *(S 34 11.162 E 022 09.369, Point Rd, ☎021-449-2400, May-Sept: 10am-3pm Mon-Fri, adult R16, child R8)* offers spectacular ocean views from the top of the 1864 lighthouse tower. Just below the lighthouse is Cape St Blaize Cave, a staggeringly large cavern that faces the sea. Indigenous people in the area have used the cave for 160,000 years.

WESTERN CAPE

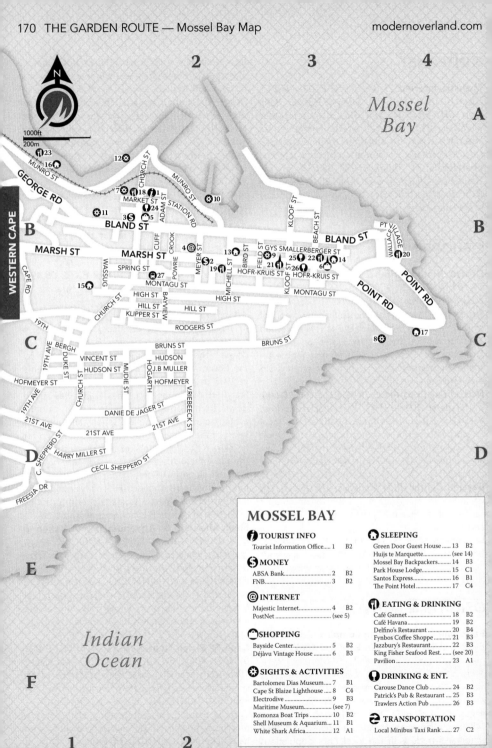

MOSSEL BAY

TOURIST INFO
Tourist Information Office..... 1   B2

MONEY
ABSA Bank.............................. 2   B2
FNB.. 3   B2

@ INTERNET
Majestic Internet..................... 4   B2
PostNet .... (see 5)

SHOPPING
Bayside Center......................... 5   B2
Déjàvu Vintage House 6   B3

SIGHTS & ACTIVITIES
Bartolomeu Dias Museum..... 7   B1
Cape St Blaize Lighthouse 8   C4
Electrodive 9   B3
Maritime Museum................ (see 7)
Romonza Boat Trips 10   B2
Shell Museum & Aquarium .. 11   B1
White Shark Africa................ 12   A1

SLEEPING
Green Door Guest House 13   B2
Huijs te Marquette................. (see 14)
Mossel Bay Backpackers........ 14   B3
Park House Lodge.................. 15   C1
Santos Express...................... 16   B1
The Point Hotel 17   C4

EATING & DRINKING
Café Gannet 18   B2
Café Havana.......................... 19   B2
Delfino's Restaurant 20   B4
Fynbos Coffee Shoppe 21   B3
Jazzbury's Restaurant............ 22   B3
King Fisher Seafood Rest. ...... (see 20)
Pavilion 23   A1

DRINKING & ENT.
Carouse Dance Club.............. 24   B2
Patrick's Pub & Restaurant ... 25   B3
Trawlers Action Pub 26   B3

TRANSPORTATION
Local Minibus Taxi Rank 27   C2

White Shark Africa (*S 34 10.730 E 022 08.500, Quay 4 Commercial Slipway, Mossel Bay Harbour,* ☏*044-691-3796* or ☏*082-455-2438, www.whitesharkafrica.com, R1,200*) offers cage diving trips that include a light breakfast before departing and 3-4hr on the boat along with lunch. The boat departs from the harbor and heads to Seal Island about 5 km away where sharks are common.

Romonza Boat Trips (*S 34 10.803 E 022 08.821, Mossel Bay Harbour,* ☏*044-690-3101, www. mosselbay.co.za/romonza/*) does trips to Seal Island (*year-round, 1hr, adult R110, child R55*), where you can see the colony of 3,000 Cape Fur seals and whale watching (*Jul-Oct, 1.5-3hr, adult R580, child R300*) with guaranteed sightings, and sunset cruises (*Nov-Apr, 2hr adult R190, child R90*).

Skydive Mossel Bay (*S 34 09.496 E 022 03.690, Mossel Bay Airfield,* ☏*082-824-8599* or ☏*086-510-4754, www.skydivemosselbay.com, R1,500*) offers tandem jumps at 10,000 feet above sea level, with a 40-second 250-km/hr fall followed by a gradual descent and beach landing.

Deepsea Adventures (☏*072-454-2988* or ☏*083-260-2222, www.deepseaadventures.co.za,* adult R550, child 450) is an established deep sea fishing operator that offers chartered day trips on their fully rigged, 8-meter boat.

Electrodive (*S 34 10.958 E 022 08.965, cnr Field St & Marsh St,* ☏*082-561-1259* or ☏*072-130-9489, www.electrodive.co.za*) offers shore-based and boat dive trips to the Santos shipwreck and to a number of area reefs. They also offer diving certification courses and gear and equipment sales and rental. Prices vary depending on the type of excursion you're interested in, so stop by their office to check out the array of trips they offer and get specific pricing.

✪SLEEPING

BUDGET

Mossel Bay Backpackers (*S 34 10.956 E 022 09.213, 1 Marsh St,* ☏*044-691-3182, www. mosselbayhostel.co.za,* camping R80/person, dm R120, d R320-380, bar, Baz Bus, Internet, swimming pool*) is a lively backpacker favorite with a large lounge room, full bar, braai and patio. The friendly staff will ensure that you enjoy your stay and can book all sorts of area activities, tours and extreme sports.

Santos Express (*S 34 10.711 E 022 08.237, Santos Beach,* ☏*044-691-1995, www.santosexpress.co.za,* dm R100, train compartment w/ shared bathroom R130-190/person, caboose R380-450, Baz Bus, breakfast included*) is exactly what you've been looking for if you've always dreamed of sleeping on a train on the beach. Though the standard compartments don't offer much elbowroom, you can hear the crashing of the waves through your window, roll out of your bunk in the morning and go for a swim. The caboose is a much more spacious, if expensive, option.

Park House Lodge (*S 34 11.037 E 022 08.416, 121 High St,* ☏*044-691-1937, www.parkhouselodge. co.za,* dm R130-150, guesthouse d R270-600, Baz Bus*) is a backpackers and guesthouse built inside the rambling manor house of a Victorian-era ostrich baron. Both dorms and various-sized en suite rooms are clean, tasteful and furnished with antiques. Outside, there's a plenitude of hammocks, cozy garden nooks and a fire pit where the owner's son conducts drum circles upon request.

De Bakke Caravan Park (*S 34 10.384 E 022 07.782, Santos Beach,* ☏*044-691-2915,* camping R110-320, chalets R350-850*) is the best of the city's caravan parks. Located right next to Santos Beach, it offers impressive views across the bay. Seafront camping is slightly more expensive than the back row, but well worth it. They also have one- to three-bedroom self-catering chalets.

MID-RANGE

B@Home Guest House (*S 34 10.457 E 022 07.724, 94 Long St,* ☏*044-690-5385,* or ☏*079-497-7679, www.b-at-home.co.za,* s R450-500 d R700-800, breakfast included, Internet*) is a pleasant five-bedroom guesthouse situated 150 m from the beach. Rooms are spacious with dark hardwood furniture and good-sized bathrooms, TV and AC. There is also a large living room with full window views of the ocean where you can whale watch from the couch.

Huijs te Marquette (*S 34 10.979 E 022 09.193, Marsh St,* ☏*044-691-3182, www.marquette. co.za,* s R480-530 d R780-960, breakfast included, Internet/wifi, secure parking, swimming pool*) is a small, clean and traditional guesthouse in the center of town. The common areas have small atriums where hummingbirds come to feed regularly and rooms surround a nicely landscaped pool area.

WESTERN CAPE

Green Door Guest House *(S 34 10.961 E 022 08.874, 49 Marsh St,* ☎*044-691-3820, greendoorbb@mweb.co.za, dm 100, s R325-425, d R400-600, breakfast included, parking)* is centrally located on Marsh Street in a heritage building with original architectural details. Guests can nab a sundowner from the cocktail bar to drink on the deck overlooking the ocean. Rooms span the spectrum of dorms to family-sized second-story rooms with private balconies overlooking the ocean.

TOP END

The Point Hotel *(S 34 11.140 E 022 09.492, Point Rd,* ☎*044-691-3512, www.pointhotel.co.za, breakfast included, Internet/wifi, secure parking, s R980, d R1,300)* is reputed to be one of the best hotels in town, presumably for the magnificent location rather than the standard rooms. Wake up to surf crashing just below your balcony and swim laps in the tide pools during high tide, but avoid the first-floor rooms, which open out to a view of the rock face instead of open sea. The Point also has an upscale restaurant and bar attached.

ⓘ EATING

Café Gannet *(S 34 10.803 E 022 08.543, cnr Church St & Market St,* ☎*044-691-1885, www.oldposttree.co.za/htm/ganetindex.htm, 7am-11pm, mains R80-180)* is without a doubt the best restaurant in town. Its chic decor, airy patio and harbor views are complemented well by the fusion of Mediterranean and African flavors on the menu. It's stylish without being stuffy and has deliciously creative food.

Jazzbury's Restaurant *(S 34 10.974 E 022 09.147, 11 Marsh St,* ☎*044-691-1923, 6pm-10pm, mains R80-120)* is a quaint restaurant with just over a dozen candlelit tables in three rooms. The food is a modern interpretation of traditional South African cuisine. Its house specialty, the ostrich fillet, is delicious and they have a decent selection of potjies and fresh seafood.

Delfino's Restaurant *(S 34 10.973 E 022 09.423, Point Village, Point Rd,* ☎*044-690-5247, www.delfinos.co.za, 7am-11pm, mains R25-60)* is standard Italian fare with beachside dining and an incredible view of the ocean. Walk right through the pizza joint's bland front dining room to the chic lounge area in the back, where sand-covered floors and weathered antiques add romance to the wads of cheddar cheese that most everything is covered with.

King Fisher Seafood Restaurant *(S 34 10.973 E 022 09.423, Point Village, Point Rd,* ☎*044-690-6390, www.thekingfisher.co.za, 11am-11pm, mains R45-100)* is upstairs from Delfino's and by the same owner. It serves up large portions of fish and shellfish and has a gorgeous view of the ocean from its wide balcony. You can often see seals playing in the waves below.

Fynbos Coffee Shoppe *(S 34 10.968 E 022 09.009, 31 Marsh St,* ☎*044-691-1366, 8:30am-5pm Mon-Fri, 9:30am-1pm Sat, mains R20-50)* serves breakfast and lunch in a beautiful Victorian sunroom and backyard. The fussy tearoom vibe isn't for everyone, but the simply prepared fare and baked goods are a welcome change from Mossel Bay's plethora of fried food. Next door is Fynbos Shoppe, a catacomb of gifts and home décor.

Pavilion *(S 34 10.599 E 022 08.158, Santos Beach,* ☎*044-690-4567, mains R50-140)* was closed for remodeling after a recent interior fire when we stopped by, but is a popular spot located right on the beach.

Café Havana *(S 34 10.973, E 022 08.845, 38 Marsh St,* ☎*044-690-4640, 11am-late, mains R70-*

110) is decked out with photos of Che and does a decent job of putting together the Havana look in Mossel Bay. The food won't inspire a revolution, but the solid variety of mostly fried appetizers, such as lemon garlic chicken strips or onion rings and steaks can solidly pave your stomach for a night of raucous drinking. Upstairs is the Havana cocktail bar, with a good selection of drinks and cheap flavored cigars.

❶ DRINKING & ENTERTAINMENT

Patrick's Pub & Restaurant (S 34 10.973 E 022 09.112, 17 Marsh St, ☎044-691-0077, www. patrickspub.co.za, 9am-2am) is an Irish pub that has been a Mossel Bay institution for many years. Recently under new management, this place pulls in a hearty festive crowd of locals, bikers and tourists most days of the week. They also are a restaurant that serves pub grub and steak.

Carouse Dance Club (S 34 10.822 E 022 08.575, cnr Church St & Market St, ☎044-690-5867, 8am-4am) is the only dance club in town and the place to be on Wednesday, Friday and Saturday nights. But catch it on any other night of the week and it may be just a few guys playing pool and more people in the DJ booth than on the dance floor.

Trawlers Action Pub (S 34 10.986 E 022 09.120, 18 Marsh St, ☎044-691-3073, 10am-2am) is not looking to impress but is a popular place with locals, bikers and "action seekers" passing through. You can watch Mossel Bay go by as you quench your thirst from picnic tables on the deck. They also serve some fried pub fare.

❷ TRANSPORTATION

❸ Bus

Long distances buses do not come all the way into Mossel Bay, but pick up and drop off passengers at the **Voorbaai Shell filling station** (S 34 08.682 E 022 06.061, R102) located about 8 km north of town. **City-to-City** (☎021-449-3333, www.translux. co.za), **Intercape** (☎0861-287-287, www.intercape. co.za), and **Greyhound** (☎021-505-6363, www. greyhound.co.za) will take you along the coast in either direction. From the filling station you can take one of the local taxis that are often parked outside or a minibus into town (R7).

❹ Minibus Taxi

Local Minibus Taxi Rank (S 34 10.997 E 022 08.606, cnr Zietsman St & Ernest Robertson St) is located behind the Shoprite on the corner of Marsh & Church Streets and taxis run around town and to nearby George. For all other destinations head to the **Long Distance Minibus Taxi Rank** (S 34 10.946 E 022 06.790, cnr R102 & Mossel St) located 3.5 km west of town where you can catch daily transport to Cape Town (R150), Oudtshoorn, and surrounding cities.

KNYSNA

GPS: S 34 02.297 E 023 02.739
pop. 52,000 | elevation 5 m/16 ft

The City of Knysna is strung across the coast of a shimmering lagoon, which feeds into the ocean through a rocky pass called The Heads. Knysna's commercial and touristic center is in its downtown area at the base of the lagoon, where visitors and locals can enjoy a host of great restaurants and poke around the arty shops of the town's hippie culture. The farther you get from the city center, the slower you'll find the pace - Thesen Island has a distinct upmarket beach town vibe, and Leisure Island, its woodsy counterpart, feels far from the urban bustle. There are many ways to explore the area's gorgeous waters, forests and wildlife, but you'll have to head out of town to appreciate Knysna's best aspects.

❺ TOURIST INFORMATION

Knysna Tourism (S 34 02.093 E 023 02.746, 40 Main Rd, ☎044-382-5510, www.visitknysna.co.za, 8am-5pm Mon-Fri, 8:30am-1pm Sat) has a friendly helpful staff that can give you brochures on just about everything in town.

❻ MONEY

ABSA (S 34 02.122 E 023 02.793, cnr of Main Rd and Grey St) and **FNB** (S 34 02.120 E 023 02.775, cnr of Main Rd & Grey St) are located across the street from each other and both have a bureau de change and ATMs. There is also a **Standard Bank** and **Travelex** in the **Knysna Mall** (S 34 02. 104 E 023 02.755, Main Rd). The Travelex offers traveler's checks, cash passport cards and money exchange. FNB has an ATM at the Waterfront.

@INTERNET

3@1 (S 34 02.105 E 023 02.744, Knysna Mall, Shop no. 2, Main Rd, ☎044-382-2057, www.3@1.co.az, 8am-6pm Mon-Fri, 9am-2pm Sat, 10am-1pm Sun, R10/15min) has seven updated computers with two connections for laptops. They offer all the usual services, including printing, CD/DVD burning and Skype headsets/webcams.

PostNet (S 34 02.065 E 023 02.667, Shop 16, Mulberry Gardens, Main St, ☎044-382-0616, knysna@postnet.co.az, 8am-5pm Mon-Fri, 8:30am-12:30pm Sat, R7/15min) offers the largest LCDs in town on six workstations. No laptop connectivity, however.

⊙SHOPPING

IMPACT **The Muse Factory** (S 34 02.166 E 023 03.044, Old Gaol Complex, Queen St, ☎044-382-0499, muse@cyberperk.co.za) is a local community arts project where women learn to bead and sell high-quality handmade and made-to-order jewelry.

Woodmill Lane (S 34 02.167 E 023 02.919, cnr Main Rd & Long St, www.woodmillane.co.za) is an upscale shopping center just before the entrance to Thesen Island.

Knysna Book Exchange (S 34 02.065 E 023 02.679, Pledge Square, ☎044-382-2480) is a small second-floor bookshop where you can upgrade your reads before you head to a quiet spot near the lagoon.

IMPACT **Knysna African Arts & Craft Market** (S 34 02.787 E 023 04.224, cnr George Rex Dr & Vigilance Dr, ☎083-595-7239, 9am-3pm Sat-Sun) is a growing market of locally made goods, including wire art, sculptures and kitchen items. The market is a community development project of Knysna Municipality.

⊛SIGHTS & ACTIVITIES

Featherbed Nature Reserve cruises and nature walks with **Featherbed Company** (S 34

Knysna Festivals

Knysna loves its festivals. During the popular *Knysna Oyster Festival* in July, the city fills up for a marathon and two weeks of arts, crafts and oyster-eating contests (**www.oysterfestival.co.za**). The *Pink Loerie Mardi Gras* hits Knysna between late April and early May, an outrageous weeklong gay carnival that claims to be Africa's biggest, boldest and most colorful (**www.pinkloerie.com**). Late September's *Gastronomica Festival* is a haute spot for gourmets and gourmands to unabashedly stuff their faces (**www.gastronomicakny.co.za**).

02.343 E 023 02.457, Waterfront Dr, ☎044-382-1693, www.featherbed.co.za) will take you for a trip across the lagoon and provide a buffet lunch (4hr, depart 10am & 11:30am, adult R395, child R180). The company has a small fleet including a paddleboat and catamaran, so visit the website to find a ferry that suits your fancy.

Knysna Charters (S 34 02.919 E 023 02.840, Shop 22, Safron St, Thesen Island, ☎082-892-0469, www.knysnacharters.com) also offers lagoon tours, including one to oyster beds to see how oysters are cultivated (1.5hr, R330).

Mitchell's Knysna Brewery (S 34 02.721 E 023 04.393, Arend St, Knysna Industria, ☎044-382-4685, www.mitchellsknysnabrewery.com, tours: 10:30am & 3pm Mon-Fri, R50, tastings: 8:30am-4:30pm Mon-Fri, 9:30am-12:30pm Sat, R20) is the original location of the brewery established in 1983 by Lex Mitchell. Stop in for a tasting and ask to try out their specialty mixes, which include the "Mother-in-Law," a mix of Bosuns Bitter and Raven Stout, or the "Milkwood Mild" that combines Forester's Draught and Bosuns Bitter. After your tasting, check out the Frost Brothers classic car showroom next door to see an assortment of vintage MGs, Triumphs, and Jaguars available for sale and export as your perfect souvenir from South Africa.

Knysna Museum (S 34 02.243 E 023 03.054, Queen St, ☎044-302-6320, 9:30am-4:30pm Mon-Fri, 9:30am-12:30pm Sat, donation) is a small multi-building complex of historic buildings that are part archive and part hodge-podge historical recreation. The site includes Millwood House, an original home from the nearby gold-mining village of Millwood, which is now a ghost town.

KNYSNA

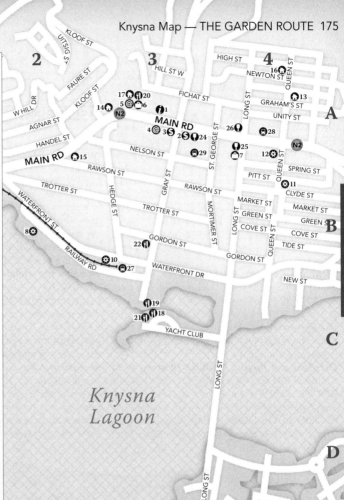

IMPACT **Knysna Elephant Park** (*S 34 02.274 E 023 16.169, N2,* 044-532-7732, *www.knysna elephantpark.co.za, 8:30am-5pm, excursions start from adult R682, child R330*) is a rehabilitation center and home to a family of orphaned elephants that will let you ride and walk with them. Sunrise and sunset safaris are also available.

Hippo Dive Campus (082-923-0267, *www. hippodivecampus.co.za, R800 gear not included*) will teach you the basics of scuba diving and take you out on a half-day diving trip into the lagoon.

Knysna Forest Tours (*S 34 02.393 E 023 02.593, Remembrance Ave,* 044-382-6130, *www. knysnaforesttours.co.za*) can arrange guided mountain bike tours, kitesurfing and canoeing trips.

Southern Comfort Western Horse Ranch (*S 34 01.507 E 023 13.628, Fisanthoek exit from N2,* 044-532-7885, *www.schranch.co.za, depart 8:30am & 2:30pm daily, 1hr R170/person, 1.5hr R240/person, 2hr 280/person*) is 17 km from both Plettenberg Bay and Knysna and offers twice-daily horse rides through the Knysna Forest.

Old Gaol and Knysna Maritime Museum (*S 34 02.166 E 023 03.044, cnr Main St & Queen St,* 044-302-6320, *9:30am-4:30pm Mon-Fri, 9:30am-1pm Sat, free*) is housed in the town's old jail but has little to see besides a few walls dedicated to the town's seafaring history, jailed life, local elephants, and (inexplicably) the sinking of the Titanic.

⚙ SLEEPING

BUDGET
Highfields Backpackers (*S 34 02.063 E 023 03.087, 2 Graham St,* 044-382-6266, *www. highfieldsbackpackers.co.za, dm R100, d R270, bar, Baz Bus, Internet, swimming pool*) occupies a rambling historic house just above the center of town. This is a backpackers with a lot of love put into the clean and well-finished rooms. Cozy details like an original wood burning fireplace in the common area make it easy to settle in.

Woodbourne Holiday Resort (*S 34 04.277 E 023 04.153, George Rex Dr,* 044-384-0316, *gardenroute.co.za/Woodbourne, camping: R240-320 first 2 people, R35-45/additional person, chalets: R390-470 first 2 people, R90-110/additional person, parking, swimming pool*) is a sweeping farmstead of chalets and campgrounds that employees will claim once belonged to George Rex, rumored to be the illegitimate son of King George III. Self-catering chalets for two or four people are well outfitted, and campgrounds have access to hot water showers, electricity, bathrooms and spigots. Note that prices are significantly higher in December and January.

House of Judah Rastafarians in Khayalethu South Township

The House of Judah is South Africa's largest Rastafarian community - with about 80 Niyabinghi Rastafarians. The community is located in Judah Square just outside of the city of Knysna in the Khayalethu South Township. Visitors are welcome to come for the day or spend the night and check out the community, learn about their culture, the Rastafarian way of life, play music and dance and just chill out.

The House of Judah has a binghi, or holy day, on the first Saturday of the month and it is held at Judah Square every other month. If you are fortunate enough to visit when they are hosting the binghi, you can take part in the religious ceremony. It involves chants to Ethiopian Emperor Haile Selassie, singing, dancing, smoking, beating drums, and sermons extolling the virtues of Rastafarianism.

Accommodation is available within the community at *Sister Keri's B&B* (083-502-2229, R120/person) in a separate house just next to her home. It has two bunk beds, a toilet and a sink. Vegetarian meals can be prepared upon request.

If you're interested in visiting the community, call one of the following community members and they can come into Knysna and pick you up or make plans for meeting you at Judah Square.

Brother Maxi (084-205-8305)   *Brother Zebulon* (076-649-1034)
Sister Keri (083-502-2229)   *Brother Paul* (073-117-6103)

WESTERN CAPE

Knysna Backpackers (*S 34 02.012 E 023 03.066*, 42 Queen St, 044-382-2554, *www.knysnabackpackers.co.za*, dm R110, s R280, d R300-380, breakfast included, Baz Bus, parking) is in a Victorian house in the hills behind downtown Knysna. It's easy to love for its short distance from major in-town attractions and friendly staff.

Island Vibe (*S 34 02.169 E 023 02.517*, 67 Main Rd, 044-382-1728, *www.islandvibe.co.za*, dm R100-110, d R320-350, t R420-460, bar, Baz Bus, Internet, secure parking, splash pool) is a chill backpackers near the lagoon within walking distance of downtown Knysna. Like its big sister in Jeffreys Bay, this Island Vibe is built around its funky common areas, which makes for a great party scene. The dorm is so close to the pool and bar that you can hold a conversation from your bunk bed, so if you have an early start the next day, consider a double room.

MID-RANGE

Azure house (*S 34 02.067 E 023 02.001*, 65 Circular Dr, 044-382-1221, *www.azurehouse.com*, s R450, d R580-750, Dec-Feb: s/d R850, breakfast included, Internet, secure parking, swimming pool) is a whitewashed and beachy guesthouse with a breathtaking view of the lagoon. Each room is spacious and fresh, has facilities for self-catering and guests take breakfast on their individual porches.

Inyathi Guest Lodge (*S 34 02.065 E 023 02.620*, 52 Main Rd, 044-382-7768, *www.inyathiguestlodge.co.za*, s R380, d R760, breakfast included, wifi, secure parking) is a series of earthy African-themed cottages built into a former craft village. Each room is furnished with reclaimed architectural accents, which makes for an exotic and eclectic experience, just steps from the city center. Ask for Room #6, which has the best outdoor area and layout.

Cunningham's Island Guest House (*S 34 04.052 E 023 03.811*, 3 Kingsway, Leisure Isle, 044-384-1319, *www.islandhouse.co.za*, s/d R695-795, breakfast included, wifi, secure parking, swimming pool) is a friendly B&B on the low-key and woodsy Leisure Island. A large porch overlooks the pool, and the house is so cozy that you'll feel like you're stealing time in a well-off friend's vacation home.

Wayside Inn (*S 34 02.058 E 023 02.669*, Pledge Square, 48 Main Rd, 044-382-6011, *www.waysideinn.co.za*, s R400, d R600, breakfast included, secure parking) is a simple, colonial style B&B that provides basic luxuries and convenience at a decent price. Rooms are within walking distance to all Knysna's in-town attractions and there are two great restaurants in the same square.

TOP END

IMPACT The Phantom Forest (*S 34 01.383 E 022 59.150*, Phantom Forest, 044-386-0046, *www.phantomforest.com*, s R1,900-2,200, d R2,800-3,400, breakfast included, parking, swimming

WESTERN CAPE

pool) is a luxurious and sustainable hideaway in the Phantom Forest Eco Reserve. The beautifully outfitted open-plan suites are built in and around the trees and overlook the lush canopy top. Guests here can feel close to nature without losing any of civilization's perks as they swim in the fern lined pool, dine at one of the hotel's two restaurants, or receive an organic spa treatment.

Villa Afrikana (S 34 02.026 E 023 01.903, 13 Watsonia Dr, Paradise, ☎044-382-4989, www.villaafrikana.com, s R850-950, d R1,700-1,800, breakfast included, wifi, secure parking, swimming pool) is a 5-star, ultramodern guesthouse on Paradise Hill overlooking the lagoon. The striking white geometric mansion boasts some of the most spacious suites in town, with fireplaces, private balconies and original artwork.

Under Milk Wood (S 34 04.534 E 023 03.747, 13 George Rex Dr, ☎044-384-0745, www.milkwood.co.za, s/d R940-3,675, wifi, secure parking) is a collection of 16 deluxe self-catering log cabins for two or four people with swimming access to the water and dramatic views of the Heads. Though just minutes from town, lush foliage and large private decks make this spot feel like a secret enclave all your own. If you're up for adventure, borrow a canoe to explore the lagoon.

Lightleys Holiday Houseboats (S 34 01.244 E 022 59.142, Phantom Pass Rd, ☎044-386-0007, www.houseboats.co.za, 2-person boat R1,025-1,375, 4-person boat R1,395-1,750, 6-person boat R1,495-2,075) has the best waterfront rooms you'll find in Knysna in their self-drive charters. Two to six-person boats are fully self-catering and an easy and beautiful way to visit Knysna's most scenic points along the water.

🍴EATING

Sirocco (S 34 02.949 E 023 02.869, Thesen Harbour Town, ☎044-382-4874, www.sirocco.co.za, 12pm-5pm, 6pm-10pm, bar open late, mains R90-400) is one of the best seafood restaurants in the city. Airy and elegant, with sweeping views of the Heads, it's no wonder that Sirocco is a favored spot of well-to-do weekenders.

Catembe Bar (S 34 02.065 E 023 02.679, Pledge Square, Main Rd, ☎044-382-6641, 5pm-10pm, bar 2am, mains R40-70) is a new Mozambican joint with flavorful food, strong drinks and gregarious owners. Start off with a dharwa (similar to a

caipirinha, with a big stick to beat the lime with). Though the place strives to be a main libation destination in town, the food is just too good to not be the main attraction - spicy fresh offerings like Piri Piri chicken are a great value and the menu changes daily on the wall-sized blackboard.

Cornuti Knysna (S 34 04.619 E 023 03.636, George Rex Dr, East Head, ☎044-384-0408, cornutiknysna@telkomsa.net, 12pm-10pm, mains R50-130) is the last stand between civilization and the Heads, a narrow pass the British army once described as the most dangerous in the world. Enjoy a gourmet pizza or a sundowner at this sophisticated restaurant, and lounge while rooting for boats trying to navigate the rough waters.

Mon Petit Pain (S 34 02.352 E 023 02.719, cnr Gray St & Gordon St, ☎044-302-5767, 7:30am-3pm Mon-Fri, 7:30am-1pm Sat, mains R20-50) is the smaller sister bakery to the perpetually popular Il de Pain on Thesen Island. This casual café near the Quays serves up delicious light meals and baked goods in a space that feels as fresh as its bread. Snag a spot on the patio for the best people watching.

The Drydock Food Company (S 34 02.505 E 023 02.695, Knysna Quays, 12pm-10pm Mon-Fri, mains R80-140) has the best view in downtown Knysna. Situated at the tip of the Quays, it offers a variety of seafood as wide as its panorama of the lagoon. Sit outside and enjoy your meal while watching boats make their way in and out of the harbor.

Caffe Mario (S 34 02.476 E 023 02.703, Shop No 7, Waterfront Dr, ☎044-382-7250, caffemario@mweb.co.za, 7am-11pm, mains R20-80) possesses the mythic restaurant trifecta – great food, great prices, great location. Enjoy an array of Italian specialties or brunch delights from the banks of the narrow canal off the waterfront.

34 South (S 34 02.495 E 023 02.732, Knysna Quays, Waterfront Drive, ☎044-382-7331, www.34-south.com, 9am-10pm, mains R60-120) is one of the most popular restaurants on the Quays for its extensive seafood menu and perfect positioning along the canal leading into the Knysna Lagoon. The restaurant also has a deli, sushi counter and boutique.

Cruise Café (S 34 02.343 E 023 02.457, Remembrance Ln, ☎044-382-1693, www.featherbed.co.za, 8am-11pm, mains R80-170) has one of the most beautiful seaside views in downtown and the short distance from the quays make for a much more mellow dining experience. The upscale café serves contemporary meals with an emphasis on seafood. This is also the dock location of Featherbed Ferry Cruises and you can watch their paddleboat launch from the large terrace.

DRINKING & ENTERTAINMENT

Upstairs on Main (*S 34 02.146 E 023 02.933, Main Rd, 4pm-2am Mon-Sat*) is an eclectic, artistic lounge that brings in the expat and backpacker crowd. You could easily be in a downtown loft in a major city as you settle in with a drink inside or on the balcony, but this bar's crowd still has a beach town vibe. **Swing Café** (*S 34 02.130 E 023 02.822, Templeman Square, Main Rd,* 044-382-1771, *9am-2am Tue-Sat, 1pm-12am Sun*) is a bumping local haunt, especially on weekends. Order a round at their shooter bar or fill up on one of their burgers on the large second story patio (mains R25-55). Bands play here on Wednesday, Friday and Saturday; expect a cover (R20 and up) on nights with live music. **Zanzibar Lounge** (*S 34 02.116 E 023 02.942, Main Rd,* 044-382-0386, *8:30pm-2am Wed-Sat, R10 cover on Fri*) is an airy dance club with a crowd as mixed as its music. The sleek decor keeps this bar from taking on a seedy late-night dance floor vibe when people start breaking it down after midnight.

TRANSPORTATION

Bus

Long distance buses stop at **Knysna Toyota** (*S 34 02.144 E 023 03.012, Main Rd*), including **Greyhound** (083-915-9000, *www.greyhound. co.za*) **Intercape** (0861-287-287, *www.intercape. co.za*), and **TransLux** (021-449-3333, *www. translux.co.za*).
Knysna Station (*S 34 02.417 E 023 02.634, Station Building, Memorial Dr,* 044-382-1971) is the old train station located at the Quays. **TransLux** (021-449-3333, *www.translux.co.za*) and **Intercape** (0861-287-287, *www.intercape. co.za*) buses also stop there. Tickets for **Intercape** and **TransLux** can be purchased at the station, at **Shoprite** (*S 34 02.148 E 023 02.794, cnr Main Rd & Gray St*) or at the Checkers one block down.

Minibus

Minibus Taxi Rank (*S 34 02.175 E 023 02.816, Nelson St*) is in front of the main entrance to the Shoprite and offers frequent departures to many destinations including George (*30min, R40*) and Plettenberg Bay (*30min, R20*).

PLETTENBERG BAY

GPS: S 34 03.381 E 023 22.322
pop. 35,000 | elevation 86 m/282 ft

Plettenberg Bay is an exquisite coastal resort town that draws droves of visitors for its beaches, natural wonders and kick-back elegance. Though the town has its share of surfers and beach bunnies, a stroll down Main Street is enough to see that Plett attracts a ritzier crowd. To love it here, you'll have to stray from downtown and explore the lagoon, strand and indigenous forests that inspired early Portuguese explorers to dub the area "Bahia Formosa" or "beautiful bay."

TOURIST INFORMATION

Plett Tourism (*Melville's Corner, Main St,* 044-533-4065, *www.plettenbergbay.co.za*, *8.30am-5pm Mon-Fri, Apr-Oct: additional 9am-1pm Sat*) is straightforward and helpful, with brochures on everything in town.

MONEY

Standard Bank (*S 34 03.361 E 023 22.296, Melville's Corner, cnr Main St & Marine Way*) is located on the upper level of the Melville's Corner Shopping Center. It offers several ATMs and a bureau de change. FNB has an ATM there as well.

INTERNET

Plett Computers (*S 34 03.361 E 023 22.296, Melville's Corner, Main St,* 044-533-6828, *8:30am-5pm Mon-Thu, 8:30am-4pm Fri, 9am-12pm Sat, R10/12min*) has four updated computers and laptop connectivity. Printing, CD/DVD burning, and webcams are also available.
PostNet (*S 34 03.361 E 023 22.296, Melville's*

WESTERN CAPE

WESTERN CAPE

PLETTENBERG BAY

🛈 TOURIST INFO
Plett Tourism 1 D3

💲 MONEY
Standard Bank .... (see 1)

@ INTERNET
Plett Computers .... (see 1)
PostNet .... (see 1)

🛍 SHOPPING
Market Square 2 B3
Old Nick Village 3 A4

✲ SIGHTS & ACTIVITIES
Ocean Blue Adventures 4 D4

🛌 SLEEPING
Albergo for Backpackers 5 C3
Amakaya Backpackers 6 D3
Anlin Beach House 7 F4
Bay Lodge 8 D4
Beacon Lodge 9 B3
Cornerway House 10 F3
Nothando Backpackers 11 D3
The Plettenberg 12 C4
Sandbanks Luxury Retreat ... 13 C3
10 Swallow's Nest 14 B3

🍴 EATING & DRINKING
Kappa Cheeno .... (see 1)
LM in Plett 15 D4
The Lookout Deck 16 C4
The Med Seafood Bistro 17 C3
Miguel's Restaurant & Cocktail
Terrace .... (see 1)
Plett Market on Main 18 D4

🍷 DRINKING & ENT.
Cubar 19 D4
Flashbacks 20 D3

⇄ TRANSPORTATION
Minibus Taxi Rank 21 D3
Shell Ultra City Garage 22 C2

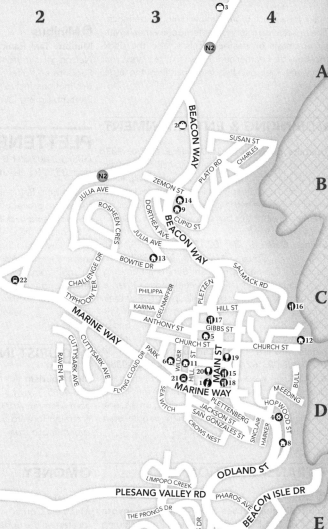

Cruise The Crags

The Crags (S 33 57.399 E 023 28.341, off the N2) are a tourist enclave just outside of Plettenberg Bay with several wildlife and adventure parks that make up the majority of things to see in the area surrounding town. You can easily spend a day or more exploring the area, but keep in mind that these attractions are geared toward tourists, are very child-friendly and can border on tacky at times. That said, here are a few spots worth checking out. For a complete guide to the Crags, head over to Plett Tourism.

Elephant Sanctuary (S 33 57.649 E 023 28.926, The Crags, 044-534-8145, **www.elephantsanctuary.co.za**, 8am-5pm) is a family-friendly elephant reserve where people of all ages can feed, groom (75min, adult R350, child R175), walk "trunk-in-hand" (1hr, adult R295, child R150) and ride elephants (75min, adult R670, child R350, includes walk).

Monkeyland (S 33 57.890 E 023 28.969, The Crags, 044-534-8906, **www.monkeyland.co.za**, 8am-5pm) is a forest sanctuary home to 16 species of primates. It's free to enter Monkeyland but in order to go beyond the viewing deck you must hire a ranger for an hour-long monkey safari (adult R115-125, child R57.50-62.50). As part of the tour, you cross a 118-meter suspension bridge above the forest canopy. *Birds of Eden* (**www.birdsofeden.co.za**, adult R116-125, child R57.50-62.50), just next door to Monkeyland, allows you to bird watch inside a 2-hectare dome that spans over a gorge of indigenous forest. There is a similar but shorter canopy walk inside. Guests can wander Birds of Eden freely, but guided tours are available for R100. If you plan to visit both, you'll save money by purchasing a combo entrance ticket (adult R184-200, child R92-100).

IMPACT *Tenikwa Wildlife Awareness Center* (S 33 57.900 E 023 29.417, Forest Hall Rd, The Crags, 044-534-8170, **www.tenikwa.co.za**) is a wildcat rehabilitation center that offers incredible animal encounters to fund their work. One-hour guided tours throughout the day (every 30min between 9am-4:30pm, adult R150, child R70) let visitors get up close to cheetah, leopard and other endangered wildlife. Book ahead for sunrise and sunset cheetah walks to lead the cats through the fynbos and forest (adult R350, child R250).

Corner, Main St, ☎044-533-6201, 8:30am-5pm Mon-Fri, 9am-1pm Sat, R10/15min) has two computers available, but no hookups for laptops.

⊙ SHOPPING

Plettenberg's downtown area, Main Street, is lined with boutiques and surfing stores.
Market Square (S 34 02.535 E 023 22.233, Beacon Way) is a large shopping mall on the edge of town. It has a Pick 'n Pay, Woolworths and a cinema.
Old Nick Village (S 34 02.068 E 023 22.342, N2, ☎044-533-1395, www.oldnickvillage.co.za, shops 9am-5pm, workshops and studios 9am-5pm Mon-Fri) has shops, galleries and craft and art workshops inside a historic cape settlement among indigenous gardens.

✪ SIGHTS & ACTIVITIES

IMPACT **Ocean Blue Adventures** (S 34 03.471 E 023 22.601, 5 Hopwood St, ☎044-533-5083, www.oceanadventures.co.za) offers year-round whale watching and marine life tours (2hr, adult R650, child R350), sea kayaking (2hr, R300) and Qolweni township walking tours (1hr, R150). The company is also carbon neutral and leading a community-wide effort to offset carbon emissions in the area. Horseback riding is available through **Equitrailing** (☎044-533-0599, ride@pletthorsetrails.co.za), which offers half-day trail rides (R400/person), moonlight and champagne breakfast trail rides (R500/person) and shorter rides (R150/person).
Southern Comfort Western Horse Ranch (S 34 01.507 E 023 13.628, Fisanthoek exit off the N2, ☎044-532-7885, www.schranch.co.za, 1hr R170/person, 1.5hr R240/person, 2hr 280/person, depart 8:30am & 2:30pm daily) is 17 km from both Plettenberg Bay and Knysna and offers twice-daily horse rides through the Knysna Forest.
Plettenberg Bay Game Reserve (S 33 56.753 E 023 21.028, off the R340, ☎044-535-0000, www.plettgamereserve.com) has 2,000 hectares just 15 minutes outside of Plettenberg Bay. The reserve offers game drives (2hr, adult R345, child R95) and horse safaris (2hr, adult R345, child R345) where you can try to spot lions, giraffe, hippo and buffalo. There is also a lodge and restaurant in the reserve.
IMPACT **Sky Dive Plettenberg Bay** (S 34 05.288

E 023 19.527, Plettenberg Airport, ☎*082-905-7440, www.skydiveplett.com, tandem jump R1,600)* offers first-timers the chance to jump with an instructor above Plett's gorgeous coastlines. The company has been certified to be carbon neutral.

Learn 2 Surf (☎*083-414-0567, www.learn2surf. co.za)* offers two-hour surfing lessons on Robberg Beach. Private lessons are R450 and group lessons of up to four people are R300. The school also rents out surf gear.

⊙SLEEPING

BUDGET
Nothando Backpackers *(S 34 03.293 E 023 22.184, 5 Wilder St,* ☎*044-533-0220, www. nothando.co.za, dm R105-125, d R300-550, bar, Baz Bus, Internet, secure parking)* spoils weary budget travelers with its comfortable beds and deliciously clean linens. The owner's homey touches combined with the fact that Nothando is only a few blocks from Plett's main strip makes this a surefire bet for those who want beach time combined with a restful night's sleep.

IMPACT **Albergo for Backpackers** *(S 34 03.220 E 023 22.281, 6 & 8 Church St,* ☎*044-533-4434, www.albergo.co.za, camping R70, dm R120, d R340-400, bar, Baz Bus, Internet/wifi, secure parking)* is the closest hostel you can get to both the beach and town, which makes it a favorite for the surfer contingent. The place's mellow surfer vibe is reinforced with worn-in, breezy rooms, board rentals and a plentitude of hammocks, but only the dorms have ocean views. Albergo is also a carbon-neutral business, and regularly plants trees to offset its carbon emissions.

Amakaya Backpackers *(S 34 03.309 E 023 22.143, 1 Park Lane,* ☎*044-533-4010 or* ☎*072-290-0821, www.amakaya.co.za, dm R110-150, d R350, bar, Baz Bus, Internet, secure parking, swimming pool)* is a modern take on the beach bum's shack – travelers roam barefoot through the bright and airy rooms or lounge at the rooftop bar and pool. The hostel has onsite surfboard and wetsuit rentals for R150.

MID-RANGE
Cornerway House *(S 34 04.285 E 023 22.059, 61 Longships Dr,* ☎*044-533-3190, www. cornerwayhouse.co.za, s R275-460, d R550-920, breakfast included, Internet/wifi, secure parking,*

swimming pool) is a quiet cottage in the suburbs about 15 minutes drive outside of town. The guesthouse and newly built self-catering rooms are cozy and plush, and the neat grounds feel straight out of the English countryside.

Swallow's Nest *(S 34 02.738 E 023 22.151, 61 Beacon Way,* ☎*044-533-4059, www.swallowsnest. co.za, breakfast included, wifi, secure parking, swimming pool)* is a retro beach home that's been nicely renovated. The 4-star guesthouse abuts the lagoon and is just a short walk from the beach.

Beacon Lodge *(S 34 02.760 E 023 22.134, 57 Beacon Way,* ☎*044-533-2614, www.beaconlodge. co.za, s R200-300, d R400-600, breakfast included, parking)* is a clean neat guesthouse with just two rooms. A great pick for its value, tranquility and proximity to the beach.

Anlin Beach House *(S 34 04.096 E 023 22.370, 33 Roche Bonne Ave,* ☎*044-533-3694, www. anlinbeachhouse.co.za, s R420-730, d R840-1,460, wifi, secure parking)* is a sleek collection of self-catering rooms, just a short walk from the beach in Plett's nearby suburbs. A cool palate of glass, steel and slate keep even the mountain-facing rooms feeling fresh, but Anlin's real attraction is the expansive patios and views from its ocean-facing rooms.

Sandbanks Luxury Retreat *(S 34 02.946 E 023 22.076, 13 Bowtie Dr,* ☎*044-533-3592, www. sandbanks.co.za, d R500-1,500, breakfast included,* ☎*secure parking, swimming pool)* is located on a hill just outside of town, which makes for a stunning view from the large infinity pool. Rooms vary from ultimate luxury to comfortable and quaint. Self-catering rooms with communal living and cooking spaces make it an ideal option for groups of people traveling together.

TOP END
The Plettenberg *(S 34 03.235 E 023 22.650, 40 Church St,* ☎*044-533-2030, www.plettenberg.com, s R1,650-2,400, d R2,250-4,000, breakfast included, Internet/wifi, secure parking, swimming pool)* is a luxurious, Relais & Chateaux rated hotel perched on a cliff overlooking the ocean. Each room is spacious, plush and uniquely decorated and the hotel's two infinity pools couldn't be more inviting for a dip. Ask for a room just across the street in the Annex, which is a bit more quiet and private than the main building.

Bay Lodge *(S 34 03.543 E 023 22.599, 15 Hopwood St,* ☎*044-533-4977, www.baylodge.net,* standard R2,500, luxury R3,700-R4,750, breakfast included, Internet/wifi, secure parking, swimming pool) is a chic oasis just outside of town. Each luxury room either opens up onto a private sun-filled balcony or is outfitted with a fireplace at the foot of your bed. The infinity pool, complete with waterfall, overlooks the waterfront, and rooftop cabanas let you unwind in style.

⑪ EATING

The Lookout Deck (S 34 03.109 E 023 22.643, Lookout Rocks off Formosa St, ☎044-533-1379, www.lookout.co.za, 9am-10pm, mains R50-130) is a casual seafood joint perched on a cliff overlooking the strand. Stunning views bring a crowd most times of the day, so prepare to enjoy your sundowner or fried seafood shoulder to shoulder with rambunctious new friends. Bring your suit for a dip at the small beach just below the restaurant.

LM in Plett (S 34 03.315 E 023 22.338, 6 Yellowwood Centre, Main St, ☎044-533-1420, 12pm-10pm, bar until 11pm, mains R60-150) is an upscale Mozambican restaurant specializing in Lourenco Marques prawns. But just as outstanding are the meats presented skewered and marinated in Piri-piri sauce. The best kick-back spot is at the picnic tables on the front terrace where you can people watch while you eat.

Miguel's Restaurant & Cocktail Terrace (S 34 03.367 E 023 22.315, Melville's Corner, Main St, ☎044-533-5056, www.miguels.co.za, 9am-late, mains R100-145) is a Portuguese restaurant and lounge popular for its well-seasoned main dishes and for the huge covered terrace that overlooks Plett's main street and the beach beyond. It's one of the few ocean-view establishments in town that features seafood more sophisticated than the usual fried fare.

Kappa Cheeno (S 34 03.367 E 023 22.315, 1A Melville's Corner, Main St, ☎044-533-1471, 7:30am-5pm Mon-Fri, 8am-2pm Sat, 9am-1pm Sun, mains R25-50) is a great breakfast spot to start your day. Take a seat on the patio to watch the world go by and enjoy live music on weekends.

The Med Seafood Bistro (S 34 03.162 E 023 22.311, Village Square, Main St, ☎044-533-3102, www.med-seafoodbistro.co.za, Mon-Fri 12pm-2pm, 6pm-9:30pm, Sat 6pm-late, mains R80-120) is a basement-level seafood restaurant known for having some of the best fish in town. The seafood options are plentiful and the venue is cozy for a chilly night.

Plett Market on Main (S 34 03.345 E 023.22.340, Main St, ☎044-533-1630, 8am-7pm) is a small outdoor collection of food and boutique stalls in the center of town. The French and Italian eateries offer cheap and tasty breakfast options, and on Fridays locals crowd in for dinner and live music.

❶ DRINKING & ENTERTAINMENT

Flashbacks (S 34 03.306 E 023 22.316, Main St, ☎044-533-4714, www.flashbacks.co.za, 12pm-2am Mon-Sat, 5pm-2am Sun) is a restaurant by day that turns into the town's hottest bar and dance club at night. The Top 40 playlist and a younger crowd make this the closest Plett comes to a bona fide frat party.

Cubar (S 34 03.282 E 023 22.301, Main St, ☎044-533-4314, 7pm-2am Mon-Sat) is where party-going grown-ups go. The resident DJs spin primarily house and trance music; head to the back patio bar if you want to chat over your cocktails.

❷ TRANSPORTATION

❸ Bus

Long Distance Buses passing through Plettenberg Bay stop at the **Shell Ultra City Garage** (S 34 03.022 E 023 21.494, cnr N2 and Marine Dr). **Greyhound** (☎083-915-9000, www.greyhound.co.za), **Intercape** (☎0861-287-287, www.intercape.co.za) and **TransLux/City-to-City** (☎021-449-3333, www.translux.co.za) can all take you along the coast in either direction. Stops for Intercape include Cape Town (R225-R275), Mossel Bay (R152) and Port Elizabeth (R170). City-to-City is your cheapest bus option and hits almost all the same places including Cape Town (R190), Port Elizabeth (R100) and Durban (R300). Tickets can be purchased at the **Checkers** (S 34 03.251 E 023 22.348, Main St).

❹ Minibus Taxi

Minibus Taxi Rank (S 34 03.339 E 023 22.197, cnr Kloof St & High St) offers you cheapest and quickest transport to Knysna (20min, R18), but most minibuses also stop at the Shell Ultra City.

WEST COAST

The west coast doesn't get as much foot traffic as the rest of the province, which makes it all the more sublime for those who do make it there. The shores just north of Cape Town are well-known to kiteboarders given their ideal ocean and wind conditions. Extreme sports aside, it is an exceptional region for those looking to unplug and enjoy a simpler life. There are a handful of small fishing towns that haven't changed much in the last few decades; the fishermen are on the beach early each morning hauling in their daily catch, the pace of life is slow and the town's restaurants serve up seafood that couldn't be fresher.

LANGEBAAN

GPS: S 33 05.468 E 018 01.923
pop. 8,000 | elevation 7 m/23 ft

Langebaan is a small beach town with a big following for its wind-fueled sports. Its glassy lagoon and reliable winds make it an ideal spot for windsurfing and kiteboarding between September and April. Langebaan's downtown is just a few shops and restaurants along Bree Street and Main Road, but the beaches and streets fill up on the weekends when visitors from Cape Town head up along the west coast for a quick dose of R&R.

ⓘ TOURIST INFORMATION

The Tourist Information Office (*S 33 05.468 E 018 01.977, Municipal Building, Bree St,* ☎*022-772-1515,* www.langebaaninfo.com, *8am-1pm*

& 1:30pm-4:30pm Mon-Fri) has information and brochures for area accommodation, activities and restaurants.

ⓢ MONEY

There is an **ABSA Bank** and **ATM** (*S 33 05.455 E 018 01.915, Marra Square, cnr Main Rd & Bree St*).

@ INTERNET

F.R.I.E.N.D.S. (*S 33 05.455 E 018 01.915, Marra Square, cnr Bree St & Suffren St,* ☎*022-772-0159, 8am-5pm Mon-Fri, 8am-4pm Sat, R10/15min*) is a fully licensed Internet café and bar with three computers and wireless vouchers that can be used anywhere in Marra Square as well as at Pearly's Restaurant, which stays open later.

⊙SHOPPING

The three blocks of Bree St that form the downtown area near the intersection of Main Road have a few small shopping centers and a handful of craft shops and galleries. A much larger shopping center, just around the corner from Bree Street is the **Koewheni Center** (*S 33 05.421 E 018 02.042, Oosterwal St*), which has a SuperSpar, bottle shop, pharmacy, Standard Bank and FNB and ABSA ATMs.

⊙SIGHTS & ACTIVITIES

Cape Sports Center (*S 33 04.930 E 018 01.947, Main Rd,* 022-772-1114 *or* 082-940-2309, *www. capesports.co.za*) is stocked with the latest gear for kiteboarding, windsurfing, kayaking and mountain biking. In addition to gear rental, they also provide lessons.

Horseback riding is available at **Oliphantskop Farm Inn** (*S 33 03.037 E 018 03.338, Olifantskop,* 022-772-2326, *www.oliphantskop.co.za, R150/hr*) where scenic rides take you up through the surrounding hills for views over the Langebaan lagoon. Rides depart daily at 9:30am, 11am, 2:30pm and 4pm. Booking is recommended.

⊙SLEEPING

BUDGET

Oliphantskop Farm Inn (*S 33 03.037 E 018 03.338, Olifantskop,* 022-772-2326, *www.oliphantskop.co.za, s R280 d R330-480, 4-person R420-680, swimming pool*) is a renovated 120-year-old farmhouse and horse stables on the outskirts of town. The farm's rustic architecture is at once charming and impressive. Self-catering fieldstone chalets are built on top of outcropped boulders and en suite rooms in the main farmhouse have 2-foot-thick stone walls. The farm also has a restaurant and bar.

MID-RANGE

Gecko Beach House (*S 33 05.205 E 018 01.856, 134 Beach Rd,* 022-772-1586, *www.geckobeachhouse.com, d R990-1,190, breakfast included, wifi, parking*) is a lovely, recently built

four-bedroom guesthouse located just beside the beach. Each room has an extra-long luxuriously dressed bed, a modern bathroom and a private patio that opens out to views of the lagoon.

Friday Island (*S 33 04.948 E 018 01.919, Main St,* 022-772-2506 *or* 082-640-9319, *www.fridayisland.co.za, courtyard: s R350-450, d R600-720, sea-facing: s R450-650, d R700-1,000*) is located right on the beach. A handful of the 12 rooms face the lagoon and have patios with lounge chairs, otherwise you can make your way out to the small private beach. The lodge has an attached restaurant and Cape Sports Center is just next door.

⊙EATING

Froggy's (*S 33 05.303 E 018 01.878, 29 Main St,* 022-772-1869, *6:30pm-9pm Tue-Sat, lunch by booking only Wed-Sun, mains R85-110*) is an intimate restaurant and art gallery and by far the best eatery in town. Though the restaurant has a host of delectable seafood dishes and their Moroccan lamb shank is killer, try to hold out for one of its famed curries and save room for dessert. Reservations are suggested.

Pearly's Restaurant (*S 33 05.478 E 018 01.848, 46 Beach Rd,* 022-772-2734, *9am-late, mains R50-100*) is just steps from the water. It's a casual eatery with indoor and outdoor seating and a range of menu options including seafood, pizza, pasta and salads. You can frequently see kite surfers in action while you dine.

WESTERN CAPE

West Coast Fossil Park

West Coast Fossil Park (S 32 56.784 E 018 05.830, Hopefield Rd/R45, *022-766-1606*, **www.iziko.org.za/iziko/partners/wcfp.html**, 8am-4pm Mon-Fri, 9am-12pm Sat-Sun, adult R10, child R5) is a former phosphate mining site where bones of over 200 animals - many of which are now extinct - have been partially unearthed by paleontologists so that visitors can view the fossils in their original state. Some of the more impressive findings include an early Sahara Bear and sabre-toothed cats. Mining operations stopped in 1993 and in 1998 the 14-hectare fossil-rich site was declared a National Heritage site. Full two-hour tours (11:30am, Mon-Fri, adult R50, child R15, entrance fee included) include a slide presentation of the history of the site and a guided tour of the dig sites. Shorter tours to the dig sites can also be arranged.

Windstone Backpackers (S 32 56.670 E 018 05.730, Hopefield Rd/R45, *022-766-1645* or *083-477-1756*, **www.windstone.co.za**, dm R100 d R270, Internet) has four dorm rooms and private flats in a pretty, rustic lodge beside the West Coast Fossil Park. There is a self-catering kitchen, lounge area and an indoor solar-heated pool. They also offer horseback riding lessons, day rides and overnight camping trips.

Die Strandloper (*S 33 04.327 E 018 02.345, on the beach off Oosterwal St, ☎083-227-7195 or ☎022-772-2490, www.strandloper.com, 12pm-4pm Wed & Fri-Sun, 6pm dinner Fri-Sat by booking R190*) is more a regular event than a restaurant. Located on the beach just north of Langebaan, they offer a set 10-course seafood meal, grilling everything from mussels to crayfish over an open fire pit, while a beach-going local strums the guitar. The open-air dining room and bench seating are littered with requisite nautical accoutrements and drinks are available at the bar or BYOB. Reservations are required and you should expect to spend the entire afternoon. It's a great place for kids.

Black Velvet Coffee Café (*S 33 05.472 E 018 01.861, Shop 3, Waterfront Centre, Bree St, ☎ 022-772-2422, 8am-5pm, mains R30-R50*) is a cute outdoor eatery with picnic table dining right on the street. They serve breakfast all day as well as sandwiches, packed spuds with toppings galore, sweets, smoothies and gourmet coffee.

⮐ TRANSPORTATION

Minibus Taxi

Minibus Taxi Rank (*S 33 04.945 E 018 02.205, Oosterwal St*) is across the street from the Seven Eleven and has transport to Vredenburg (R20). To get to Cape Town, take a minibus to Vredenburg and then from Vredenburg to Cape Town (R70).

PATERNOSTER

GPS: S 32 48.568 E 017 53.437
pop. 700 | elevation 13 m/43 ft

Paternoster is a quaint fisherman's village of whitewashed huts beside the Cape Columbine Nature Reserve. While much of the town's livelihood has changed its focus to tourism, seafaring traditions live on and you can still see fishermen returning with their daily catch in the early mornings. Crayfish is particularly popular and delicious in Paternoster, but avoid purchasing them from locals on the street, as most of these have been illegally caught and overfishing threatens the local crayfish population.

❼ TOURIST INFORMATION

Paternoster Village Tourism Information Center (*S 32 48.589 E 017 53.701, cnr St Augustine Rd & Mosselbank St/R45, ☎022-752-2323, www.paternoster.info, 9am-5pm Mon-Fri, 10am-3pm Sat*) has brochures and information on area accommodation and activities.

⑤ MONEY

There is an FNB ATM at the **Paternoster Food Market** (*S 32 48.643 E 017 53.676, Mosselbank St/R45*).

@ INTERNET

There is no public Internet available in Paternoster and it is unlikely that any will be popping up soon.

⟳ SHOPPING

There is no real central part of town, but there

are a few shops and galleries along St Augustine Road.

✹SIGHTS & ACTIVITIES

Cape Columbine Nature Reserve *(S 32 49.036 E 017 51.946, off St Augustine Way,* ☎*022-752-2718, 7am-7pm, adult R11, child R7)* is a 263-hectare park located just 3 km outside of Paternoster. There are 60 beachside campsites within the reserve, as well as guesthouse lodging in the homes of former lighthouse keepers (see below).

Cape Columbine Lighthouse *(S 32 49.626 E 017 51.385, Cape Columbine Nature Reserve,* ☎*022-752-2705, 10am-12pm & 12:30pm-3pm Mon-Fri, R16/person)* is the main attraction within the reserve. Visitors can climb up a series of ladders within the lighthouse to the top, where massive optics intensify a light beam so that it can be seen for 32 nautical miles. Built in 1936, this was the last manually operated lighthouse to be installed along the South African coast.

Fishing, crayfish catching and hiking or walking throughout the nature reserve are also popular activities.

Guided sea-kayaking and wildflower walks can be arranged through **The Beach Camp** *(S 32 49.122 E 017 51.319,* ☎*082-926-2267, www.beachcamp.co.za)* just inside the Cape Columbine Nature Reserve.

☽ SLEEPING

BUDGET
The Beach Camp *(S 32 49.122 E 017 51.319, Cape Columbine Nature Reserve,* ☎*082-926-2267, www.beachcamp.co.za, s/d R200, A-frames R250)* feels like the Lost Boys camp from Peter Pan. Six A-frames that face the beach and permanent tents with beds inside (bring your own bedding and a flashlight – there is no electricity) are bordered by a playful fortress of fishing nets and beach gear. There is an impressive beach bar, braai facilities and a full self-catering kitchen. Meals can be prepared for you. The lodging rate includes entrance into the nature reserve, and use of kayaks and canoes. If you don't have your own transport, call to see if they can arrange a shuttle for you.

Cape Columbine Nature Reserve campsite *(S 32 50.373 E 017 51.723, Cape Columbine Nature Reserve , camping R90)* has many sites on the beach within feet of the water and a central bathroom with solar-heated showers. There are also a number of more private campsites next to the ocean and farther away from the main camp. There are fire pits (bring your own wood) and water taps, but no electricity.

MID-RANGE
Paternoster Dunes Guesthouse *(S 32 48.582 E 017 53.038, 18 Sonkwas St,* ☎*022-752-2217, www.paternosterdunes.co.za, courtyard: s R600-800,*

WESTERN CAPE

d R900-1,300, sea facing: s R700-1,100, d R1,100-1,900, breakfast included, wifi, splash pool) is a beachside six-room guesthouse. Some rooms have breathtaking ocean views and others surround a small courtyard and splash pool. The upstairs lounge is light and spacious, with a bar overlooking the ocean for breakfast and sundowners.

Cape Columbine Lighthouse Guesthouse (S 32 49.626 E 017 51.385, Cape Columbine Nature Reserve, ☎022-752-2705, Sept-Apr R600-995/house, May-Aug R500-700/house) is a most unique accommodation option within the reserve. The simple two and three-bedroom guesthouses were the homes of former lighthouse keepers who maintained the lighthouse before the beam was automated. There are three cottages surrounding the lighthouse with full kitchens and an outdoor braai area.

Baywatch Villas (S 32 48.253 E 017 53.949, 6 Ambyl Rd, Mosselbank, ☎022-752-2039, www.baywatchvilla.co.za, s R435-695, d R620-990, breakfast included, villas: d R470-695, 4-person R695-1,250) is a collection of spotlessly outfitted bright white beach houses. Choose from en suite rooms in the central house, self-catering two-bedroom villas that have lounges and deck braai areas or a penthouse unit on the beach.

⑪EATING

Noisy Oyster (S 32 48.582 E 017 53.629, 62 St Augustine Rd, ☎022-752-2196 or ☎079-491-5765, 12pm-3pm & 6pm-9pm Wed-Sat, 12pm-3pm Sun, mains R65-180) is an intimate courtyard restaurant with a menu that changes daily. The restaurant boasts the freshest oysters and mussels in the country and was voted the most romantic dining destination in the west coast.

Paternoster Lodge Restaurant (S 32 48.560 E 017 53.405, 64 St Augustine Rd, ☎022-752-2023, www.paternosterlodge.co.za, 7am-9:30pm, mains R40-130) is one of Paternoster's better restaurants, known for their fresh seafood and steaks. The restaurant overlooks the beach where local fishing boats unload their daily catch, and has panoramic views of the bay.

Paternoster Hotel Restaurant (S 32 48.587 E 017 53.507, St Augustine Rd, ☎022-752-2703, www.paternosterhotel.co.za, 8am-9:30pm Mon-Sat, 8am-4pm & 6:30pm-9pm Sun, mains R50-100) is popular with the locals for its seafood, especially the freshly caught Paternoster crayfish. They also have burgers, sandwiches and breakfast.

Voorstrandt Restaurant (S 32 48.463 E 017 53.605, Strandloper Rd, ☎022-752-2038, www.voorstrandt.com, 10am-10pm, mains R50-R150) serves up seafood specialties, and on a deck that's as close as you can get to the ocean without being in it. There is also a small beach bar attached if you're interested in stopping over for drinks.

❶DRINKING & ENTERTAINMENT

Paternoster Hotel Restaurant (S 32 48.587 E 017 53.507, St Augustine Rd, ☎022-752-2703, www.paternosterhotel.co.za, 7pm-late) is known for its "Panty Bar" where - you guessed it - the ceiling is hung with underwear. In 1974, the bar owner started a collection of "honeymoon panties", which has since been revived by his son and co-owner. This is a Paternoster Institution and it is not uncommon for locals to show up at 8am and continue drinking throughout the day.

⮂TRANSPORTATION

There is not a lot of public transport in and out of Paternoster, but minibus taxis that come through stop near the **Tourism Information Center** *(S 32 48.589 E 017 53.701, cnr St Augustine Rd & Mosselbank St)* and head to Vredenburg (R20). To get to Cape Town, take a minibus to Vredenburg and then from Vredenburg to Cape Town (R70).

CLANWILLIAM
& AROUND
GPS: S 32 10.544 E 018 53.556
pop. 3,000 | elevation 84 m/276 ft

Clanwilliam is a historic town situated at the base of the Cederberg Mountains that is best known as the home of Rooibos Tea. It makes for a good base to explore the Cederberg region, especially during August and September when millions of indigenous flowers spring up and carpet the fields. The nearby Clanwilliam Dam also draws water sports enthusiasts.

❶ TOURIST INFORMATION

Tourist Information Office *(S 32 10.844 E 018 53.613, Main St,* ☎*027-482-2024, www.clanwilliam. info, 8:30am-5pm Mon-Fri, 8:30am-12:30pm Sat)* has helpful staff that will take the time to tell you about the town and provide a list of options for area accommodation and activities.

❸ MONEY

Main Street is lined with the major banks. **ABSA** *(S 32 10.700 E 018 53.599, Main St)* has an ATM and a bureau de change, but there is also a Standard Bank, NedBank and FNB within three blocks.

@ INTERNET

Internet Café & Coffee Shop *(S 32 10.572 E 018 53.571, cnr of Augsburg St/R364 & Main St,* ☎*027-482-2021, 8am-5pm Mon-Fri, 8am-1pm Sat, R15/30min)* is a coffee shop with a handful of computers available for Internet use, but laptops are not allowed.

⬚ SHOPPING

Most of the retail shops in Clanwilliams are located within a five-block area of Main Road. There is a **SuperSpar shopping center** *(S 32 10.630 E 018 53.562, Main Rd)* that has the largest collection of shops in town.

✱ SIGHTS & ACTIVITIES

Rooibos Ltd *(S 32 11.205 E 018 53.361, Old Cape Rd,* ☎*027-482-2155, www.rooibosltd.co.za)* has been producing Rooibos Tea - grown almost exclusively in the neighboring Cederburg area - since 1954 and is one of the main manufacturers and distributors of the product today. The factory stopped giving tours a couple years ago, but you can still go to the visitor center and watch a 15-minute video on tea production (shown at 10am, 11:30am, 2pm and 3:30pm Mon-Fri) and purchase Rooibos Tea products. **Strassberger Veldskoen Factory** *(S 32 11.145 E*

WESTERN CAPE

018 53.450, Old Cape Rd, ☎027-482-2140, www.strassberger.co.za, 8am-12pm & 1pm-3:30pm Mon-Fri) has been hand-making soft leather shoes, or veldskoen, since 1834. Here you can see the entire production process of these shoes and boots, from tanned hide to the box on the store floor.

☾SLEEPING

BUDGET
Daisy Cottage (S 32 10.644 E 018 53.662, Fosters St, ☎027-482-1603 or ☎079-497-8996, liciae@telkomsa.net, R175/person) is a charming thatched roof cottage that has a bedroom and a loft. The cottage sleeps four and is on a residential street just one block east of Main Street. The cottage has AC, a full kitchen and a patio in the back with a large yard.

MID-RANGE
Clanwilliam Hotel (S 32 10.757 E 018 53.598, Main St, ☎027-482-1101, www.clanwilliamhotel.co.za, s R250-R300, d R390-490, secure parking, swimming pool) is Clanwilliam's largest hotel, with 55 rooms on the main drag. Some of the newer rooms in the back are self-catering and there is a restaurant and bar downstairs.
Yellow-Aloe (S 32 10.840 E 018 53.642, 1 Park St, ☎027-482-2018 or ☎082-893-4899, www.cyberall.co.za/webpages/yellowaloe.html, s R400, d R640, breakfast included, wifi, splash pool) is a simple and elegant three-room guesthouse where the highlight of your stay could be sleeping in one of their luxuriously outfitted beds. On the guesthouse grounds there is also a plant nursery, coffee shop and boutique open to the public.

☾EATING

Reinhold's (S 32 10.753 E 018 53.612, Main St, ☎027-482-2163, 7pm-9pm Tue-Sat, mains R95-175) is the best restaurant in town. Situated in a historical building dating back to 1905, they serve good home-cooked meals of primarily fish, steak and pasta and have a mouthwatering selection of hors d'oeuvres. There is a small cocktail bar inside, where you can enjoy a pre- or post-dinner drink.
Olifantshuis Restaurant (S 32 10.549 E 018 53.574, cnr Augsburg St/R364 & Main St, ☎027-482-2301, 6:30pm-10pm Mon-Sat, mains R70-100) is a family restaurant run by head chef Jaco Slabber, a Rooibos enthusiast. At the time of research, Jaco was revamping his menu of classic steaks, fish and pizza to include some Rooibos inspired dishes as well. Dine indoors or in the tree-shaded garden, or just stop by for a drink at the bar.
De Kelder Pub & Grill (S 32 10.542 E 018 53.473, Graafwater Way/R364, ☎027-482-1037, 5pm-2am Mon, 12pm-2am Tue-Sat, mains R50-90) is the locals' restaurant, just next to the pub. It's a cozy place that serves mostly steaks, but it also has a selection of salads, burgers and seafood, all at a good value.

DRINKING & ENTERTAINMENT

De Kelder Pub & Grill (S 32 10.542 E 018 53.473, Graafwater Way/R364, ☎027-482-1037, 5pm-2am Mon, 12pm-2am Tue-Sat, mains R50-90) is the only place in town that fills up with a healthy crowd of patrons every night. This is a no-frills sports bar where you can grab a spot on a stool near the tap or at a picnic table.

☾TRANSPORTATION

Minibus Taxi Rank (S 32 10.572 E 018 53.555, cnr Main St & Voortrekker St) is located on the corner beside the Spar, next to the Police Station and just off of the R364. The rank has transport to Vredenburg (R120), Citrusdal (R80), Malmesbury (R100) and Cape Town (R180).

CEDERBERG
WILDERNESS AREA
GPS: S 32 22.448 E 019 03.574
elevation 522 m/1,713 ft

Cederberg Wilderness Area (S 32 22.448 E 019 03.574, Off the N7, ☎027-482-2404, www.capenature.org.za, entrance R40/person) spans 710 square kilometers of rugged Cederberg Mountains, their spectacular rock formations and waterfalls, the endangered Clanwilliam cedar tree, and many impressively preserved San rock art sites. During August and September, wildflowers bloom and carpet the landscape with color.
   The Cederberg Wilderness Area is divided up

into three separate sections to preserve the park's secluded atmosphere and limit visitor impact. Each area covers roughly 24,000 hectares and is limited to 50 visitors per day. Permits can be purchased from the Cape Nature Reserve office at the **Algeria Camp** (*S 32 22.448 E 019 03.574,* ☎*027-482-2404,* *www.capenature.org.za*) or from the private accommodation locations within the area.

The most common animals in the Cederberg area are baboons, rock dassies, various antelope and more than 100 species of birds. Less common but still present are the honey badger, porcupine, leopard, fox and snakes such as the puff adder and black spitting cobra.

☉SIGHTS & ACTIVITIES

Hiking and rock climbing (*free with entrance permit*) are the Cederberg's most popular activities. Day visitors are permitted to go on hikes throughout the reserve with a minimum of two people. **Overnight hikes** (*permit R60-65/night*) require a minimum of three people and the park allows camping anywhere within the reserve or in basic huts along the trails. Detailed topographical maps of the Cederberg are available at the Cape Nature Reserve Algeria Camp.
The Wolfberg Arch (*S 32 26.571 E 019 15.194*) is a fantastically massive rock arch, and the **Maltese Cross** (*S 32 30.798 E 019 10.143*), a 30-meter high vaguely cross-shaped rock, are two of the more impressive rock formations within the Cederberg. Both are located in the southern section of the wilderness area and can be reached on day hikes.
Rock art is well preserved within the hundreds of caves and rock overhangs throughout the area. The paintings are believed to be between 300-6,000 years old. There are many rock art sites both on the hiking trails and off the road, which are convenient to explore on your own.

☉SLEEPING

Algeria Camp (*S 32 22.448 E 019 03.574,* ☎*027-482-2404,* *www.capenature.org.za,* *camping R165-185, 4-person cottage R420-640*) is the main campsite administered by Cape Nature. It has 48 campsites and seven cottages situated near the Rondegat River. There is a small shop and information office onsite and the camp is perfectly situated for day hikes to see nearby waterfalls and San rock art. Algeria Camp can get busy at times so if you're interested in something a bit more tranquil, you can ask at the office about some of the other Cape Nature campsites within the reserve or one of the private lodges bordering the wilderness area.
Jamaka Organic Farm (*S 32 20.471 E 019 01.723,* ☎*027-482-2801* or ☎*082-466-4331,* *www.jamaka. co.za, camping R120, chalets R360-450*) is a family-run organic citrus and mango farm with seven fully equipped freestanding self-catering cottages that sleep 4-6 people each. The campsites are located away from the cottages on the banks of the Rondegat River with braai areas and a number of natural rock pools nearby for swimming. The farm is located just outside the wilderness area boundary on the road between Clanwilliam and the Algeria Camp, roughly 4.5 km north of the Algeria Camp.
IMPACT **Gecko Creek Wilderness Lodge** (*S 32 23.766 E 018 59.149,* ☎*027-482-1300* or ☎*083-234-1112,* *www.geckocreek.com, camping R130/ person, s R200-290, d R400-580*) is the perfect place to escape into rustic beauty situated in a large private nature reserve bordering the wilderness area. Tents can be supplied for camping, or take one of three private cabins, each with a hammock strung from the front deck. Lighting and hot water are solar powered and there is a large central lapa, fire pit and braai area for guests. Children under 16 are not allowed out of concern that Hoka, the resident timber wolf, may get a bit playful. The lodge is located off the main road between the N7 and Algeria Camp, follow the signed turn (at *S 32 22.107 E 018 58.907*) and head south for 3.4 km to the lodge.

⮌TRANSPORTATION

There are a handful of routes into the Cederberg Wilderness Area between Citrusdal and Clanwilliam. The main road into the Cederberg is off the N7 (*at S 32 21.833 E 018 56.366*) with signs directing you to the Algeria Camp and main office. There is no public transport into the wilderness area.

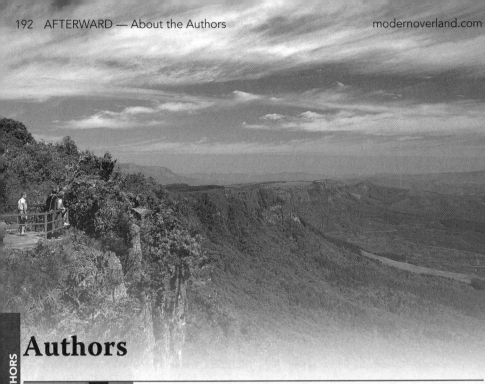

Authors

John Bradley

John set out on his first solo overland trip hitching south across the Sahara Desert into central Africa. Over the next decade he traveled through more than 75 countries before returning to Chicago where he worked in mergers and acquisitions. He recently returned to his favorite continent where he spent over a year traveling in circles soaking up the different cultures of South Africa, trekking into the highlands of Lesotho and living off the grid in rural Swaziland. In between working on Modern Overland guides and traveling, John is based in Madison, Wisconsin.

Liz Bradley

Liz fell in love with South Africa when she first paddled the Orange River as a youngster in 1997. She jumped at the opportunity to take a break from her life in New York City to help write Modern Overland's South Africa, Lesotho & Swaziland guidebook. Her time in South Africa allowed her to rekindle her inner-history nerd and trust unexpected adventures. When not playing with penguins, she works at a nonprofit committed to social justice and human rights.

Victoria Fine

Victoria is originally from Los Angeles and regularly globetrots as a humanitarian journalist and a managing editor at The Huffington Post. South Africa most definitely has her three destination must-haves -- great culture, great beaches and great food. Her biggest lesson learned while working on this guide? An ostrich is not to be messed with, unless it is in your burger.

Jon Vidar

Jon is a passionate traveler, explorer, photographer and writer who maintains a constant foothold in his home city of Los Angeles. During the past 10 years, his travels have taken him to six continents, from working on archaeological excavations in Turkey and Greece, to running new media training programs in Rwanda and Iraq. His experience in South Africa was unlike any country he had seen before. He simultaneously fell in love with the majestic scenery of the Drakensberg Mountains and the wine of the Stellenbosch region.

AUTHORS

Modern Overland Authors

Our adventurous and independent authors are passionate travelers and writers. They work hard interviewing thousands of locals, exploring all that South Africa has to offer and distilling it down to the very best. They strive to get to know and write about locations not covered in other guidebooks, such as the vibrant South African townships, city center districts on the verge of regeneration and destinations that reach beyond off-the-beaten-path.

From spot on GPS coordinates to exact opening times, current prices and directions, they take pride in getting the details right. With a tell it like it is approach they provide in depth coverage of the best sights and adventure activities, budget hostels, luxury hotels and top restaurants. But it is not all just about sights, hotels and restaurants. After a full day of research our authors head out to pubs, nightclubs, music venues, comedy clubs and cocktail lounges in order to provide solid coverage on the best local nightlife and entertainment hot spots.

Think you have what it takes to be a Modern Overland author? Check out: modernoverland.com/jobs

Credits

Managing Editor Victoria Fine
Editor Mary Dudley
Assistant Editors Rachel Grischke, Georgiana Ceausu
Contributing Authors Margaret Dudley, Steve Schultz, Julia Burke, Leah Yurasek, Sara Vidar
Art Director Eric Olason
Cartographic Designer Eric Olason
Layout Designer Eric Olason
Cover Designers Stefan Chinof
Image Editor Eric Olason
Photo Editors Ben Sommers-Dehaney, Stephanie Mann
Online Jon Vidar, Georgiana Ceausu
Marketing & Publicity Mary Dudley, Sara Schwartz

CREDITS

Modern Overland
PO Box 2320
Madison WI 53701   USA

Photo Credits

CREDITS

Index

INDEX

INDEX

ModernOverland.com

Modern Overland
PO Box 2320
Madison WI 53701 USA

Printed by Fabulous Printers Pte Ltd
Printed in Singapore

Send Us Your Feedback

We would love to hear from you – our authors read everything that is sent in from our readers. If you have an update, something you think we've missed, or something new, please let us know. Each person who sends us useful information is thanked in the next edition of our book and those who send in especially useful information will be rewarded with a free book.

To send us your update, opinion, comment or suggestion visit modernoverland.com/contact

Note: we may edit, reproduce and incorporate your comments in Modern Overland products such as guidebooks, websites, and digital products, so let us know if you don't want your comments reproduced or your name acknowledged. For a copy of our privacy policy visit modernoverland.com/privacy-policy